CHAPTER I

INTRODUCTION

THERE IS MORE AGREEMENT today than at any earlier period on the need for some change in the traditional international system of a community of sovereign states. Unlimited sovereignty is no longer automatically accepted as the most prized possession or even as a desirable attribute of states. The postwar revulsion against war and against an international system in which war is not only possible but tolerated is stronger as our most recent experience with war is more frightful. The potentialities of atomic warfare give more widespread support to the effort to exercise greater ingenuity, to achieve more success, in the science of politics. It is natural that some minds seek a complete change through the immediate creation of a world government. Others would prefer to build more slowly through the medium of what is generally called international organization or administration, now typified by the United Nations. One point of agreement may be found in all plans and proposals, whether they come from statesmen or from laymen, from experts or from novices. That common point is the necessity for an adequate international law. This feeling is naturally the more pronounced in countries devoted to the slogan that government should be of laws and not of men. International lawyers and laymen alike admit or assert defects in the present system of international law. Some deny that any such system even has an existence. Leaving that argument momentarily aside, it may be conceded that there is at this time both need and opportunity for the development of a modern law of nations.

No system of law springs into existence full-panoplied. All legal systems from the most primitive to the most advanced have their backgrounds and roots in the society which they govern. It is therefore not enough for the future of the international society to say that we must have a rule governing the use of atomic bombs and other weapons of mass destruction. It is not enough merely to have a law

CONTENTS

TO
L. K. J.

A MODERN LAW
OF NATIONS

— AN INTRODUCTION —

BY

PHILIP C. JESSUP

THE MACMILLAN COMPANY
NEW YORK   1948

A Modern Law Of NationsAn Introduction

making war illegal. Such rules, even if backed by an adequate form of organization or government, would fail to create a well-ordered international society, the existence of which is a prerequisite to the successful functioning of any legal system. If there be no adequate body of law governing the solution of the conflicts which are inherent in any human relations, frictions and tensions will develop to a point which will bring about breaches of the primary rules about weapons and wars; even in the most highly developed societies, underlying inequities and resulting strains produce riots, revolutions, and civil wars.

It is the purpose of this book to explore some of the possible bases for a modern law of nations. The exploration proceeds upon the basis of an examination of the way in which peoples and nations have attempted, however inadequately, in the past to govern their interrelationships. It proceeds upon the assumption that progress must and can be made in the social sciences to come abreast of the new advances in the physical sciences. Two points in particular are singled out as keystones of a revised international legal order. The first is the point that international law, like national law, must be directly applicable to the individual. It must not continue to be remote from him, as is the traditional international law, which is considered to be applicable to states alone and not to individuals. The second point is that there must be basic recognition of the interest which the whole international society has in the observance of its law. Breaches of the law must no longer be considered the concern of only the state directly and primarily affected. There must be something equivalent to the national concept of criminal law, in which the community as such brings its combined power to bear upon the violator of those parts of the law which are necessary to the preservation of the public peace.

Sovereignty, in its meaning of an absolute, uncontrolled state will, ultimately free to resort to the final arbitrament of war, is the quicksand upon which the foundations of traditional international law are built. Until the world achieves some form of international government in which a collective will takes precedence over the individual will of the sovereign state, the ultimate function of law, which is the elimination of force for the solution of human conflicts, will not be fulfilled. There must be organs empowered to lay down rules (a legislature); there must be judicial organs to interpret and apply those rules (a judiciary); and there must be organs with power to compel compliance with the rules (a police force). These organizational developments must take place, and if this volume does not concern itself primarily with the solution of such problems, this is not because of any doubt concerning their importance. This work is dedicated to the solution of another problem: granted that the necessary organization is perfected, what is to be the nature of the body of law which is to be laid down, applied, and enforced?

Law is indeed a human necessity. The current spate of writing about the need for world government avows the need for law. The Romans put it tersely—*ubi societas ibi ius*. The Charter of the United Nations recognizes the fact. It is asserted in the roundly phrased orations of heads of state and of foreign ministers [1] and in the crusading columns of the *New Yorker* magazine. Opinions will continue to differ enormously about the type of world government or world organization demanded by an atomic age the exact potentialities of which are too vast to be kept in the common consciousness. There is as much disagreement about the means for achieving the desired end and about the tempo of the progress which is practicable. There are advocates of more government and of less government in human affairs, but only the most detached philosophic minds contemplate the utopia of anarchy, that perfection of the human spirit in which no rules and no controls are necessary to enable human beings to live together in peace and harmony. Law must govern world relationships if they are to be peaceful, whether those relationships continue to be organized on the present order of sovereign states, whether there is to be a world confederation, or whether there is to be one unitary world state. The differences of opinion lie far more in the necessary agencies and methods of enforcement of law than in the actual rules to govern human conduct.

There is no such dichotomy as one writer suggests between law and diplomacy.[2] They are not mutually exclusive procedures. To be sure, both procedures may be abused; the lawyer may become legalistic, the diplomat may become Machiavellian. But the successful practicing attorney is as much a negotiator as a citer of precedents,

---

[1] Cf. Jessup, "International Law in the Post-War World," *Am. Soc. Int. L., Proc.* (1942), 46.

[2] Morgenthau, "Diplomacy," 55 *Yale L.J.* (1946), 1067.

whether he be dealing with a corporate reorganization, a divorce suit, or the protection of national interests abroad.

As in arguments about many other matters, differences of opinion about law are frequently found to rest upon definitions. X may use the word "law" to include moral law, religious law, and rules of social intercourse, as well as the statutes enacted by a legislature, while Y may be using the same word to include only the last category. In legal literature there is voluminous debate about the proper definition. There are still devotees of the simple Austinian concept based upon uncomplicated observation of the most usual manifestations of law—rules laid down by a superior power (legislature), enforced by a superior power (police). There are more modern concepts which have been evolved largely as the result of consideration of the Anglo-American system of the development of common law through court decisions. Thus it is said that law is a prophecy of the action of agencies of society; it is "the law" that I must not steal or break my contract, in the sense that if I do the forbidden thing, agents of society—policemen or courts and their marshals—will arrest me or seize and sell my goods to pay a determined amount of damages.

There is a tendency to assume that there is such a thing as one correct definition for any one word or concept. In the physical sciences, in mathematics, this was generally thought to be true. Water was always H_2O and 2 plus 2 equaled 4. But even in the physical sciences such old fundamentals as Newtonian physics and Euclidean geometry have had to yield their sacrosanct character in the light of such ideas as relativity and the retesting of basic assumptions against a broader field of observation. Frederick S. Dunn pointed out fifteen years ago that the time had come for a similar challenge of underlying assumptions in international law and relations.[8] In the social sciences surely an old Chinese proverb is much to the point: "It is always well to have in the background of one's mind a multiplicity of definitions covering the subject at hand to prevent oneself from accepting the most obvious." A definition is useful only to the extent to which it records an accurate observation, whether of natural phenomena, literary usage, or social conduct. "Law and obedience to law," wrote Judge Cardozo, "are facts confirmed every day to us all in our expe-

[8] Dunn, *The Protection of Nationals* (1932), 7.

rience of life. If the result of a definition is to make them seem to be illusions, so much the worse for the definition; we must enlarge it till it is broad enough to answer realities." [4]

International law, or the law of nations, is a term which has been used for over three hundred years to record certain observations of the conduct of human beings grouped together in what we call states. There is a vast literature on the subject, and courts have examined that literature and based decisions upon it. The works of the writers, the United States Supreme Court has said, "are resorted to by judicial tribunals, not for the speculations of their authors concerning what the law ought to be, but for trustworthy evidence of what the law really is." [5] The debate about the propriety of using the word "law" in the term "international law" is as old as the term. Much of that debate is fruitless because it rests upon the undeclared differences in underlying definition. If to X the word "law" cannot properly be applied to any rules behind which there is not a sanction or power of enforcement by an overall authority, then X is correct in denying that international law is "law." Although the Supreme Court of the United States asserted in *Virginia v. West Virginia* [6] the power to enforce its judgments against one of the states of the Union, federal force has never been used for such a purpose. If it were used against a resisting state, it would be difficult to distinguish the situation from rebellion or civil war. Under Article 94 of the Charter of the United Nations, the Security Council could direct the use of force against a state which failed to perform the obligations incumbent on it under a judgment rendered by the International Court of Justice; such a situation would resemble international war or civil war within the United Nations. The vindication of "rights"—i.e legal rights under international law—has frequently throughout modern history been advanced as the justification for resort to war. It is clearly a kind of enforcement very different from that of the ordinary police action: it is power against power, North against South, United Nations against Axis. One side is "right" and the other side is "wrong," and these are not merely moral judgments, but also

[4] Cardozo, *The Nature of the Judicial Process* (1928), 127.
[5] The Paquete Habana, 175 *U.S.* 677, 700 (1900).
[6] 246 *U.S.* 565 (1918). See Rosenberg, "Brutum Fulmen: A Precedent for a World Court," 25 *Col. L. Rev.* (1925), 783, 794; Freeman and Paullin, *Coercion of States: In Federal Unions* (1943).

reflections of conviction that certain rules, certain standards of conduct, have been violated.

The significant question to ask about international law is whether the use of that term is in accordance with an accurate observation and study of the conduct of states in the world community. Superficially, the negative reply comes easily. Wars, breaches of treaties, oppression of the weak by the strong, are the headlines of the daily press and of the history textbooks. The superficial observer has not noted the steady observance of such treaties as that under which letters are carried all over the world at rates fixed by the Universal Postal Union. He ignores the fact that there is scarcely an instance in two hundred years in which an ambassador has been subjected to suit in courts of the country where he is stationed. The recording of the observation of this last fact is stated in legal terms by saying that under international law an ambassador has diplomatic immunities. The superficial observer has not read the hundreds of decisions handed down by international courts called Mixed Claims Commissions, which have awarded money damages duly paid by the defendant states. Perhaps he has not even read the sixty-odd decisions and opinions of the Permanent Court of International Justice or noted the subsequent history of the observance of those pronouncements as recorded for example in the writings of Judge Manley O. Hudson.[7] He may be unfamiliar with the extent to which international law has been incorporated in national law and has thus secured an enforcement agency through the ordinary governmental machinery of the national states. Perhaps he forgets that the Constitution of the United States gives Congress the power to "define and punish . . . Offences against the Law of Nations" and that the Supreme Court has sustained the constitutionality of the exercise of that power by determining that the duty to prevent the counterfeiting of foreign currency is a duty imposed upon the United States by international law.[8] He may not be familiar with such classic statements as that of Mr. Justice Gray: "International law is part of our law, and must be ascertained and administered by the courts of justice of appropriate jurisdiction, as often as questions of right depending upon it are duly presented

[7] E.g. *The Permanent Court of International Justice 1920-1942* (1943); *World Court Reports* (2 vols., 1934, 1935).
[8] *United States v. Arjona*, 120 U.S. 479 (1887).

for their determination." [9] He may not have examined the counterparts of these United States positions in the constitutions and judicial decisions of the courts of other countries.[10] Always he will come back, with his own definition of law in mind, to the undeniable fact that international law has been unable in the past to check resort to war because the international society lacks its own overall police force. As in our own individual relations, it is the instances of lawless conduct and of violence that dominate the memory. We are accustomed to think that the United States is a community governed by law, but violence and the failure of government controls in labor relations are "facts confirmed every day to us all in our experience of life." Indeed, the parallelisms between labor relations within states and international relations among states are striking. It is said that it was experience with labor problems that led William Jennings Bryan as Secretary of State to negotiate a series of treaties providing for "cooling-off periods" and fact-finding commissions.[11] If such devices have not succeeded in eliminating international conflicts, this is not surprising in view of their comparable inadequacy within the framework of a highly developed national legal system.

Those who have taken the pains to become familiar with the way in which governments behave in their relations with other governments reach no such discouraging conclusions as those which obsess the minds of the headline-readers. One of the wisest and most experienced of them all, John Bassett Moore, has recorded his observation that on the whole international law is as well observed as national law.[12] The Director of the Yale Institute of International Studies has recently remarked that those "who make light of treaty commitments in general seem to ignore the fact that the vast majority of such engagements are continuously, honestly, and regularly observed even under adverse conditions and at considerable inconvenience to the parties." [13] It is not without significance that foreign offices throughout the world have, and have had through the course of at least two centuries, staffs of legal advisers, most of whose time is devoted to

[9] The Paquete Habana, 175 U.S. 677, 700 (1900).
[10] See Masters, *International Law in National Courts* (1932).
[11] Scott, "Remarks," *Am. Soc. Int. L., Proc.* (1929), 172.
[12] Moore, *International Law and Some Current Illusions* (1924), 300.
[13] Brodie (ed.), *The Absolute Weapon: Atomic Power and World Order*, (1946), 8.

problems of international law. When a controversy develops between two governments (a controversy of the ordinary day-to-day type) the legal adviser either drafts or has a hand in drafting the correspondence. If one skims such diplomatic correspondence written over the course of many decades, one is bound to be struck by the frequency, the habitual frequency, with which governments support and defend their international actions by appeal to legal arguments, arguments based on international law.[14] It is immaterial for the purposes of this discussion whether such legal arguments are hypocritical or are contradicted by subsequent conduct. The fact remains that they reflect the basic human conviction of the necessity of law and bear witness to the evolution through the years of a body of customary and treaty international law, invoked by governments and applied by courts. The record proves that there is a "law habit" in international relations. It is not immaterial to add that the instances in which judgments of international tribunals have been flouted are so rare that the headline-reader may well place them in the man-bites-dog category.

It is true, as Hall said in a passage quoted with approval by the Judicial Committee of the Privy Council in 1934, that "Looking back over the last couple of centuries, we see international law at the close of each fifty years in a more solid position than that which it occupied at the beginning of the period. Progressively it has taken firmer hold, it has extended its sphere of operation, it has ceased to trouble itself about trivial formalities, it has more and more dared to grapple in detail with the fundamental facts in the relations of States." [15]

Among the defects of the existing international legal system, two have been mentioned as the basis of this study. They stand out as obstacles to progress. The first is the fundamental tenet of traditional international law that it is a law only between states, not between individuals or between individuals and states. The individual has been one stage removed from the application of international law, the legal jargon being that he is not a "subject" of the law but only an

---

[14] Jessup, "The Reality of International Law," 18 *Foreign Affairs* (1940), 244.

[15] Viscount Sankey, L. C., In Re Piracy Jure Gentium [1934], *A.C.* 586, 591, citing the preface to the third edition of Hall, *International Law* (1889).

"object." International law affects him only through the medium of the state. Perhaps the most striking example of the weight of the dead hand of this juridical concept is to be found in that branch of international law known as the Responsibility of States for Injuries to Aliens, or the Diplomatic Protection of Citizens Abroad.[16] The concepts of alienage and citizenship are based on the notion that the individual has no legal significance from the standpoint of international law save as he is related to one state through the bond of citizenship or nationality and thus stands in relation to other states in the role of alien. The responsibility of the state for injuries to an individual is owed under international law to another state and not to the individual. Thus there is no responsibility if the injured individual is stateless, that is, has no nationality. To explain the legal basis of responsibility to another state, international law for some two centuries has made use of a fiction invented by Vattel to the effect that a state is injured through the injury to its citizen. If this were the true basis of responsibility, the measure of damages to be paid for an injury would vary with the importance of the role played by the injured individual in the life of the state of which he is a citizen. Actually, in the hundreds of claims cases which have been adjudicated by international tribunals, lip service only is paid to the fiction, and decisions are made upon the inescapable realization that it is really John Smith or François Picaud who has been physically injured or whose widow and children have been left destitute. The alleged indirect loss to the state is forgotten until the final judgment is expressed in terms of an obligation of the defendant state to pay a sum of money to the claimant state, the usually unexpressed assumption being that the latter will pay the money over to the proper individuals. Many tortuous bits of judicial reasoning would have been eliminated if it were agreed that the individual himself is protected by the rule of law.

There is a considerable literature on the question whether this fundamental basis of the traditional law as a law between states only, is juridically and philosophically sound.[17] It is frequently asserted that the principle is not an absolute one, since it admits of exceptions, notably in the case of piracy, where the pirate is said to be *hostis*

[16] This topic is explored in detail in Chap. V.
[17] See Chap. II.

humani generis, punishable by any state that apprehends him. The trials of war criminals have elicited learned discussions along the same lines. It is not intended here to continue such debates concerning the existing law. It is rather the purpose to take as a hypothesis the general acceptance of the thesis that internaional law *does* apply directly to the individual, that it does or can bind him as well as states directly, and in the light of that hypothesis to re-examine the existing law as it has developed through the centuries to see what changes, what modifications would need to be made to fit the law to the new basis. Much of the current discussion of world government concerns itself with this problem of the direct application of international law to the individual, but the nature of the changes which such a concept would need to work in international relations does not appear to have been fully explored.

A second characteristic of the traditional international legal system requires the same kind of thorough re-examination. As already noted, international law resembles tort law rather than criminal law in the national legal system. The significance of this comparison is that under the traditional international legal system, a breach of international law is considered to be a matter which concerns only the state whose rights are directly infringed; and no other state, nor the community of states, is entitled to remonstrate or object or take action. "No nation," said Judge Story, "has a right to infringe the law of nations, so as thereby to produce an injury to any other nation. But if it does, this is understood to be an injury, not against all nations, which all are bound or permitted to redress; but which concerns alone the nation injured." [18] In contrasting international and national law Elihu Root remarked that we "are all familiar with the distinction in the municipal law of all civilized countries, between private and public rights and the remedies for the protection or enforcement of them. Ordinary injuries and breaches of contract are redressed only at the instance of the injured person, and other persons are not deemed entitled to interfere. It is no concern of theirs. On the other hand, certain flagrant wrongs the prevalence of which would threaten the order and security of the community are deemed to be everybody's business . . . [robbery or assault]. Every citizen is deemed to be injured by the breach of the law because the law is

[18] La Jeune Eugénie, Fed. Case No. 15,551 (C.C., D. Mass. 1822).

his protection, and if the law be violated with impunity, his protection will disappear. . . . Up to this time breaches of international law have been treated as we treat wrongs under civil procedure, as if they concerned nobody except the particular nation upon which the injury was inflicted and the nation inflicting it. There has been no general recognition of the right of other nations to object. . . . If the law of nations is to be binding, if the decisions of tribunals charged with the application of that law to international controversies are to be respected, there must be a change in theory, and violations of the law of such a character as to threaten the peace and order of the community of nations must be deemed to be a violation of the right of every civilized nation to have the law maintained and a legal injury to every nation." [19]

Article 11 of the Covenant of the League of Nations was hailed as marking an innovation in this respect by declaring: "Any war or threat of war, whether immediately affecting any of the Members of the League or not, is hereby declared a matter of concern to the whole League. . . ." Some have hailed the Briand-Kellogg Pact as another step in the same direction. The American Republics at the Lima Conference of 1938 recorded their conviction that "Each State is interested in the preservation of world order under law, in peace with justice, and in the social and economic welfare of mankind." [20] The philosophy underlying the Charter of the United Nations clearly embraces the notion of the community interest in matters affecting international peace. For example, under Article 34, "The Security Council may investigate any dispute, or any situation which might lead to international friction or give rise to a dispute. . . ." Article 35 empowers any Member of the United Nations to bring to the attention of the Security Council or of the General Assembly any such dispute or situation. This is sound political principle governing the operations of the international organization. Yet the traditional legal foundations of unilateralism remain largely unshaken. The Charter provisions may be applicable to what Root called "flagrant wrongs" where the danger to peace is apparent. It is not clear that international

[19] Root, "The Outlook for International Law," *Am. Soc. Int. L., Proc.* (1915), 7–9.
[20] *Report of the Delegation of the United States of America to the Eighth International Conference of American States,* Dept. of State Pub. 1624 (1941), 191.

law yet embodies the principle that because the law is the protection of all states, all are interested in any breach or weakening of that law. How far should such a principle extend? [21] Are there some breaches of international law that should still be the concern only of the state immediately injured? According to Article 62 of the Statute of the International Court of Justice, a state may request from the Court permission to intervene in any case if it considers that "it has an interest of a legal nature which may be affected by the decision in the case." Has a state such a legal interest, for example, in the vindication of the law of diplomatic immunities? Presumably there will always be breaches of law that do not involve the general community interest, just as the trespass of my neighbor's cow concerns me alone and is to be remedied by my individual lawsuit, without the intervention of third parties and without the community processes of arrest and criminal prosecution. The definition of "matters which are essentially within the domestic jurisdiction of any state," which are reserved under Article 2 of the Charter, is a cognate problem.

In some instances the acceptance of the concept of community interest would be comparable, as Root contemplated, to substituting for the present tort basis of international law a basis more comparable to that of criminal law, in which the community takes cognizance of law violations. In other instances, however, the change would be a shift in the direction of more extended governmental functions of an organized international community, as would be true if processes of collective recognition should be substituted for the present unilateral action.

It is the purpose of this volume to examine traditional international law in an attempt to suggest to what portions of a developed international legal system the concept of community interest might well apply. For this purpose again, the discussion will proceed on the hypothesis that a new principle is accepted, in this instance the principle of community interest in the prevention of breaches of international law.

Implicit in the adoption of the two hypotheses upon which this work is based is the questioning of the archfiction of international law—absolute state sovereignty. "Sovereignty is essentially a concept

[21] Cf. Postulate 4, *The International Law of the Future*, Carnegie Endowment for International Peace (1944), 32.

of completeness. It is also a legal creation, and as such, is a paradox, if not an absolute impossibility, for if a state is a sovereign in the complete sense, it knows no law and therefore abolishes, at the moment of its creation, the jural creator which gave it being."[22] "Legal fiction," says Morris Cohen, "is the mask that progress must wear to pass the faithful but blear-eyed watchers of our ancient legal treasures. But though legal fictions are useful in thus mitigating or absorbing the shock of innovation, they work havoc in the form of intellectual confusion."[23] The establishment of the United Nations presents an opportunity for innovations. The development of the organization of the international community suggests the ultimate possibility of substituting some kind of joint sovereignty, the supremacy of the common will, for the old single state sovereignty. The official proposals of the United States with reference to the international control of atomic energy rests on an altered attitude toward the fiction of sovereignty. Mr. Baruch, in his presentation of these proposals to the United Nations Commission, declared that the peoples of the democracies "are unwilling to be fobbed off by mouthings about narrow sovereignty . . ."[24] But in the same Commission the Soviet representative declared that the "principle of sovereignty is one of the cornerstones on which the United Nations structure is built; if this were touched the whole existence and future of the United Nations would be threatened."[25] The path to progress may be long and thorny; this book does not seek to catalogue the obstacles or to hazard guesses on how soon they may be surmounted.

The two hypotheses taken as the basis of the present re-examination of international law would involve an alteration of the traditional notion of sovereignty. They do not exhaust the needs or possibilities of the situation, and their preliminary development here is advanced with no claim to completeness or exclusiveness. If they constitute an introduction to a much larger task, they will serve the purpose for which they are designed. Article 13 of the Charter of the United Nations imposes upon the General Assembly the duty to

[22] Jessup, op. cit., supra note 1, p. 49.
[23] Cohen, Law and the Social Order (1933), 126.
[24] UN Atomic Energy Commission, Official Records, No. 1 (June 14, 1946), 6.
[25] The International Control of Atomic Energy: Growth of a Policy, Dept. of State Pub. 2702 (1946), 219.

"initiate studies and make recommendations for the purpose of . . . encouraging the progressive development of international law and its codification." There are abundant opportunities for fruitful work in discharge of this obligation.[26] Such development can best proceed by utilizing the experience of the past centuries, reviewed in the light of new concepts. As Chief Justice Stone pointed out, "the problem . . . of jurisprudence in the modern world is the reconciliation of the demands . . . that law shall at once have continuity with the past and adaptability to the present and the future." [27] Ignorance of the progress already achieved in the development of international law over the past three centuries and blindness to the still primitive character of the international legal system are equally inimical to the further progress which must be made if all civilization is not to go the way of Hiroshima and Nagasaki.

[26] See Eagleton, "International Law and the Charter of the United Nations," 39 Am. J. Int. L. (1945), 751; Jessup, Development of International Law by the United Nations, ibid., 754.

[27] Stone, "The Common Law in the United States," 50 Harv. L. Rev. (1936), 4, 11.

CHAPTER II

THE SUBJECTS OF A MODERN
LAW OF NATIONS

INTERNATIONAL LAW is generally defined or described as law applicable to relations between states. States are said to be the subjects of international law and individuals only its "objects." Treatises on international law accordingly usually proceed at the very outset to examine the nature and essential characteristics of the fictitious jural person known as the state.

But there has welled up through the years a growing opposition to this traditional concept. Numerous writers have attacked the dogma from a variety of approaches. Duguit, Krabbe, Kelsen, and others have impugned the philosophical and juridical basis of the concept.[1] Georges Scelle has called the traditional view "une vue fausse, une abstraction anthropomorphique, historiquement responsable du caractère fictif et de la paralysie de la science traditionelle du droit des gens." [2] The record of progress toward the goal of acknowledging the international legal position of the individual has been traced by many jurists.[3] Politis has graphically said: "Formerly

[1] Duguit, 1 *Traité de droit constitutionnel* (3rd ed. 1927), 713, Krabbe "L'Idée moderne de l'état," 13 *Hague recueil des cours* (1926), Vol. III, 514; *The Modern Idea of the State* (1922); Kelsen, *General Theory of Law and the State* (1945).

[2] Scelle, "Règles générales du droit de la paix," 46 *Hague recueil des cours* (1933), Vol. IV, 343. Cf. Dunn, "The International Rights of Individuals," *Am. Soc. Int. L., Proc.* (1941), 14, 16.

[3] Cf. e.g. Segal, *L'Individu en droit international positif* (1932); Politis, *The New Aspects of International Law* (1928); Le Fur, "Le Développement historique du droit international," 41 *Hague recueil des cours* (1932), Vol. III, 505; Ténékidès, *L'Individu dans l'ordre juridique international* (1933); Lauterpacht, *Private Law Sources and Analogies of International Law* (1927), 73 ff., 305. See also Garner, "Le Développement et les tendances récentes du droit international," 35 *Hague recueil des cours* (1931), Vol. I, esp. 695 n. 1; Aufricht, "Personality in International Law," 37 *Am. Pol. Sci. Rev.* (1943), 217 ff.; Pintor, "Les Sujets du droit international autres que les états," 41 *Hague recueil des cours* (1932), Vol. III.

the sovereign State was an iron cage for its citizens from which they were obliged to communicate with the outside world, in a legal sense, through very close-set bars. Yielding to the logic of events, the bars are beginning to open. The cage is becoming shaky and will finally collapse. Men will then be able to hold free and untrammelled communication with each other across their respective frontiers." [4]

Since this discussion starts with the hypothesis that a change in the old fundamental doctrine has been accepted and proceeds from that point to consider certain modifications in the traditional body of international law which would be desirable or necessary if individuals as well as states were considered subjects of the law of nations, there is no occasion here to continue the debate as to whether under existing international law individuals are subjects of the law or only its "destinataires." [5] Those who will may consider some of the observations here as *lex lata*, while others will deal with them as made *de lege ferenda*. It remains true, as Sir John Fischer Williams has said, that it "is obvious that international relations are not limited to relations between states." [6] The function of international law is to provide a legal basis for the orderly management of international relations. The traditional nature of that law was keyed to the actualities of past centuries in which international relations were interstate relations. The actualities have changed; the law is changing.[7] The conclusion may be that states remain the organs for conducting even those international relations which involve individuals, and it may also be true, as the same able writer has said, that when "the world is more fully organized politically . . . the disappearance of the State as we know it will mean that international law will either be wholly absorbed into a general body of law or will preserve a separate existence only as a

[4] Politis, *op. cit., supra* note 3, p. 31.
[5] Cf. Spiropoulos, *Traité théorique et pratique de droit international public* (1933), 42 ff.
[6] Williams, *Aspects of Modern International Law* (1939), 18.
[7] "The existence of rules of international law governing relations between states and foreign individuals is not inconceivable, but their existence has not been proved, and, if it should be proved the contents of the rules will necessarily differ from those rules which concern relations between sovereigns." Feilchenfeld, *Public Debts and State Succession* (1931), 582. As indicated above, this discussion assumes the proof by way of hypothesis and proceeds to consider the content of the international law of the future.

branch of a general system." [8] But one may also agree with him that de Madariaga's insistence that we want to supplant *international* law by "world law, or to use a fine Roman expression, *jus gentium, le droit des gens,* the law of the World Commonwealth," involves merely a superficial change of name.[9] The term "Modern Law of Nations" has been used here nevertheless to suggest the point that the acceptance of the hypothesis on which this discussion proceeds involves a break with the past.

For the purposes of this context, therefore, international law or the law of nations must be defined as law applicable to states in their mutual relations and to individuals in their relations with states.[10] International law may also, under this hypothesis, be applicable to certain interrelationships of individuals themselves, where such inter-relationships involve matters of international concern. So long, how-ever, as the international community is composed of states, it is only through an exercise of their will, as expressed through treaty or agreement or as laid down by an international authority deriving its power from states, that a rule of law becomes binding upon an indi-vidual.[11] When there is created some kind of international constitu-ent assembly or world parliament representative of the people of the world and having authority to legislate, it will then be possible to assert that international law derives authority from a source ex-ternal to the states. This would be true even though states might well have been the original creators of such a representative legislature. The inescapable fact is that the world is today organized on the basis of the coexistence of states, and that fundamental changes will take place only through state action, whether affirmative or negative.[12]

[8] Williams, *Chapter on Current International Law and the League of Nations* (1929), 19, 20. Cf. Schucking, *The International Union of the Hague Conferences* (1918), 147, 150.

[9] Williams, *op. cit., supra* note 6, pp. 18, 20, and cf. his *Chapter on Current International Law and the League of Nations,* 7, note 2.

[10] Cf. Spiropoulos, *op. cit., supra* note 5, p. 43.

[11] Cf. Borchard, "The Access of Individuals to International Courts," 24 *Am. Soc. Int. L.* (1930), 359. Many writers distinguish the individual as a sub-ject of international law from the individual as a creator of norms; cf. e.g. Rundstein, "L'Arbitrage international en matière privée," 23 *Hague recueil des cours* (1928), Vol. III, 331; Strupp, "Les Règles générales du droit de la paix," 47 *ibid.* (1934), Vol. I, 263; Akzin, *Problèmes fondamentaux du droit inter-national public* (1929), 125 ff.

[12] 1 Hyde, sec. 11A-C, 38 ff.

The only possible alternative would be revolution on a world scale which would circumvent the existing system of states as national revolutions have circumvented pre-existing constitutional or governmental law and procedure. It is true to say that states themselves operate by virtue of the will of individuals and that the individual is thus the ultimate source of authority. Yet so firmly rooted is the international state system that we are accustomed to think in terms of the state itself as the ultimate authority and sole actor.

There is no novelty in the suggestion that states may delegate the exercise of some of their customary attributes. The classic case is that of the European Commission of the Danube established under the Treaty of Paris of March 30, 1856. The Commission was given legislative, administrative, and judicial powers.[13] The Central Commission for the Navigation of the Rhine established under Article 109 of the Final Act of Vienna of 1815 had comparable powers.[14] The regulations of these commissions were directly applicable to individuals, and individual infractions of the rules were directly cognizable by the Commissions. Thus the international bodies dealt directly with individuals in the same manner in which national bodies customarily deal with them. The same remark may be made in regard to those exceptional cases in which individuals have been given by treaty the right to appear before international tribunals.[15] The notable cases are those of the Central American Court of Justice established in 1907, the Mixed Arbitral Tribunals established by the peace treaties at the end of World War I, and the Arbitral Tribunal for dealing with the rights of minorities in Upper Silesia under the Geneva Convention of 1922 between Poland and Germany. In such cases the international tribunal acted directly upon the claim of an individual and the judgment ran in favor of the individual. It is not yet clear to what extent the powers delegated to the organs of the United Nations will be

[13] See Ténékidès, *L'Individu dans l'ordre juridique international* (1933), 84; Hostie, "Examen de quelques règles du droit international dans le domaine des communications et du transit," 40 *Hague recueil des cours* (1932), Vol. II, 488 ff.; Chamberlain, *The Regime of International Rivers: Danube and Rhine* (1923), c. 3, p. 47. See also P.C.I.J. Ser. B, No. 14, Adv. Op. on Jurisdiction of European Commission.

[14] Hostie, *loc. cit.*, note 13.

[15] The question of individuals as beneficiaries of treaty provisions is discussed in Chap. VI.

exercised directly upon the individual. The measures of enforcement ordered by the Security Council may be directly applicable to individuals.[16] The development of the Trusteeship Council and the Commission on Human Rights may produce similar situations. Current proposals for the establishment of a United Nations Atomic Energy Commission may well lead to the creation, by special treaty to which states will be parties, of a rule-making authority which will enact rules directly binding on individuals. Thus it may become a rule of international law that no state shall use atomic bombs; it may also become a rule of international law that no state *or individual* shall without international license manufacture, possess, or traffic in atomic bombs or fissionable materials.[17]

States may agree to separate the legislative function from the law-enforcing function so far as international agencies are concerned. Enforcement may be left to national authorities as is customary under treaties for the protection of fisheries, the control of the slave trade, and the traffic in narcotics. The degree of delegation does not affect the principle. Just as a national legislature may delegate certain regulatory authority and powers to an administrative commission or officer, so the community of states may delegate to an international authority. Although one may in both cases trace the authority back to its original source, the individual will deal with the immediate and not the remote source and will regard the former as the origin of his rights and duties.[18]

In using the term "individual" in connection with the hypothesis here under discussion, it should be understood that various types of groups or associations of individuals are included. International law, particularly in claims cases, is accustomed to dealing with corporations as "citizens" or "nationals" of states in the same way in which it deals with natural persons. So long as national law creates these

[16] But the national state may be the intermediary through which measures are brought home to the individual, cf. Eagleton, "The Individual and International Law," *Am. Soc. Int. L., Proc.* (1946), 22, 24, citing Public Law 264, 79th Cong. 1st Sess., 59 Stat. 619 (1945) on enforcement of United Nations measures by the President.

[17] See the recommendations of the report of the Atomic Energy Commission to the Security Council, contemplating the definition of international crimes in connection with the use of atomic weapons and the punishment of both persons and nations, 15 Dept. of State *Bulletin* (1946), 1090.

[18] Cf. Balladore Palliere, *Diritto internazionale pubblico* (1937), 286.

juristic persons, international law must deal with them as individuals.[19] Accordingly, under the hypothesis, corporations or partnerships may also be subjects of international law. In this instance, however, the fiction of the juristic person introduces new complications in the international field, since a corporation may be created under the law of State A, may have its principal place of business in State B, may have directors who are nationals of State C and stockholders who are nationals of State D.[20] Problems resulting from such situations will be further considered in Chapter IV.

Special mention should be made of the problem created by the growing tendency of the state to assume and to discharge functions which in the formative period of international law were normally considered to be the function of private interests.[21] Where the state, for example, sets up a government corporation to manage a fleet of merchant vessels or to operate a government monopoly in matches or tobacco, international law has tended toward the acceptance of a rule which would distinguish the corporation from the state. The development has taken place especially in connection with the law of sovereign immunity before the courts of another state; such immunity is denied to government corporations in the jurisprudence of many countries.[22] Even where no governmental corporation is interposed, the sovereign character of the state has not been recognized by some courts when the state acts as a private trader.[23] In a socialized state it would seem to be distinctly to the advantage of the state to separate

[19] "Every system of law that has attained a certain stage of development seems compelled by the ever-increasing complexity of human affairs to add to the number of persons provided for it by the natural world, to create persons who are not men." Pollock and Maitland, I, *History of English Law* (1st ed.), 469, quoted by Fischer Williams in "The Legal Character of the Bank of International Settlements," 24 *Am. J. Int. L.* (1930), 665, 666.

[20] See Timberg, "Corporate Fictions: Logical, Social, and International Implications," 46 *Col. L. Rev.* (1946), 533, 572.

[21] See Friedmann, "The Growth of State Control over the Individual, and Its Effect upon the Rules of International State Responsibility," 19 *Brit. Y. B. Int. L.* (1938), 118.

[22] "Harvard Research in International Law, Draft Convention on Competence of Courts in Regard to Foreign States," Art. 12 and Comment, 26 *Am. J. Int. L. Supp.* (1932), 641.

[23] See *ibid.*, Art. 11 and Comment, 597 ff. and cf. the changing view of the Supreme Court of the United States as reflected in Republic of Mexico v. Hoffman, 324 *U.S.* 30 (1945).

its political character from its business functions in order that economic relations may be carried on without the frictions and prestige considerations which may be involved if the business is handled on a political level. Perhaps the Soviet corporations fulfill this function.[24] It has been found useful, for example, for European railway administrations, both public and private, to arrange their affairs through the Union of International Transport by Rail, before whose arbitral tribunal no distinction is made between the governmental and the private administration.[25] The formation of international corporate bodies in finance, such as the International Bank for Reconstruction and Development and the International Monetary Fund, in the development of atomic energy, as in the proposed United Nations Atomic Energy Commission, and in other fields, may serve in international economic relations to reduce the number of instances in which private individual and public governmental interests have clashed on the international level.[26] There is a corresponding possibility that all clashes of interest would be raised at once to the level of national interests with ensuing complications in international relations. The recognition of the international legal personality of corporate or other bodies, whether private, governmental, or intergovernmental, would tend to bring their interrelationships under normal international legal controls, exercised by appropriate international organizations and procedures which would need to be established.

Since statehood is not here an essential criterion for a subject of international law, there ceases to be any difficulty about the legal

[24] See Hazard, "Soviet Government Corporations" (1943), 41 Mich. L. Rev. 850. Cf. the view expressed by Lord Maugham in The Cristina, 54 Times Law Reports 512 (1938), 32 Am. J. Int. L., 825, 848 (1938): "The Soviet Republic has apparently adopted the admirable practice of owning its merchant ships through limited companies, and does not claim—even if it could, which for my part I should doubt—any immunity whatever in relation to such ships."

[25] See Hudson and Sohn, "Fifty Years of Arbitration in the Union of International Transport by Rail," 37 Am. J. Int. L., 600 (1943).

[26] See Timberg, op. cit., supra note 20, 556: "Communication of the Delegation of the United States to the Secretary-General of the United Nations (Sept. 24, 1946)," 15 Dept. of State Bulletin 659; Finer, "The T.V.A., Lessons for International Application" (1944), I.L.O. Studies and Reports, Ser. B. No. 37; Schmitthoff, "The International Corporation," 30 Transactions of the Grotius Society (1945), 165. It is interesting to note that fifteen governments have agreed to organize a "Caribbean Tourist Development Association" which is to be a Delaware corporation; 15 Dept. of State Bulletin (1946), 735.

personality of various other entities. In traditional international law there has been debate about the status of the Holy See, the great chartered companies of an earlier period, various "semi-independent" political entities, and international organizations. The Dutch East India Company and the British East India Company had the power to make war and peace and to conclude treaties on which their states relied as the basis of rights. Because of the traditional concept that only states were international persons, Judge Huber as sole arbitrator in the Palmas Island case between the United States and the Netherlands felt compelled to hold that the agreements made by these companies were not "in the international law sense, treaties or conventions capable of creating rights and obligations such as may, in international law, arise out of treaties." But at the same time he felt impelled to attribute to them certain legal significance which is hardly distinguishable in fact from that which they would have had if he had called them international law treaties.[27] Under traditional international law, third states did not attribute the quality of statehood to the native princes of India although, perhaps as a matter of domestic policy, the British courts treated them as such.[28] In the United States, although the Supreme Court has applied the international law rules concerning treaties to agreements with the Indian tribes, their status was early determined by Chief Justice Marshall to be that of "domestic dependent nations." [29] An international tribunal has held that the Cayuga Indians had no standing before it save as represented by a state.[30] Under the hypothesis here taken, these entities may also be subjects of international law, as may other national minority groups which may come under the protection of special provisions in treaties.

Colonies and other political subdivisions have long been admitted

[27] Scott, *Hague Court Reports*, 2d Ser. (1932), 115 ff.; cf. Lawrence, *The Principles of International Law* (4th ed., 1910), 73 ff.; Wheaton, *Elements of International Law* (8th ed., 1936), 26.

[28] Mighell v. Sultan of Johore [1894], 1 Q.B. 149; Duff Development Co. v. Kelantan [1924], A.C. 797. A parallel situation is presented by the recognition of the status of the Philippine Commonwealth in courts of the United States: Bradford v. Chase National Bank 24 F. Supp. 28 (1938); Hooven and Allison Co. v. Evatt, 324 U.S. 652 (1945).

[29] Cherokee Nation v. Georgia, 5 Peters 1, 17 (1831).

[30] Great Britain (The Cayuga Indians Claim) v. United States, "United States Great Britain Arbitration," *Nielsen's Report* (1926), 272, 307.

as members of various international unions such as the Universal Postal Union and the International Institute of Refrigeration. Under Article 1 of the Covenant of the League of Nations they could also become members of the League if they were "fully self-governing"; the provision was designed to provide for the membership of the British dominions and India. This situation has necessitated fine legal distinctions, since the entities were not states and yet had a certain international position.[81] According to Schwarzenberger, "The attempts which have been made to decide in the abstract whether entities which are not states are subjects or objects of international law do not lead beyond mutually contradictory assertions. The only premise which it is safe to state, is that the existing subjects of international law are free to extend the application of international law to any entity whom they see fit to admit to the realm of the international legal system." [82] All such entities are here recognized as subjects of international law.

There has been debate also about the status of various international organizations.[83] Whether or not the League of Nations should be considered an international person was hotly debated, the juridical arguments reflecting the political controversy over the question whether the League was to be considered a "super-state." [84] Sir John Fischer Williams calls attention to the striking case of the international personality of the Reparations Commission established under the Treaty of Versailles. Once created by states, the Commission enjoyed a large degree of independence. It could not be ordered by the Allied Government "not to give Germany 'a just opportunity to be heard.'" A delegate on the Commission was not in legal contemplation the agent of his government and was not paid by his government; he could be recalled by his government, but his acts were not subject to governmental ratification. The judicial decisions of the

[81] Cf. the solution of Strupp, *Éléments du droit international public universel, européen et américain* (1927), 22–3.

[82] Schwarzenberger, 1 *International Law* (1945), 62.

[83] Cf. Brierly, "Le Fondement du caractère obligatoire du droit international," 23 *Hague recueil des cours* (1928), 526.

[84] "The League of Nations appeared before the Court of Appeal of Geneva as an 'international organism' enjoying privileges and immunities exempting it from the jurisdiction of local courts." Allen, *The Position of Foreign States before National Courts* (1933), 6. See also Pfankuchen, *A Documentary Textbook of International Law* (1940), 52.

Commission bound the states, and majority rule applied in reaching decisions.[35]

In the formation of the various United Nations organizations, it has become customary to insert in their constitutions or charters some reference to their legal status. Thus for example Article XV of the Constitution of the Food and Agriculture Organization provides: "The Organization shall have the capacity of a legal person to perform any legal act appropriate to its purpose which is not beyond the powers granted to it by this Constitution." [36] In general the history of the drafting of these provisions suggests that the drafters were concerned chiefly with the legal status of such organizations under national law: could they take title to real and personal property, make contracts, and sue in national courts? In regard to the United Nations Organization itself, there was evident a distinct reluctance to include in the Charter any provision relative to the international status of the Organization. Thus Article 104 merely provides: "The Organization shall enjoy in the territory of each of its members such legal capacity as may be necessary for the exercise of its functions and the fulfillment of its purposes." The subcommittee of .Committee IV/2 of the San Francisco Conference, in reporting this text, stated: "As regards the question of international juridical personality, the Subcommittee has considered it superfluous to make this the subject of a text. In effect, it will be determined implicitly from the provisions

[35] Fischer Williams, "A Legal Footnote to the Story of German Reparations," 1932 *Brit. Y. B. Int. L.*, 34. See also the same author's article cited, *supra* note 19, and Hudson, *International Tribunals, Past and Future* (1944), 67, where the Bank for International Settlements is mentioned in the same connection as having the right under treaties to appear as a party before international tribunals.

[36] Food and Agricultural Organization of the United Nations, *Report of the First Session of the Conference* (1945), 87. Cf. Art. 47 of the *Convention on International Civil Aviation* (1944), Dept. of State Pub. 2282, 72; Art. 66 of the *Constitution of the World Health Organization: Final Acts of the International Health Conference, 1946*, United Nations Doc. E/155; Art. IX of the *Articles of Agreement of the International Monetary Fund* and Art. VII of the *Articles of Agreement of the International Bank for Reconstruction and Development*, Dept. of State Pub. 2187, 42 and 88; Art. XII of the *Constitution of UNESCO*, Dept. of State Pub. 2457, 21; Art. 73 of the *Suggested Charter for an International Trade Organization of the United Nations*, Dept. of State Pub 2598, 44; Art. IX, sec. 1, of the "Draft Convention for an Inter-Governmental Maritime Consultative Organization," 15 Dept. of State *Bulletin* (1946) 1096.

of the Charter taken as a whole." [37] Yet under Article 43 it is clear that the Organizations may make agreements with states, and there is no reason to believe that the agreement-making power will not be exercised also in other connections, as, for example, the current proposals for an agreement between the United Nations and the state in which its headquarters are to be located.[38]

As Borchard has suggested, we now have "autonomous corporations formed under a constitution which assures their perpetuity, grants them immunities from taxation and other local burdens, and yet subjects them to judicial responsibility for their business activities. . . . These are no longer mere agencies of the constituent states. hampered by the unanimity rule of sovereignty." [39]

The reasons why international organizations do not have a *locus standi* before the International Court of Justice are more political than juridical. The Statute of the Court retains the provision in Article 34 of the Statute of the Permanent Court of International Justice that only states may be parties in cases before the Court. A determined effort was made in the United Nations Committee of Jurists which drafted the Statute in Washington, and later in Committee IV/1 of the San Francisco Conference, to amend this article so as to permit intergovernmental organizations to have direct access to the Court as parties.[40] The International Labour Organization was the body which naturally came first to mind in this connection, and the relations between it and the Soviet Union had not been brought into adjustment. Under the Statute of the Permanent Court, the ILO was to be at liberty to furnish information in contentious labor cases, but no such case arose. In advisory proceedings, international organizations were permitted to furnish information "and even to take part in the oral proceedings which were almost invariably held." [41] The

[37] See Reiff, *Work of the United Nations Legal Committees*, 15 Dept. of State *Bulletin*, 3, 12; Preuss, "The International Organizations Immunities Act," 40 *Am. J. Int. L.* (1946), 332, 341.

[38] See UN Doc. A/67, 1 Sept. 1946, 23.

[39] Borchard, "Relation of Bretton Woods Agreements to Other Types of International Organization," Money and the Law, *Supplement N.Y.U. L. Rev.* (1945), 99, 110. Cf. Sumberg, "Financing International Institutions," 13 *Soc. Res.* (1946), 276, 278.

[40] "UNIO," 14 *Documents of the United Nations Conference on International Organization, San Francisco, 1945* (1945), 133 ff.; Vol. 13, 233, 270.

[41] Hudson, *op. cit., supra* note 35, pp. 68–9.

committee vote in both Washington and San Francisco was against the proposals for amending Article 34, but the door was left open for international organizations, if authorized by the General Assembly, to request advisory opinions.[42] Under Articles 34 and 66 of the new Statute, international organizations may furnish information to the Court in appropriate cases. The United Nations itself, represented by its Security Council or General Assembly,[43] may request advisory opinions, as could the Council and Assembly of the League of Nations under the old statute, but the United Nations could not be a party to a contested case before the Court. The result has no significance in law or logic relating to the legal personality of international organizations. The consequence of the reluctance to accord them standing before the International Court of Justice is revealed by a provision in the Working Draft of the proposed "Convention/Agreement between the United Nations and the United States of America" relative to the location of the United Nations headquarters in the United States. Under Article 38 of the Draft, disputes concerning interpretation or application are to be referred to a special tribunal of three arbitrators, the third member in case of deadlock to be selected by the President of the International Court of Justice.[44]

THE DOCTRINE OF EQUALITY

The proposition that such individuals, groups, or bodies have legal personality and are subjects of international law does not necessarily imply that they have equal rights and duties. A fundamental document such as the Charter of the United Nations may confine membership in that organization to states, thus excluding from membership individuals, corporations, and various types of dependencies.[45]

[42] Art. 96 of the Charter.
[43] The Economic and Social Council was given the right to request advisory opinions by a resolution of the General Assembly adopted on Dec. 11, 1946, under the authority of Art. 96 of the Charter; UN Doc. A/201. A similar right has been given to specialized agencies; Hudson, "The Twenty-fifth Year of the World Court," 41 Am. J. Int. L. (1947), 1, 14.
[44] UN Doc. A/67, 1 Sept., 1946, 23. See also Domke, "The Settlement of Disputes in International Agencies," 1 (New Series) The Arb. J., 145.
[45] But see Kelsen, "Membership in the United Nations," 46 Col. L. Rev. (1946), 391, 392 on the question whether the original members of the United Nations are all states.

But another instrument of like origin may create an international organization composed of states, dependencies and corporations, or individuals. A treaty would thus no longer be properly defined as an agreement between states; it may be an agreement between a state and an individual.[46] The criterion distinguishing a treaty from what has usually heretofore been called a contract is whether the agreement imposes obligations and confers rights under international or under municipal law. There have been examples of agreements between states which were municipal law contracts, as, for instance, the usual type of contract of State A to purchase land from State B for the erection of an embassy and some loan contracts such as the Inter-Allied loans of World War I, which are couched in terms of municipal law and not of international.[47] A concession contract from a state to a national (individual or corporation) of another state or to a stateless person may also, under our hypothesis, be an international law agreement, thus eliminating the type of controversy revealed in certain decisions of Mixed Claims Commissions.[48] Special international tribunals may be established for the adjudication of controversies arising out of such contracts between a state and an individual, and other international tribunals may be open only to states, as is prescribed by Article 34 of the Statute of the International Court of Justice.

It is thus apparent that much of the existing law concerning the nature and qualifications of states as international persons is still pertinent, regardless of the acceptance of the hypothesis that individuals are also subjects of the same law. But certain concepts stand in need of clarification. The principle of the equality of states is among the principles which need to be reappraised. In saying that states are equal, the assumption is implicit that all the subjects of international law enjoy equality, one with another. As Dickinson has pointed out, this statement is true of equality in the sense of "equality before the law" or "equal protection of the law," which is a matter of status, but not necessarily true of equality used in the sense of "equality of

[46] This subject is more fully explored in Chap. VI.

[47] See Mann, "The Law Governing State Contracts," 1944 *Brit. Y. B. Int. L.,* 11.

[48] See Judge Nielsen's dissent in United States of America on behalf of International Fisheries Company v. United Mexican States, Nielsen, *International Law Applied to Reclamations* (1933), 520.

capacity for rights," which he notes is not essential to the reign of law.[49] In Dickinson's sense, equality would still appertain to all subjects of international law, whether individuals or states; both would enjoy the equal protection of the law. But the actual existing inequalities of capacity for rights which is apparent in the present international state system would continue and be sharpened with reference to the differences between states and individuals.

As is also true of other parts of international law, the writings on the subject of equality often fail to distinguish between the legal principle and the political maxim. There was a historical period in which the doctrine of equality of states had to make its way as the national state emerged in Europe out of the collapse of the empire, but for a century at least statesmen and international politicians have been able to assert the existence of the principle without fear of verbal contradiction but with some certainty that, while equality is preached, inequality will be practiced. The international problem of equality is the result of the coexistence of two facts:

1. States are not factually equal; their power differs; ·
2. States have "feelings," and the psychological factor cannot be ignored in international politics.

Power may be overcome by superior power or checked by an equivalence of power. From this principle there has evolved, in the interest of maintaining the peace, the plan of the balance of power. Power may be surrendered, and from this principle stem plans for disarmament, for an international police force, and for a world state. Power may be utilized by those who have it for the general advantage of the international community as a result of a conviction of self-interest in such utilization. This is the theoretical basis of the United Nations Charter, which recognizes the existence of power and entrusts its exercise, under agreed limitations, to those who possess it.

Just as within states the last hundred years reveals a growth of

[49] Dickinson, *The Equality of States in International Law* (1920), 4. As Kelsen, *op. cit., supra* note 45, p. 398 points out, Art. 35 of the Statute of the International Court of Justice recognizes the principle of equality between Members of the United Nations and non-Members, by requiring that conditions on which the court is to be open to "other states" shall not "place the parties in a position of inequality before the Court."

social consciousness and of a public conscience, so has it been, in lesser degree, in the international community. Contrasting the Congress of Vienna of 1815 and its aftermath with the Paris Peace Conference of 1919 and its aftermath, one finds in both situations the original dominance of the Great Powers, but in the latter period, as the League of Nations developed, there is a growing participation and, comparatively, a growing influence of the middle and small powers commanding a world audience through the Geneva forum. Moving on to the San Francisco Conference of 1945 and the early stages of the United Nations, one observes that the voice of the middle and small powers is louder, more insistent, and, again comparatively, more productive of results.

The psychological factor may properly be called the prestige factor. This is not universally true, as for example when the small riparian states on the Danube have demanded representation on a river commission with a view to exercising at least some influence over decisions that vitally affect them. Here a legal interest may be involved and appeal made to the legal principle of equality before the law. But the insistence of certain diminutive states at the Hague Peace Conference of 1907 on permanent and equal representation on the bench of the proposed International Court of Arbitral Justice was much less genuinely a reflection of legal interest than of prestige considerations.

As one examines the manifestations of the doctrine of equality of states in international relations, one seems to detect the emergence of a notion that it does no violence to the doctrine if unequal rights or privileges are accorded on the basis of a formula which fairly reflects a recognizable degree of interest. One may compare the United States constitutional doctrine that a reasonable classification of persons affected saves a statute from doing violence to the constitutional guarantee of the equal protection of the laws. Examples of this emergent notion are abundant in connection with various international organizations. For instance, in the International Institute of Agriculture voting was determined by membership in one of five classes, members of Class I having five votes and members of Class V having one vote. Equality was admitted in the sense that each state was free to choose the class to which it wished to belong, but membership in Class I involved an assessment of 16 units of the budgetary base, and membership in Class V involved the assessment of only one unit.[50] A comparable plan in the Bretton Woods agreement led states to seek a larger allotment of shares in the Fund in order to be entitled to larger credit facilities, and to avoid larger allotments of shares in the Bank, with resulting larger obligations to subscribe capital.

It is relatively easy to find formulae for inequalities in voting power and in representation in technical international organizations, where interest can be measured by statistics or factual criteria. It is supremely difficult to find acceptable formulae in political organizations, where the prestige factor and problems of political existence may be at stake. Great powers have power because they are great and not because a skillful draftsman has invented an ingenious formula. The platform of the League to Enforce Peace suggested in 1918 that "The representation of the different nations in the organs of the League should be in proportion to the responsibilities and obligations they assume." This suggestion is not dissimilar to the actual basis of five-great-powers control of the Security Council of the United Nations. The provisions of the Charter on regional arrangements reflect in large part the wide concessions which the United States, in pursuance of the Good Neighbor Policy, has actually made to the principle of political equality in the Americas. The United Nations organization is affirmed by the Charter to be "based upon the principle of the sovereign equality of all its Members," but no one can deny that unequal rights, privileges, and responsibilities are also recognized throughout the Charter.[51] Some of the factual inequalities are based on the more readily measurable types of interest, as in the composition of the Trusteeship Council. Some, as in the voting formula for the Security Council, are based on the inescapable fact of power differentials. It is true, as Woodrow Wilson said, that "all nations are equally interested in the peace of the world"; it is not true that all can make equal contribution to its maintenance.[52]

[50] A similar plan had been utilized in the agreement of December 1907 creating the International Office of Public Health.

[51] In his fable *Animal Farm* (1946) George Orwell describes the amendment of the animals' principle "All Animals are Equal" by the addition of the words "But Some Animals are More Equal than Others." The Charter might realistically be amended in the same way.

[52] The above discussion of equality is based largely on the writer's introduction to a series of studies on the subject prepared in the graduate seminar in

The doctrine of equality of states has been championed by small states and their spokesmen. It is they who see in it a safeguard against encroachments by the greater powers. The great powers have their divisions among themselves within their small circle, but in a major sense the conflict of interest in terms of designing international organization or world government has been between the great powers on the one side and the small and middle powers on the other. When the international community lacked any form of internationally democratic organization, there was no other safeguard to which the smaller powers could appeal.[58] With the development of international organization, even in the still relatively primitive form which the United Nations takes, there is a possibility that the function of equality as a legal and political principle may be fulfilled by a doctrine of community interest, the acceptance of which is taken as a second hypothesis in this discussion. Given the forum of the General Assembly and also of the Security Council, to which any state may appeal, and given the extension of the acceptance of the compulsory jurisdiction of the International Court of Justice, all operating on the basis of the acceptance of the principle of community interest in the maintenance of a developed law of nations, the safeguards of the international organization may suffice to protect the legal interests of all subjects of international law, whether states or individuals. Thus all subjects of the law would be guaranteed equal protection of the law, although equal capacity for rights would still differ with factual criteria. The prestige factor would still need to be taken into account as a matter of international politics, as is true in any social relationships, but it would tend to become more clearly recognized in its true light, stripped of confusion with the sound legal principle of equality. States would still seek the prestige of representation on various international commissions and other bodies, but progress could be made

---

International Law at Columbia University; Peterson, "Political Inequality at the Congress of Vienna," 60 *Pol. Sci. Q.* (1945), 527. Herrera, "Evolution of Equality of States in the Inter-American System," 61 *ibid.* (1946), 90. The writer has also had the benefit of other unpublished studies of the seminar, especially Lande, *Revindication of the Principle of Legal Equality of States in the Period Between the Franco-Prussian War and the First World War.* The first installment of Dr. Lande's study has been published in 62 *Pol. Sci. Q.* (1947), 258.

[58] As Lande, *op. cit., supra* note 52 points out, the small states have at times been the beneficiaries of the rivalries among the Great Powers.

along the lines of the development of an international civil service in which individuals would be selected on the basis of their competence rather than on that of state representation. The formula already in use in UNRRA and in the Charter (Article 101)—"Due regard shall be paid to the importance of recruiting the staff on as wide a geographical basis as possible"—would still represent a sound principle of administrative organization.

The acceptance of the adaptation of the legal principle of equality of states to the principle of equality of subjects of the law, whether states or individuals, is necessary to the development of new doctrines of human rights under the Charter of the United Nations.[54]

It is not impossible to accord equal protection of the law to states and to individuals when these two different subjects of international law appear before an international forum. The experiment has been tried with some success in the special regime for the protection of the minorities in Upper Silesia. Kaeckenbeeck, in his excellent analysis of this regime, says: "Even when, as a result of what is almost a fiction, a state and a private person stand side by side as parties before an international tribunal—a new and still quite exceptional departure—it is essential that the impartiality of the judge should not be affected by the difference in the importance of the parties, if I may put it in this way, and in this connection it is essential that the judge should treat the parties as equals. But from another standpoint, if we are not to lose touch with reality, it must be admitted that the interests of a state and the interests of an individual are not on the same level, and further, that the feelings of a nation, with their consequences, both national and international, are not commensurate with the psychological and material satisfaction which an individual receives when his strict rights are recognized." [55] He notes that in the matter of costs of the judicial or arbitral procedure, for example, the state is in a very different position from the individual and that "costly justice . . . would upset the balance very strongly in favour of the State." Similarly in the matter of language, which is always a diffi-

---

[54] See Chap. IV.
[55] Kaeckenbeeck, The International Experiment of Upper Silesia (1942), 78. Cf. in the same sense Ténékidès, L'Individu dans l'ordre juridique international (1933), 35.

culty for any international body, states are in a position to hire skill-ful attorneys to plead in any required language, whereas the individ-ual would be at a complete loss unless his own language could be used.[56] Kaeckenbeeck's observations are directed to a pioneering experiment in the field of international recognition of individual rights, and it was essential to the success of that experiment that com-promise and adjustment should play a large part. Similarly in con-nection with the Mixed Arbitral Tribunals established under the Peace Treaties at the end of World War I, it has been noted that, while the individual could appear in his own right before the tribunal, there was no procedure open to him for the collection of a judgment rendered in his favor save through the assistance of his government.[57] As the law develops and the world community becomes more familiar with the problem and its possible solutions, the difficulties will tend to minimize themselves, although they may never be wholly obliterated. One difficulty inherent in the minority regimes was that they were imposed only on certain countries and did not represent a principle accepted by the whole world and notably by the great states. When the position of the individual is internationally recog-nized and the rights of man are placed under international protec-tion against both the small and the great states, equality before the law may be insisted on with respect to both states and in-dividuals.

It has been said that "big commercial and industrial enterprises increasingly often deal with States on a footing of complete equality," and the arbitration between the Lena Goldfields Company Ltd. and the Soviet Union has been cited in this connection.[58] In some in-stances the private corporation may even be factually in a more advantageous position than the government with which it deals.[59]

[56] Kaeckenbeeck, *op. cit., supra* note 55, p. 500
[57] Blühdorn, "Le Fonctionnement et la jurisprudence des tribunaux arbi-traux mixtes créés par les traités de Paris," 41 *Hague recueil des cours* (1932), Vol. III, 141.
[58] Cf. Schwarzenberger, *op. cit., supra* note 32, p. 215. The Arbitral award in this case is summarized in *Annual Dig. of Pub. Int. L. Cases* (1929-30), Case No. 1.
[59] The United Fruit Company might be suggested as an example; see Kepner, *Social Aspects of the Banana Industry* (1936) and sources there cited; also the statement of allegations in American Banana Co. v. United Fruit Co. 213 U. S. 347 (1909).

The necessity for considering the problem of equality in such international commercial relationships would take a different form but would not be eliminated if there should be "international incorporation of private business firms conducting business operations on an international or world scale." [60]

If the foregoing be now factually true regarding the relations between private corporations and states, there is no reason why a modern law of nations should not embody the result in an appropriately qualified rule of law. *A fortiori*, equality between states and international organizations presents no legal difficulty if both are considered subjects of the law of nations.

A modern law of nations must also take account of the principle of equality as applied to relations between and among individuals who are nationals of different states, whether those states be "sovereign" equals or political subdivisions of a world government. Some aspects of traditional international law are illuminating in this connection even though they have been conceived in terms of interstate rights and duties with respect to individuals characterized as citizens and aliens.

In the history of the law of responsibility of states for injuries to aliens, it has been urged, notably by Latin-American jurists, that the standard of treatment of aliens should be equality with nationals. This standard has been accepted by some other states, such as the United States, only as a minimum. This latter point of view is supported by invoking the doctrine of the international standard. Thus it is maintained that if the treatment of nationals in country X falls below the minimum standard, equality of treatment is no defense to a claim on behalf of an injured alien. [61]

In commercial treaties there is a standard clause known as the national treatment clause, much used especially in connection with shipping, which assures to the nationals of one contracting party

---

[60] Studies of the need for and methods of such incorporation were suggested by the delegation of the United States to the Secretary-General of the United Nations on September 24, 1946. 15 Dept. of State *Bulletin,* 659.

[61] See Chap. V. But the Montevideo Convention of 1933 on Rights and Duties of States declares in Article 9: "Nationals and foreigners are under the same protection of the law and the national authorities, and the foreigners may not claim rights other or more extensive than those of nationals." *U.S. Treaty Ser.,* No. 881.

equality with the nationals of the other in specified matters.[62] Such national treatment clauses are to be contrasted with most-favored-nation clauses, which use as a standard equality with the most favorable treatment accorded to nationals of another state.[63]

The same principle of legal equality is to be found in the law restraining states from certain types of discrimination. This is a subject on which adequate monographic studies are lacking, but certain examples may be noted.[64] Thus the United States Immigration Act of 1924 was questioned by various foreign governments on the ground that it contained improper discrimination against their nationals. The Japanese objection was specifically based on the ground that the proposed law was "obviously aimed against Japanese as a nation." [65]

By no means all examples of discriminatory treatment are illegal under international law; states have wide latitude to accord or withhold special privileges, and this latitude may be used for bargaining purposes. The British-American Claims Commission under the Treaty of August 18, 1910 properly refused to award compensation, even under its equity powers, when the United States had compensated some but not all cable companies damaged by its cutting submarine cables during the Spanish-American war, the original destruction having been a lawful exercise of belligerent rights.[66] A tribunal of the Permanent Court of Arbitration in 1904 held in the Venezuelan Preferential Claims case that the three countries, Germany, Great Britain, and Italy, which had resorted to force to compel Venezuela

[62] See McClure, *A New American Commercial Policy* (1924), 62; Cutler, "The Treatment of Foreigners," 27 *Am. J. Int. L.* (1933), 225, 226. Cf. Art. 15 of the Chicago Convention on International Civil Aviation, International Civil Aviation Conference, 1944, Dept. of State Pub. 2282, 59.

[63] "The Most Favored Nation clause embodies the principle of equality of treatment in international economic relations." Snyder, "The Most Favored Nation Clause and Recent Trade Practices," 55 *Pol. Sci. Q.* (1940), 77. Cf. *Art. 8, Suggested Charter for an International Trade Organization of the United Nations* (1946), Dept. of State Pub. 2598.

[64] See *ibid.,* Arts. 21, 22.

[65] "The Japanese Ambassador to the Secretary of State, April 10, 1924," 1924 *U. S. For. Rel.,* II, 369, 372; "The Secretary of State to President Coolidge, May 23, 1924," *ibid.,* 39. Cf. Garis, *Immigration Restriction* (1927), 263 ff., 349; Fenwick, *International Law* (1924), 177.

[66] Great Britain (Eastern Extension, Australasia & China Telegraph Co. Claim) *v.* United States (1923), *Nielsen's Report*, 73.

to pay the claims of their nationals, were entitled to priority over other creditor states in the distribution of earmarked Venezuelan assets.[67]

Inequality or discrimination as between local and foreign creditors, particularly in bankruptcy proceedings, has been so widely recognized as an injurious trade barrier that numerous bipartite and multipartite treaties have dealt with the matter. The fact that in many of these instances the distinctions are based on residence rather than on nationality is illustrative of the point that the merging of the sovereign state system into a world government would not be a panacea and would not eliminate the need for international law. There is a sufficient unanimity in the views expressed by various international bodies, business and legal, governmental and private, to warrant the devotion of early attention to this problem when the proposed International Trade Organization is established. As has been suggested, such an effort might well proceed on the principle stated by Mr. Justice Jackson that "we cannot successfully cooperate with the rest of the world in establishing a reign of law unless we are prepared to have that law sometimes operate against what would be our national advantage." [68]

INDEPENDENCE AND INTERDEPENDENCE

Independence is another quality or characteristic which states are commonly said to possess under international law. Historically this concept has been convenient because it helped to differentiate those

[67] Scott, *The Hague Court Reports* (1916), 55. In his argument before the tribunal, Wayne MacVeagh as counsel for the United States said: "It is not enough that the conduct of the Allies in making war upon Venezuela was equally meritorious with the policy pursued by the other creditor nations in abstaining from war and in seeking to collect the claims presented by them by peaceful methods. Before you can award preferential treatment to their claims, you must declare their conduct to be more meritorious than the conduct of those nations which abstained from making war; for equality of treatment is the rule, and preferential treatment can only be accorded as an award of merit." *The Venezuelan Arbitration before the Hague Tribunal, 1903, Sen. Doc.* 119, 58th Cong. 3d Sess., 1133.

[68] Nadelmann, "Legal Treatment of Foreign and Domestic Creditors," 11 *Law and Contemporary Problems* (1946), 696, 709. This article is an excellent discussion of the whole subject and contains ample citations on the points that have been noted here.

political groupings which determined their own policies, especially in international relations, from those which acknowledged a certain subordination to other groups. Only fully independent groups were considered to be "states," although the terms "semi-independent state" and even "sovereign dependency" have had currency. The doctrine had additional importance, however, as a basis for those rules of international law which sought to restrict interferences by one state in the affairs of another. An interference in the affairs of a vassal, a protectorate, a colony, or other unit in a position of political subordination to a state might be justified by that relationship, whereas it would not be justified if the other unit were also an independent state. The doctrine of independence of states is thus also linked to the development of a legal system for the protection of the weak against the strong, and in this respect it is akin to the doctrine of equality. To that extent the acceptance of the principle of community interest and the perfection of forms of international organization will tend to diminish the importance of the concept of independence, although it will remain one of the criteria for identifying a state in cases where that classification retains its importance. In this connection Chapter XI of the Charter of the United Nations with its "Declaration Regarding Non-Self-Governing Territories" and Chapters XII and XIII on the Trusteeship System and the Trusteeship Council are significant indications of the acceptance already accorded to the community interest in nonindependent groups.

It may be suggested that it would be more conformable both to the realities and to the desiderata of the international community if, instead of emphasizing that each state is independent of every other, it were frankly asserted that each state is *dependent* on all other states, linked together in the society of nations or in a world government. But the terms "dependent" and "dependence" have connotations which would clearly make them unacceptable in this connection. The same thought is conveyed by the acceptance of the hypothesis of community interest. The thought might be expressed concisely by saying that every state has the quality of "interdependence" with every other state. Interdependence would connote both rights and duties. The rights would include respect for its territorial integrity and its safety and observance toward it by all other states of the rules of international law designed for mutual well-being. The duties would include the obligation to accord to other states reciprocal respect and observance.

Limited interdependence, through cosignature of multipartite treaties, is a familiar aspect of traditional international law. For example, Paragraph I of Article 386 of the Treaty of Versailles provided that "In the event of violation of any of the conditions of Articles 380 to 386, or of disputes as to the interpretation of these articles, any interested Power can appeal to the jurisdiction instituted for the purpose by the League of Nations." This provision was quoted by the Permanent Court of International Justice in its first judgment in the case of the S.S. *Wimbledon*, involving the right of free passage provided by the treaty as the regime for the Kiel Canal. A refusal of passage to a French vessel was the subject of proceedings against Germany before the Court. The proceedings were instituted jointly by France, Great Britain, Japan, and Italy, and Germany raised the question whether such joint application was proper, inasmuch as only France could "adduce a prejudice to any pecuniary interest." The Court held that the joint application was proper, since "each of the four Applicant Powers has a clear interest in the execution of the provisions relating to the Kiel Canal, since they all possess fleets and merchant vessels flying their respective flags." [69] If the legal quality of interdependence were recognized, the same reasoning could be applied to the interest of any maritime state in a question involving the freedom of the seas or the navigation of an international river, and it would not be necessary to show that the state asserting the interest was a party to any treaty which might be involved. This would mark a clear change from the traditional position, which has been well stated by Verdross in saying that the "merely ideal interest of the other states in maintaining the international legal order is . . . insufficient" to support a claim to act. But he admits that there may be exceptional cases where the general interest is involved, as when some state embarks on a career of lawlessness.[70] Upon the acceptance of the concept of interdependence, the exception would become the rule.[71]

[69] *P.C.I.J.*, Ser. A, No. 1, p. 20 (1931).

[70] Verdross, *Völkerrecht* (1937), 165, citing Vattel and Hefter in accord on these exceptional cases.

[71] Garner in 1925 argued that states should have "an admitted legal right to protest against violation of the law" even where no immediate injury could be shown; *Recent Developments in International Law*, 814.

Tentative assertion of such a right in connection with the common interest of all neutral states in the upholding of the law of neutral rights is to be found in the views expressed by several European governments in connection with the Trent Affair in 1861.[72] The same thought was utilized in various proposals for armed neutralities or leagues of neutrals.[73]

The history of the Concert of Europe throughout much of the nineteenth century is illustrative of the acceptance of a concept of interdependence as a legal norm in international relations, at least so far as the affairs of the European continent were concerned. It is true that this instrument was wielded by the Great Powers, often for selfish ends, and that they tended to ignore the rights of the small powers. But as the action of the Concert was frequently rationalized and defended, there was an invocation of a concept of community interest, of interdependence. Procedurally, the Great Powers asserted their right to act as the instruments of the public law of Europe. Thus Lord Salisbury defended the action of the Concert in respect of Greece by referring to "the federated action of Europe" enacting rules as a "legislature" in the interests of European peace.[74] Numerous discussions and agreements concerning the neutralization of Switzerland and other areas reflect the acceptance of the concept of interdependence.[75] The famous declaration in the treaty of Paris of March 30, 1856 is comparable in its pronouncement that the Sublime Porte was admitted to participate in the advantages of the public law and Concert of Europe. The signatory powers accordingly agreed to respect the independence and territorial integrity of the Ottoman Empire and said that they would consider any act tending to violate

[72] "Harvard Research in International Law, Draft Convention on Rights and Duties of Neutral States in Naval and Aerial War," Art. 114, commentary, 33 Am. J. Int. L. Supp. (1939), 788 ff.; French Statement in 55 British and Foreign State Papers, 610–12, and 1862 U.S. For. Rel., 307; Austrian position in 55 British and Foreign State Papers, 618 and German statement in ibid., 624; also British summary of these views in ibid., 641 ff.

[73] See Jessup, "Neutrality, Its History, Economics and Law," Vol. IV, Today and Tomorrow (1936), 160 ff.; Bülow to Lord Granville, 31 Aug. 1870, Fontes juris gentium, Ser. B. Sectio I, Tomus I, Pars I, 2.

[74] Address in the House of Lords quoted in 1 Westlake International Law (2d ed. 1910), 322; cf. Lawrence, The Principles of International Law (7th ed. 1923), 322.

[75] See "General Act of the Congress of Vienna, June 9, 1815," Articles IX, LXXXIV, XCII. 2 British and Foreign State Papers, 3; cf. Peterson, op. cit., supra note 52, p. 547.

this engagement as a question of general interest.[76] The joint interest of the powers in the "open door" for China and respect for Chinese territorial integrity may also be noted. The concept of interdependence is clearly recognized in the Covenant of the League of Nations and in the Charter of the United Nations.[77]

An interesting assertion of the right of a state to secure satisfaction because of the injury it sustains through the weakening of the international legal system through any breach of a rule of international law was made by the French Government in its case against Italy before a tribunal of the Permanent Court of Arbitration in the cases of the *Carthage* and the *Manouba*. These two French ships had been captured by the Italians during their war with Turkey; the French claims for indemnity were submitted to arbitration. In addition to material compensation for the damage to the vessels, the French Government asked for the "sum of one hundred thousand francs for the moral and political injury resulting from the failure to observe international common law and conventions binding both Italy and France." The Tribunal, correctly under the existing law, refused to make such an award, holding that the establishment by an arbitral tribunal of the fact of a breach of international legal obligations "constitutes in itself a serious penalty." [78]

SOVEREIGNTY

Sovereignty, in its meaning of an absolute, uncontrolled state will, ultimately free to resort to the final arbitrament of war, is the quicksand on which the foundations of traditional international law are built.[79] Until the world achieves some form of international government in which a collective will takes precedence over the individual will of the sovereign state, the ultimate function of law, which is the elimination of force for the solution of human conflicts, will not be fulfilled. Like the legal attribute of equality, the function of sovereignty as a legal concept was to protect the state in a world devoid of

[76] 46 *British and Foreign State Papers* (1855-56), 8.
[77] See "Commentary on the League of Nations Covenant by the British Government," reprinted in Butler, *A Handbook to the League of Nations* (2d ed. 1925), 171.
[78] Scott, *Hague Court Reports* (1906), 332, 335.
[79] See the Introductory Chap.

any alternative to self-protection. The gradual development of adequate modernized law and organization should provide such an alternative.

Because the international system has so far failed to meet the central problem of war, it is often inaccurately assumed that no progress has been made in the direction of limiting the free exercise of state will.[80] Once it is agreed that sovereignty is divisible [81] and that it therefore is not absolute, various restrictions on and relinquishments of sovereignty may be regarded as normal and not stigmatizing. The slow but steady development of majority rule in international organizations [82] bears witness to the change which is taking place. Of great significance is the contrast between the Covenant of the League of Nations, which left to each member freedom to decide whether it would participate in sanctions recommended by the Council, and Chapter VII of the Charter of the United Nations, whereby the members relinquish the power of decision to the Security Council and are bound to take action on the basis of that decision. Notable also are those numerous provisions in the Charter which recognize that the treatment of the individual citizen is no longer a matter solely of domestic concern and that the denial of fundamental human rights to a citizen can no longer be shrouded behind the impenetrable cloak of national sovereignty.[88] Sovereignty in the sense of exclusiveness of jurisdiction in certain domains, and subject to overriding precepts of constitutional force, will remain a usable and useful concept, just as in the constitutional system of the United States the forty-eight states are considered sovereign. But sovereignty in its old connotations of ultimate freedom of national will unrestricted by law is not consistent with the principles of community interest or interdependence and of the status of the individual as a subject of international law. With the development of international law regulating the state's use of force and the implementation of the spirit of those provisions of the Charter which should make any resort to war clearly illegal, sover-

[80] Cf. Postulate 3, *International Law of the Future* (1944), p. 29; Chap. VII, *infra*.
[81] See the practical argument to this effect in 1 Oppenheim, Sec. 69, p. 116.
[82] See Riches, *Majority Rule in International Organization* (1940).
[88] See Norman Wait Harris Memorial Foundation, *Proceedings 21st Institute* (1945), "The United Nations and The Organization of Peace and Security," 99, 126; Chap. IV, *infra*.

eignty would no longer constitute a major obstacle to the development of a genuine international community. Theoretical difficulties confronting the acceptance of the supremacy of international law would then disappear.

CHAPTER III

RECOGNITION

THIS CHAPTER DEALS with the recognition of states and governments
and of insurgents and belligerents. It does not deal with non-
recognition as a sanction; that subject will be considered in Chapter
VII.

Recognition of a state is the act by which another state acknowledges that the political entity recognized possesses the attributes of
statehood. The common case is one in which a community not there-
tofore accepted as a member of the international society has thrown
off a previous subservience to another state, as in the case of a revolting colony which declares its independence, or which is accorded
full autonomy by the former parent state. Less frequent are those
instances in which independent and locally well-developed groups
have at length established full contacts with the world community,
which in earlier days meant the western world; the entrance of
Japan into the family of nations is an example. The recognition
of new governments involves very different considerations and
should be sharply distinguished; it will be treated later in this
chapter.

There is broad divergence of opinion among writers as to whether
recognition is declaratory or constitutive; that is, whether a state
exists prior to recognition or whether it is brought into being by the
act of recognition. Professor Lauterpacht maintains the constitutive
view in a recent article.[1] The American Republics concluded at
Montevideo in 1933 a convention which emphatically states the
declaratory position.[2] Confusion is caused by the fact that some
writers consider recognition a purely political act, whereas others

[1] Lauterpacht, "Recognition of States in International Law," 53 *Yale L. J.*
(1944), 385.
[2] *U.S. Treaty Ser.* No. 881. The proposition was reaffirmed in Art. VII of
the Draft Declaration of the Rights and Duties of American States, approved by
the Governing Board of the Pan-American Union, July 17, 1946.

stress its legal character. Whichever view reflects more accurately the existing international law, it is clear that political opposition to the constitutive view stems from the lack of organization of the international community, inasmuch as recognition is accorded at the will of established states in a position to blackball a new aspirant to membership in the community of nations. The argument of some writers that there is a duty to recognize when an aspirant actually possesses the attributes of statehood has afforded slight satisfaction in the absence of organized international machinery to enforce the obligation.

Surely this is a situation to which the concept of community interest has clear application. The appearance on the international scene of a new state must be a matter of interest to all other states, especially in modern times, when so many contacts in trade, aviation, radio, and other human activities do not depend on geographical proximity and when there is general acknowledgment of the world-wide interest in the existence of stable and "peace-loving" governments. The traditional practice of unilateral recognition of a new state is not consistent with the hypothesis of the acceptance of the concept of community interest. Examples in the past of group recognition of a new state bear witness to the fact that recognition of states in certain areas and under certain conditions has already been acknowledged to involve such a degree of community interest as to induce joint action. This was particularly true of the period in which during the nineteenth century the Concert of Europe undertook to act in matters of common concern. Turkey was indeed recognized before it was admitted "to participate in the advantages of the public law and the Concert of Europe" by the Treaty of Paris of 1856; that treaty was rather an acknowledgment and guarantee of the integrity of the Ottoman Empire.[3] It was otherwise with the Balkan states. When Rumania declared its independence Russia considered that this created a *de facto* but not a *de jure* situation; the legal position would remain to be determined by the Powers.[4] Not until Rumania was recognized by a European congress was it believed that the new state could become a party to international

[3] See statement of Lord Salisbury in the House of Lords, 19 March 1897, reprinted in 1 Westlake, *International Law* (2d ed. 1910), 322.

[4] Lord Loftus to the Earl of Derby, 31 May 1877, *Fontes Juris Gentium*, Series B. Sectio I, Tomus II, Pars I, p. 53.

treaties.[5] By the Treaty of Berlin of 1878 the Great Powers formally recognized the independence of Rumania. But in the same treaty a split in the collective front is registered by the provision of Article XXVI relative to Montenegro, whose independence was recognized by the Sublime Porte "and by all the High Contracting Parties who have not yet admitted it." Serbia was recognized in the same manner as was Rumania.[6] After World War I the Principal Allied and Associated Powers jointly confirmed the recognition of Poland. In transmitting to Poland the treaty to be signed the President of the Peace Conference pointed to the past practices of Europe in dealing with such matters.[7] Negatively, the combined action of the Members of the League of Nations and of the United States in denying recognition to the Japanese puppet Manchukuo presents a striking example of a like attitude.[8]

Once this community interest in recognition is admitted, the problem resolves itself into one of procedure. There has been no single established procedure for according recognition. Recognition might be express or implied, unilateral or joint. It might take the form of a declaration, the conclusion of a treaty, or the exchange of diplomatic representatives. Under the League of Nations Covenant it might be accorded through the admission of a new state to membership in the League through the two-thirds vote of the Assembly required by Article 1 of the Covenant.[9] The Permanent Mandates Commission of the League adopted in 1931 a list of conditions which must be fulfilled before a mandated territory could be considered to have achieved a position in which it could be released from the mandatory regime and recognized as a state.[10]

These League of Nations precedents suggest the utility of invoking the organization of the United Nations for the establishment of a standard procedure for the recognition of new states. It is necessary first to determine whether recognition should be con-

[5] General Ghika to M. Kogalniceano, 14/26 January 1878, ibid., 12.
[6] 69 British and Foreign State Papers, 749.
[7] 112 ibid., 225ff.
[8] See 1 Oppenheim, sec. 751, and 1 Hyde, sec. 109c.
[9] See the discussion and citations in Lauterpacht's note 3, 1 Oppenheim, 122; Graham, The League of Nations and the Recognition of States (1933).
[10] Permanent Mandates Commission, Minutes of the Twentieth Session, 1931, League Doc. C. 422. M. 176. 1931. VI., VI. A. Mandates 1931. VI. A. I., 229, summarized in 1 Hackworth, Digest of Int. L., 119-120.

sidered to involve legal or political considerations. The answer must be that both types of considerations are involved. There are and should continue to be certain definite criteria for determining whether an entity has the necessary attributes of statehood—territory, population, and a sufficiently independent government able and willing to enter into international relationships and to assume and discharge international obligations. The fixing of those criteria is in the nature of a legislative act for which the Montevideo Convention of December 26, 1933 on Rights and Duties of States and the resolution of the Permanent Mandates Commission in 1931 afford models. Such a legislative act might take the form of a general convention proposed by the General Assembly and submitted to the states for ratification. It would seem preferable, however, to utilize the method found satisfactory in the Inter-American Conferences, which have adopted "declarations" embodying the conclusions of the delegates. These declarations do not require ratification and do not have the status of treaties, but they are persuasive evidence of the existence of the rule of law which they enunciate.[11] Thus at the Lima Conference of 1938, the American Republics reiterated "as a fundamental principle of the Public Law of America" the proposition that the occupation or acquisition of territory by force shall not be valid or have legal effect.[12] One may also note statements embodied in treaties which continue to have evidential value quite irrespective of the continued validity of the treaties in which they were originally embodied. For example, in a number of the liquor-smuggling conventions concluded by the United States in the 1920's there was an assertion of the three-mile rule as the limit of territorial waters, so phrased as to be an acknowledgment of the existing law rather than merely a contractual obligation in regard to the future.[18] A more

---

[11] Cf. Lauterpacht's view on the binding effect of resolutions of the Assembly of the League of Nations in 1 Oppenheim, 141 n. 3. According to Schwarzenberger, "if States have declared their intentions" in such a body as the General Assembly, "they cannot go back on the decision at which the international organ has arrived." In this connection he cites the advisory opinion of the Permanent Court of International Justice in the matter of the Jaworzina Boundary, P.C.I.J., Ser. B, No. 8 (1923), 51–53; 1 Schwarzenberger, International Law (1945), 212.

[12] Report of the Delegation of the United States of America to the Eighth International Conference of American States, Dept. of State Pub. 1624 (1941), 132.

[18] E.g.: "The High Contracting Parties declare that it is their firm intention to uphold the principle that 3 marine miles extending from the coast-line out-

famous instance is the statement in the Declaration of Paris of 1856
to the effect that "privateering is and remains abolished." [14]

Although the General Assembly of the United Nations possesses
under Chapter IV of the Charter powers which are no more than
recommendatory, it would be within its competence to adopt by the
two-thirds vote required under Article 18 for "important questions"
a declaration relative to the essential characteristics of a state and
to assert that there must be a finding of the possession of such
characteristics before any political entity is recognized as a
state. The membership of the United Nations is sufficiently
broad to lend persuasive force to such a declaration even at
this time; the weight of such declarations would be enhanced as
the membership is enlarged by the admission of new members. It
may be presumed that any new state would desire to become a
member of the United Nations. Under Article 4 of the Charter the
admission of new members takes place by a decision of the General
Assembly on the recommendation of the Security Council. The
General Assembly might well frame such a declaration as has been
suggested in the form of an indication of the standards by which it
would be guided in determining whether to admit a new member.
The criteria for membership would not be identical with the criteria
for statehood, but the latter would be included within the former,
since one requirement for membership is that the applicant shall be a
state.[15] Moreover the requirement of paragraph 1 of Article 4 that
the applicant shall be "able and willing to carry out" the obligations
of the Charter is closely akin to the general requirement that a state
shall possess a government able and willing to enter into and carry
out international obligations.[16] There would remain for the judgment of the Organization the question whether the applicant was
not only a state, but a "peace-loving" state.

---

wards and measured from low-water mark constitute the proper limits of territorial waters." *U.S. Treaty Ser.* No. 685.

[14] But the treaty itself declared that its provisions were binding only upon
the parties; 46 *British and Foreign State Papers*, 136.

[15] The nature of this requirement has already been discussed in Chap. II.

[16] "The recognition of any State must always be subject to the reservation
that the State recognised will respect the obligations imposed upon it either by
general International Law or by definite international settlements relating to its
territory." "Report of the International Committee of Jurists on the Legal
Aspects of the Aaland Islands Question," *League of Nations Off. J. Sp. Supp.*
(1920-21), No. 3, p. 18.

In one sense, the establishment of the fact that a state is "peace-loving" may be regarded as the imposition of a condition of recognition, but there is no basis for continuing the nonsensical practice which has been called "conditional recognition." Baty has properly pointed out in regard to so-called conditional recognition of a state that "Any entry into relations with the new state, as a governing authority, implies recognition of its state-hood. . . . It follows . . . that recognition cannot be conditional. . . . Either it is a fact or it is not. The very essence of recognition is that the recognizing state thereby declares that it has satisfied itself that the recognized authority possesses the distinguishing marks of a state. To say that one recognizes that it has them, subject to its conduct being satisfactory in other particulars, is sheer nonsense. It is like telling a pupil that her sum is right if she will promise to be a good girl." [17] These considerations do not exclude the possibility that a recognizing state may announce the conditions which it insists must be fulfilled before it will accord recognition, and these considerations may be informally communicated to the authority seeking recognition. The recognition of new states by the Concert of Europe was often extended on such conditions. The fulfillment of the condition was exacted as an indication that the new community possessed the attributes required of a state, including the readiness to comply with the responsibilities of its position in the society of nations. It is in this sense that one may read the Protocol of June 28, 1878, signed on behalf of Great Britain, France, Italy, and Germany, relative to the recognition of Serbia. It was said that "Serbia, who claims to enter the European family on the same basis as other States, must previously recognize the principles which are the basis of social organization in all States of Europe and accept them as a necessary condition of the favour which she asks for." [18] The condition there demanded was the recognition of the principle of religious liberty; in connection with the admission of a new state to the United Nations, the condition would be the recognition of the principles of the Charter relative to the pacific settlement of all international disputes. Obviously in connection with the applications for membership in the

---

[17] Baty, "So-called 'De Facto' Recognition," 31 Yale L. J. (1922), 469.
[18] Quoted in a letter to M. Paderewski by the President of the Paris Peace Conference on June 24, 1919, 112 British and Foreign State Papers, 225.

United Nations by established states such as Sweden, Iceland, and Eire, admission to membership is not the same as recognition. The observations made above relate to new entities which may come into existence, and may be considered applicable at this time to the cases of Outer Mongolia and Trans-Jordan, which had not been recognized by all states at the time of their applications for membership. It is also true that admission to membership in the United Nations is at present much more in the nature of a "favour" than was recognition of a new state in 1878, despite the tendency of the Concert of Europe to consider itself somewhat like an exclusive club.

The declaration of the General Assembly might well also include a statement of the position that members of the United Nations would not independently accord recognition to new states. Such a statement would be justified by the desideratum that the Organization become universal at the earliest possible time. It is a basic defect of the United Nations that the principle of universality was not accepted at the outset. It is obvious that this principle was rejected because the Charter was framed during a great war when political considerations led to the conclusion that certain states not then members of the political grouping already called "the United Nations" should not be included in the new more formal Organization. It would have been wiser political judgment to insist that the enemy states accept membership, instead of leaving them outside as the potential nucleus of a rival and hostile group.[19] It would be within the competence of the General Assembly to record its conviction of the desirability of attaining universality at the earliest possible date, and to that end to stipulate that, since the admission of a new state to the community of nations would eventually result in its admission as a member of the United Nations, recognition of new states should be only by the decision of the Organization itself.[20] The acceptance of the principle of universality might logically involve an amendment of Article 4 to eliminate the criterion "peace-loving," which is nothing more than a self-righteous declaration of

[19] See the persuasive arguments for universality in *The International Law of the Future*, Carnegie Endowment for International Peace (1944), 78.

[20] See *ibid.*, 81. Cf. the Norwegian proposal of May 3, 1945. "UNIO," 3 *Documents of the United Nations Conference on International Organization, San Francisco, 1945* (1945), 366.

tne victors in the war. But since it may be fairly said that the obligations of the Charter require every member to be "peace-loving," that term could be construed as embodying no concept different from that of ability and willingness to carry out the obligations of that covenant. The principle of universality of course does not exclude the possibility of adopting rules for the organization which would exclude certain states from the exercise of voting or other privileges. Such a penalty might be imposed, for example, on a state momentarily ruled by a government considered obnoxious by a majority of the members of the Organization. Thus if the principle of universality had been adopted in framing the Charter and if Spain had been a member in 1945 and 1946, the registered opposition of the United Nations to the Franco regime [21] might have been effectively implemented by the withdrawal of some of the privileges of membership, Spain remaining a state subject to the obligations of the Charter. There would not need to be any change in Article 5 of the Charter, which provides that "A member of the United Nations against which preventive or enforcement action has been taken by the Security Council may be suspended from the exercise of the rights and privileges of membership by the General Assembly upon the recommendation of the Security Council." But Article 6, which provides for the expulsion of a member, is not consistent with the principle of universality.

On the adoption of some such proposals as those just made, the problem of recognition of states would fall easily and naturally into the mold of common action by the organization. Since the birth of a new state possessing the necessary qualifications would automatically result in membership in the Organization, it would naturally be for the Organization itself and not for its members individually to accord recognition.

The question may be asked whether, if the criteria for statehood be established by legislative or quasi-legislative act of the General Assembly, it would not then be a judicial question whether an applicant had attained statehood. If this were true, the finding might be by the International Court of Justice instead of by the General Assem-

[21] See *Journal of the General Assembly*, First Session, No. 28, 11 Feb. 1946, 469ff.; Doc. A/241, 10 Dec. 1946. Text also in 15 Dept. of State *Bulletin* (1946), 1143.

bly. It is believed, however, that such a finding would inevitably call for the exercise of political judgment with respect to the ability and willingness of the applicant to carry out its obligations and that the matter should therefore be confided to the General Assembly, acting, as now required by the Charter, on the recommendation of the Security Council. It is not intended to enter here on a discussion of whether changes should be made in the Charter relative to the distribution of powers between the General Assembly and the Security Council. Neither is it intended at this point to consider the possible evolution of the United Nations into some more closely knit unit such as a world government. The problem of recognition of new states, and therefor that of their admission into the organized community of nations, would remain substantially the same under such circumstances.

RELATIONS WITH POLITICAL COMMUNITIES NOT RECOGNIZED AS STATES—RECOGNITION OF INSURGENCY AND BELLIGERENCY

Before a political community is recognized as a state, other states may have occasion to enter into certain relations with that community. In the past, such relations have been established and maintained. Few if any such communities now remain in the world which are not politically linked to some state in one or another form of dependence or subordination. In such cases the question of relationship becomes one for adjustment between the dominant state and other states. This is true of colonies, protectorates, and the like, even though, as suggested in the preceding chapter, such entities be considered "subjects" of international law. The constitutional or the treaty relationship between the dominant and the subordinate entities determines the extent to which the latter are free to deal with other members of the international community. But an international interest in the relationship may be recorded by joint action, as when in the Treaty of Berlin of 1878 Article I stated that Bulgaria was constituted an autonomous principality under the suzerainty of his Imperial Majesty the Sultan.[22]

It may be suggested, in line with the discussion of "subjects" of

[22] *Op. cit., supra* note 6. Such an international interest is implicit in connection with territories under mandate or trusteeship.

international law in the preceding Chapter, that the General
Assembly in a given case might conclude that an entity had not yet
developed the characteristics deemed necessary for membership in
the United Nations, but that it had achieved such a status as would
entitle it to become a member of some other international organizations such as the Universal Postal Union or other technical
bodies.

A more difficult problem is presented by a colony or other subordinate entity seeking to throw off the control of the mother
country. Under existing international law premature recognition of
a revolting colony constitutes intervention and is hostile to the
mother country.[23] The memory of the international disturbances
attending the Spanish Civil War in the 1930's, although the case did
not involve a struggle for the independence of a colony, is too fresh
to let one ignore the relationship between such intervention and
the peace of the world. The more recent struggle in the Netherlands
East Indies has not been lacking in international repercussions. The
government of dependencies and the treatment accorded their inhabitants has in the past been considered a domestic question in which
other states were not free to interfere. Chapter XI of the Charter
of the United Nations introduces a change in this position. By
Article 73, "Members of the United Nations which have or assume
responsibilities for the administration of territories whose peoples
have not yet attained a full measure of self-government recognize
the principle that the interests of the inhabitants of these territories
are paramount, and accept as a sacred trust the obligation to promote
to the utmost, within the system of international peace and security
established by the present Charter, the well-being of the inhabitants
of these territories." There follow certain specific obligations im-
plementing this general principle, including a duty to transmit reports to the Secretary-General of the United Nations. In Article 74,
"Members of the United Nations also agree that their policy in
respect of the territories to which this Chapter applies, no less than
in respect of their metropolitan areas, must be based on the general
principle of good-neighborliness, due account being taken of the
interests and well-being of the rest of the world, in social, economic,
and commercial matters." Where any such territories are placed

[23] 1 Hyde, 153.

under trusteeship, the additional obligations of the Trusteeship System under the Charter are also applicable.

These treaty obligations suffice to remove colonial questions from the realm of domestic questions and to acknowledge the general international interest in them. The United Nations may properly take cognizance of any maladministration in a colony or other dependent territory administered by a Member. A colonial revolution is now legally as well as practically a matter of concern to the whole international community.

Under traditional international law it was customary for states during a civil war to take cognizance of various stages of development of the conflict by recognizing the insurgency of the insurrectionary faction or, if that party had attained sufficient stature, the belligerency of the two contending parties. The principal consequence of a recognition of insurgency is to protect the insurgents from having their warlike activities, especially on the high seas, from being regarded as lawless acts of violence which, in the absence of recognition, might subject them to treatment as pirates. It may also sharpen the obligation of third states with respect to their duty of nonintervention in the conflict.[24] It may involve the recognition of the insurgents as the *de facto* authority in the territory they actually control, and thus lead to the maintenance of relations incidental to the protection of the rights and interests of the recognizing state.[25] When the insurgents are sufficiently well organized, conduct hostilities according to the laws of war, and have a determinate territory under their control, they may be recognized as belligerents whether or not the parent state has already actually or impliedly recognized that status, as by establishing a maritime blockade against ports under their control. With the recognition of belligerency, the third state assumes the obligations of neutrality, just as in a war between two states.

International war and the consequent status of neutrality as it has existed under traditional international law are not compatible with the hypothesis of the acceptance of the principle of community interest.[26] It is not clear what rights and duties should devolve upon members

---

[24] 1 Hyde, 203–204.
[25] 1 Oppenheim, 138.
[26] See Chaps. VII, VIII.

of the United Nations in civil war. No doubt the Security Council could determine that a civil war constituted a "threat to the peace" under Article 39 of the Charter, but if the Security Council took no action, no obligation under the Charter would be violated if a member state proclaimed its neutrality, thus recognizing the belligerency of the contending factions. Yet experience has clearly shown that legal neutrality in civil or in international wars, no matter how rigorously observed, may constitute a factual interference in the outcome of the struggle, in view of the geographic position of the contestants. Three centuries of experience with neutrality justify the conclusion that the very coexistence of belligerents and neutrals constitutes in itself a "situation which might lead to international friction or give rise to a dispute." Recognition of insurgency or belligerency should therefore be the act of the Organization, just as recognition of a new state should. Procedurally, the problem is much more difficult, in part because of the probable necessity of immediate decision, which would exclude the possibility of action by the General Assembly even though that body might be called into special session. It would seem necessary for the Security Council to act, and the general philosophy of the Charter would indicate that this is the appropriate body in such cases. If the Security Council is unable through the interposition of the veto or otherwise, to marshal the requisite vote, it would be better to delay action until the General Assembly convenes than to split the membership into opposing camps of recognizing and nonrecognizing states. Some of the legal problems which might arise in the interim are considered in Chapter VIII. Under Article 12 of the Charter the General Assembly cannot make any recommendation with regard to a dispute or situation while it is being considered by the Security Council unless the latter so requests. The General Assembly might, however, in the absence of a request from the Security Council, adopt a resolution recording its view that the contending factions were or were not entitled to recognition as belligerents. Whether all the member states would thereafter act in conformity with the view expressed would depend on the strength of the political forces which had prevented the Security Council from acting on the question. This situation reveals a defect in the organization of the United Nations; it also involves the basic difficulty of dealing on a general international level with the problems arising from domestic strife in any state. Such difficulties would not be avoided, although they might be solved, through a more perfect organization.[27]

THE RECOGNITION OF GOVERNMENTS

The traditional international system of leaving states free to accord or to withhold the recognition of new governments has frequently resulted in the exercise of undue influence or interference by a strong state in the affairs of a weaker state. The earlier history of the relations between the United States and the republics of the Caribbean area has been particularly marked by such instances.[28] Even in rudimentary forms of international organization such as the Paris Peace Conference and the Pan American Union, nonrecognition by the United States served to exclude Costa Rica, for example, from participation in the common tasks of the community of nations. The effect of nonrecognition of a country's government on its economic life may be marked, since it may find the principal financial markets and trade centers closed to it.[29] The acceptance of the principle of community interest would require a change in the traditional situation.

Confusion will be avoided if a distinction is sharply drawn between the according of recognition and the establishment of diplomatic relations. A tendency to identify the two acts has caused much difficulty, particularly in national courts when they have been called upon to determine whether a regime actually functioning in another country was or was not to be considered its government, with the right to represent the state in litigation. It has not been doubted that a state has continuity in the sense that its existence as a state is not affected by changes in government, whether or not the new government has secured recognition from other states. It is thus possible, and would be wise policy for states under the traditional

[27] The whole problem of international concern with such internal problems is the subject of a separate study to be published subsequently.

[28] See Buell, "The United States and Central American Stability," 7 *Foreign Policy Reports* (1931), 161 and "The United States and Central American Revolutions," *ibid.*, 187.

[29] See Lauterpacht, "Recognition of Governments": L 4s *Col. L. Rev.* (1945), 815, 818.

system of unilateral recognition, in appropriate cases to recognize that
a regime in *de facto* control of a state is the government of that state,
and at the same time to assert that, because of some disagreement
with the government, diplomatic relations will not be established
until there has been satisfactory adjustment of outstanding differences. There has never been any doubt that one state is free to
break off diplomatic relations with another state as a mark of dissatisfaction or displeasure when the situation in that other state is
free from the complication of a change in government. It is remarkable that wider cognizance has not been accorded the equally
clear proposition that where there is a change of government, recognition may be accorded without the establishment of diplomatic
relations or without the resumption of such relations if they have
been broken during the course of a civil conflict which has resulted
in the change of government.

The reason why the practice of according recognition without
establishing diplomatic relations has not been generally followed is to
be found in the changed character of the act of recognition. There
have been periods in which it was the usual practice of governments
to recognize new governments in other states as soon as it was clear
that the new government was *de facto* in control of the state and was
ready to discharge the international obligations of the state. In Jef-
fersonian terms, it was necessary merely to determine that the government represented "the will of the nation, substantially declared." [30]
Under such practice recognition was evidence of the establishment
of the new government. The change in practice and its effects has
been noted in two judicial pronouncements. In the Tinoco Arbitration between Great Britain and Costa Rica Chief Justice Taft as Sole
Arbitrator declared: "The non-recognition by other nations of a government claiming to be a national personality, is usually appropriate
evidence that it has not attained the independence and control
entitling it by international law to be classed as such. But when
recognition *vel non* of a government is by such nations determined
by inquiry, not into its *de facto* sovereignty and complete governmental control, but into its illegitimacy or irregularity of origin,
their non-recognition loses something of evidential weight on the
issue with which those applying the rules of international law are

[30] 1 Hyde, 161.

alone concerned." [31] Similarly Judge Cardozo, in breaking into the fictional log jam that for many years harassed the New York courts in passing on questions involving the status of the Soviet Government before its recognition by the United States in 1933, declared: "Consequences appropriate enough when recognition is withheld on the ground that rival factions are still contending for the mastery, may be in need of readjustment before they can be fitted to the practice, now a growing one, of withholding recognition wherever it is thought that a government, functioning unhampered, is unworthy of a place in the society of nations." [32] The withholding of recognition has thus become a political weapon wielded to force a new government to make concessions to the demands of the recognizing state.

The confusion resulting from this mélange of political and legal considerations has done much to bring about the present state of disagreement regarding such concepts as conditional recognition, de facto recognition, and the withdrawal of recognition. All three of these terms have been used in connection both with the recognition of governments and with the recognition of new states.

De facto recognition is a term which has been used without precision. When properly used to mean the recognition of the de facto character of a government, it is unobjectionable and indeed could be identical with the practice suggested of extending recognition without resuming diplomatic relations. It is objectionable when it connotes a modern revival of the now almost forgotten policy of European monarchical governments of contrasting "de facto" with "de jure divino," thus stigmatizing all republican or democratic governments. In modern form, the suggestion is implicit that another state should determine its recognition policy by inquiry into the legitimacy of origin of the new government, as Taft indicated in the Tinoco case. This is bad international politics and may actually put the recognizing state in the impossible position of attempting to pass on constitutional provisions of another state. [33] The withdrawal

[31] 18 Am. J. Int. L. (1924), 147. Cf. also United States (George W. Hopkins) v. Mexico, U.S.-Mexican General Claims Commissions, Opinions of Commissioners (1927), 50.

[32] Sokoloff v. National City Bank 239 N.Y. 158 (1924).

[33] Cf. Buell, "American Supervision of Elections in Nicaragua," 6 Foreign Policy Assn. Information Service (1930), 385, 399.

of recognition, like the according of conditional recognition, is also nonsense if the withdrawal is based on factors extrinsic to the consideration of the continued existence of the state or government. Recognition need never be "withdrawn," since it ceases to have vitality or jural consequences if the entity recognized goes out of existence. There is no impropriety in state Y's asserting that it has reached the conclusion that Government A in state X has been overthrown and is no longer the government of X. Thereafter, Government A would no longer be a recognized government so far as Y was concerned. Thus, the British Secretary of State for Foreign Affairs made a proper reply to an inquiry in the House of Commons in February, 1924, as to whether the authority of Russia was recognized as extending over Armenia and whether therefore the *de jure* recognition extended to Armenia in 1920 had been withdrawn. The Foreign Secretary replied that the answer was "yes" in that the authority of Russia over the Armenian territory was acknowledged, but he added "official recognition of governments which no longer exist de facto naturally lapses when they cease to function."[84]

X The group or community interest in the recognition of new governments has already been signalized in international relations. Thus the Central American treaties of 1907 and 1923, under which the five republics assumed certain obligations relative to the recognition of new governments which came into power through revolution or *coup d'état*, bore witness to the regional group interest in the then chronic political instability of those countries. Currently, the discussions in the United Nations General Assembly and Security Council relative to the Franco Government in Spain are comparable.[85] One may also cite the intergovernmental discussions among the American republics relative to governmental changes in the Argentine.[86]

In the functioning of the United Nations or any other international organization composed of states in which members of various bodies or commissions are delegates of governments, the community interest cannot be ignored. It must be faced whenever

[84] 169 Parl. Debates No. 14, p. 1293.
[85] See note 21, *supra*.
[86] See *Consultation Among the American Republics with Respect to the Argentine Situation*, Dept. of State Pub. 2473, (1946).

a credentials committee passes on the papers of a delegate accredited by a regime asserting governmental powers. In case of civil war where the supremacy is in the balance, two sets of delegates may appear and claim to represent the Member of the United Nations. In like cases the Secretary-General, in sending communications to the governments of Members, may be confronted with the necessity of determining which of two rival groups should be the addressee. The problem was illustrated in the history of the League of Nations with reference to the seating of Ethiopian representatives in the Assembly after the Italian conquest. The Credentials Committee handled the issue by invoking the provision in its Rules of Procedure which stipulated that, unless the Assembly decided otherwise, any representative to whose admission objection had been made should sit provisionally with the same rights as other representatives. The Ethiopian credentials were therefore considered sufficient to permit its delegation to be seated.[37] The fact that the Italians absented themselves from this session of the Assembly and withdrew from the League in the following year perhaps facilitated this solution. One may contrast the fact that after the Swiss recognition of the Burgos government in Spain in 1939 the Swiss government forcibly closed and sealed the office of the permanent delegation of Spain to the League of Nations, which had been in the possession of the representatives of the Nationalist government.[38] It would surely not be contemplated that when the permanent seat of the United Nations is established in New York the United States Government should be in a position to control the representation of another state through action comparable to that of Switzerland or through immigration restrictions applied to exclude alleged representatives appointed by a government which the United States had not recognized. The decision regarding the legitimacy of the representation should be made by some organ of the United Nations and not by a single state which happens to be in the geographical position to exercise control.[39]

[37] See Burton, *The Assembly of the League of Nations* (1941), 370.

[38] Padelford, *International Law and Diplomacy in the Spanish Civil Strife* (1939), 193.

[39] The draft agreement between the United Nations and the United States in Sec. 21 provides that the authorities of the United States "shall not impose any impediments to transit to and from the headquarters district by representatives

It would not be easy to provide that unilateral recognition of governments should wholly yield to collective recognition by the Organization, as in the case of the recognition of new states and of insurgents and belligerents. The actuality of situations in international relations which raise the issue is that when a revolution or *coup d'état* takes place in State X, other states are at once faced with the question whether they shall continue unbroken their diplomatic and consular contacts with the threatened regime, whether they shall deal with the new regime, or whether there must be dealings with both regimes.

The Mexican Government in 1930 evolved a practice for meeting such situations. The practice rests on political considerations but is sustained by jural argument. The practice or policy was formulated by Sr. Genaro Estrada, Secretary of Foreign Relations, and is known as the Estrada Doctrine. The formulation is, in effect, an announcement of instructions sent to the diplomatic representatives of Mexico to acquaint them with a new policy of their government. The policy is said to have had the specific endorsement of President Ortiz Rubio.

The declaration begins with several paragraphs containing the Mexican government's reflections on the practice of recognition of *de facto* governments. It is stated to be a well-known fact that Mexico suffered particularly from the consequences of the present practice of recognition whereby foreign governments assume the prerogative of passing on the legitimacy or illegitimacy of governments, thus subordinating national authority to foreign opinion. This recognition practice is said to be largely of postwar development and of particular application to the Latin-American Republics. After careful study of these matters, the Mexican government instructed its diplomatic representatives that it would no longer give any expression regarding recognition of new governments which come into power by *coups d'état* or revolution.

The reason for this new policy is the belief that recognition in-

---

of Members." UN Doc. A/67, 1 Sept. 1946. In case of doubt whether an individual carrying credentials from the alleged government of another state is or is not the representative of that state, the United States should assume the validity of the credentials pending action by an organ of the United Nations.

volves the assumption of a right to pass critically on the legal capacity of foreign regimes, a right derogatory to the sovereignty of other states. Consequently, the Mexican government confines itself to continuing or withdrawing its diplomatic representatives, and to continuing or not continuing to accept diplomatic representatives of other states, as it may deem appropriate from time to time, without any regard to accepting or not accepting any change of government. In respect of accrediting and receiving diplomatic representatives, Mexico continues to observe the established formalities.

In terms of a factual situation, the Mexican position is apparently as follows: A successful revolution takes place in State X; while other states may be considering recognizing or not recognizing the new de facto government, Mexico will merely continue its diplomatic representation without expressing any opinion as to recognition, *vel non*. If some circumstances, other than the mere change of government, gives umbrage to Mexico, the Mexican diplomats will be withdrawn.

Theoretically, there is much to be said in favor of the Estrada Doctrine. Latin-American commentators have emphasized the view that it is desirable in that it acknowledges the full sovereignty of the state and eliminates foreign interference in the internal affairs of governments which are not constantly stable. It has also been argued that the Estrada Doctrine properly assumes that diplomatic representatives should be considered as accredited to the state and not to the government. In times of revolutionary disturbance a foreign state may frequently be called upon to decide whether it owes a duty of noninterference to the disturbed state or of support to the threatened government. Witness the case of a revolution in Brazil, wherein the United States proceeded on the latter thesis just before the triumph of the revolutionary party which it recognized shortly thereafter. Of course the problem is less difficult when the belligerency of the revolutionary faction is recognized and the foreign state may be guided by the obligations of neutrality. It is said that the Estrada Doctrine is in accord with the principles of the continuity of the state and of the juridical equality of states. It is argued that governments *de facto* are necessarily *de jure* and that the Estrada Doctrine admits this reality. It is true that this new doctrine gives welcome evidence to the important distinction between recognition of a new state and recognition of a new government.

Practically, the Estrada Doctrine does not remove all difficulties, although only a few of the Latin-American commentators have remarked on this fact. Granted that the diplomatic relations remain unaffected by changes of government, with whom are the foreign diplomats to deal? Should they continue to carry on their business with the local officials who are in the capital, even if the revolutionists are in *de facto* control of all the rest of the country? Should they carry on their business with the revolutionary leaders if the latter seize the capital, although the government to which the diplomats were originally accredited retains control of all the rest of the country, including the seaports? Or should they deal with both sets of officials in respect of problems arising in areas in which they respectively exercise *de facto* control? And will the "constitutional" government be quite willing that the foreign representatives should deal with revolutionary leaders in certain parts of the country? If money payments should fall due to the state during a revolutionary disturbance, to whom should the sums be paid? Probably both factions could be looked to for the satisfaction of state obligations and for the protection of foreign interests. The Estrada Doctrine will not always save foreign governments from the necessity of choosing between rival claimants. Nor, as the Tinoco arbitration showed, would the elimination of recognition solve those difficulties which arise from the necessity of determining whether the state is bound by obligations incurred by *de facto* authorities.

Fundamentally, however, the Estrada Doctrine seems to contemplate the obliteration of the distinction between change of government by peaceful balloting and change of government by revolution or *coup d'état*. The formalities of presenting credentials of the diplomatic corps may be dismissed as relatively unimportant, but the formalities are frequently indicative of underlying reality. When a new president is elected in the United States, diplomatic relations with other states continue unbroken.[40] According to the Estrada Doctrine, the same consequences would follow a change of government by revolution, whereas at present, some states seem to

[40] Cf. Lauterpacht, *op. cit., supra* note 10, p. 810.

consider the deposed government as having gone out of existence, thus terminating the foreign missions.[41]

Since the issue of approving the credentials of one or the other of two rival governmental groups may arise not only in the General Assembly but also in other organs of the United Nations and in specialized agencies,[42] it would seem to be necessary to establish a general procedure for determining such questions. It would surely be unsatisfactory to have the representative of faction A seated in the Economic and Social Council and the representative of faction B seated in the Food and Agriculture Organization. Nor would one wish to contemplate the Board of Governors of the International Monetary Fund carrying on financial discussions with one faction while the Board of the International Bank for Reconstruction and Development negotiated with the other faction. There are not the same types of objective tests to determine which of two factions is entitled to be called the government of a state as are available to determine whether a new entity is or is not a state. Such tests might be developed, and if they were they could be applied by the International Court of Justice, for example in rendering an advisory opinion to one of the organs of the United Nations. But a change overnight in the factual or military situation might invalidate such an opinion. It would appear to be necessary in such situations to continue to deal with the established government until the success of the opposing faction is clearly demonstrated, applying the tests which international law has developed with reference to the premature recognition of a revolting colony. To adopt the language of Secre-

[41] This discussion of the Estrada Doctrine is taken largely from the author's Editorial Comment in 25 *Am. J. Int. L.* (1931), 719. See also Carneiro, "O Direito internacional E A democracia" (1943), 147ff.; Fenwick, "The Recognition of New Governments Instituted by Force," 38 *Am. J. Int. L.* (1944), 448.

[42] Although the function of a credentials committee is usually purely formal, the Commission on Credentials of the International Labour Conferences may be required to deal with extremely difficult problems under Article 389 of the Treaty with reference to the seating of the nongovernment delegates, especially those representing the workers. See for example the "Report of the Commission on Credentials to the International Labour Conference, Washington, 1919," 2 Shotwell, *The Origins of the International Labor Organization* (1934), 480. The Permanent Court of International Justice was called upon to render an advisory opinion on the question whether the Workers' Delegate for the Netherlands in the third session of the International Labour Conference was properly nominated by the government; *P.C.I.J.*, Ser. B, No. 1 (1922).

tary of State Adams in 1818, one must await the stage when the new government is established as a matter of fact so as to leave the chances of the opposite party to recover their dominion utterly desperate.[43] On such a basis, the determination of the facts might be left to the International Court of Justice.[44] If necessary, action on the seating of any delegate from the state affected or negotiations with the government of the state might be deferred until a decision was reached.

EFFECTS ON INDIVIDUALS

In connection with recognition and the events which call for its extension, the acceptance of the doctrine that individuals are subjects of international law may also have at least indirect application. Individuals themselves would not ever be "recognized"; their status does not depend on recognition. The common provisions in existing treaties for the reciprocal "recognition" of the juridical status of companies incorporated under the laws of the contracting states might well be generalized,[45] but the similarity to the recognition of states or governments is only terminological. Duties attendant on nonintervention or neutrality would devolve upon individuals (as well as upon states) directly under international law and not solely, as in the past, through the medium of national laws. The nature of such duties and of the measures to be taken for their enforcement is reserved for treatment in Chapter VII.

In litigations involving individuals in national courts, the decision by the determined organ of the international organization in regard to recognition should be conclusive without the necessity for further action by the government of the state in which the court exists. This would be true even though the group or community decision was taken by majority vote with the state in question voting in the

[43] 1 Moore, *Digest of Int. L.* (1906), 78. Cf. Lauterpacht, *op. cit., supra* note 29, pp. 823, 840 ff.

[44] See Lauterpacht, "Recognition of Governments: II," 46 *Col. L. Rev.* (1946), 37, 63.

[45] See Art. 16 of the Draft Convention on the Treatment of Foreigners, prepared by the Economic Committee of the League of Nations in 1928, League Doc. C. 36. M. 21, 1929. II, II. Economic and Financial 1929. II. 5.; Declaration approved by the Governing Board of the Pan-American Union in 1936, 3 Hackworth, *Digest of Int. L.* (1942), 706; 1 Hyde, sec. 2042.

negative. From a constitutional point of view in some states, this situation might require legislation or other general advance expression of the acceptance by the political branch of the government of such decisions. Such would be the fact where, as in the United States and Great Britain, judicial decisions have established the constitutional principle that recognition is a political function and that the courts will therefore look to the political branch of the government for information concerning the recognized or unrecognized status of a foreign government or state. The principle would be satisfied if the proper constitutional organ by some general statement once and for all informed the judicial branch that thereafter the decision of the international organization would be accepted by it as its view. It might be considered preferable procedure for the Courts still to address inquiries to the Foreign Office or Department of State, which might reply by advising the Court what position the United Nations had taken. This is merely another instance of the necessity for utilizing national or—in the international sense—local governmental agencies as instrumentalities of the international order for bringing the law home to the individual. There may well remain borderline cases in which the decision may not be clear or may not have been made by the international authority, and such cases will remain to be decided by the exercise of judicial discretion.

It will also remain for the courts to determine the legal consequences in any given case of the recognition or nonrecognition of the political entity involved.[46]

An individual may have a direct interest in the recognition of a state. If he travels abroad he is concerned with the acknowledgment of his passport issued by the authority of the state whose nationality he claims. If he is a member of an unrecognized community he may be as badly off as the stateless person, whose condition is considered in Chapter IV. Possibly the recognition of his state would be immaterial if he sought to invoke against it by appeal to an international authority his rights under an International Bill of Rights.

[46] On the proper division of functions between the political and judicial branches of the government in similar cases see Jessup: "Has the Supreme Court

RETROACTIVITY OF RECOGNITION

It may be necessary or desirable to have international agreement on the doctrine of the retroactivity of recognition which has been evolved by the Supreme Court of the United States and followed by British courts.[47] Under this doctrine, it is said "that when a government which originates in revolution or revolt is recognized by the political department of our government as the *de jure* government of the country in which it is established, such recognition is retroactive in effect and validates all the actions and conduct of the government so recognized from the commencement of its existence." [48] The sound view is stated by John Bassett Moore: "By no law, national or international, can such a statement be justified. . . . The supposition that recognition of any kind 'validates all the actions and conduct' of the government recognized is as startling as it is novel. Recognition 'validates' nothing. On the contrary, it opens the way to the diplomatic controversion of the validity of any and all 'actions and conduct' that may be regarded as illegal." [49] But the extent to which the doctrine has been repeatedly stated makes clarification desirable. It would be even more true of a collective or group recognition than of unilateral state recognition that recognition should not be considered as a "validation" of prior actions and conduct. If the opposite were true, a very heavy burden would be placed on the international organ charged with the according of recognition, and undesirable and seriously awkward delays might be involved.

It may be appropriate here to call attention to the legal situation which has developed as a result of the failure of courts to understand the process of recognition and what it involves. The point is exemplified by litigations involving the effect of nationalization decrees by foreign governments. The Soviet nationalization program was carried through by a government not recognized by the government of the United States. After recognition was extended in 1933

---

[47] See Underhill *v.* Hernandez, 168 *U.S.* 250 (1897) and other citations in 1 Hyde, sec. 45F.

[48] Oetjen *v.* Central Leather Co., 246 *U.S.* 297, 302 (1918).

[49] Moore, "The New Isolation," 27 *Am. J. Int. L.* (1933), 607, 618; cf. Nisot, "Is the Recognition of a Government Retroactive?", 21 *Canadian Bar Rev.* (1943), 627.

American courts talked in terms of the "retroactivity" of the recognition and assumed that recognition of the government has something to do with "recognition" of its decrees. Currently the Czechoslovak government is carrying through a nationalization program.[50] No question of the recognition of that government is involved. If litigation develops in the United States relative to the effect to be attributed here to such foreign laws, the Courts will have an opportunity to clarify the rules of conflicts of laws applicable to such situations without invoking nonapplicable doctrines of public international law.

[50] See 15 Dept. of State *Bulletin* (1946), 1027.

CHAPTER IV

NATIONALITY AND THE RIGHTS OF MAN

As ALREADY INDICATED in the Introductory Chapter, the concept of nationality was necessary in traditional international law to explain the connection between the individual, who had no standing under international law, and the state, which was the exclusive subject of that law.[1] Conversely, alienage was the title under which were subsumed the relations of the individual to a state of which he was not a national. The acceptance of the concept of the international personality of the individual would not eliminate the utility of the concept of nationality, but it would necessitate some changes in it.

The Permanent Court of International Justice declared in 1923 that "in the present state of international law, questions of nationality" were solely within the domestic jurisdiction of a state.[2] But this position was not inconsistent with the proposition soundly stated by the Harvard Research Draft Convention on Nationality that "under international law the power of a state to confer its nationality is not unlimited." [3] This proposition was endorsed by the Hague Codification Conference of 1930, as by the terms of Article 1 of the Convention on Certain Questions Relating to the Conflict of Nationality Laws, which stated that the law of each state on nationality "shall be recognized by other States in so far as it is consistent with international conventions, international custom, and the principles of law generally recognized with regard to nationality." [4] The limitations were prescribed by international law, not in the interest of the individual, but in the interest of other states. Con-

[1] Cf. 1 Oppenheim, Sec. 291; Koessler, "Subject," "Citizen," "National," and "Permanent Allegiance," 56 *Yale L. J.* (1946), 58.
[2] "Advisory Opinion on the Tunis-Morocco Nationality Decrees," *P.C.I.J.*, Ser. B No. 4.
[3] 23 *Am. J. Int. L. Supp.* (1929), 24.
[4] League Doc. C. 351. M. 145. 1930. V., V. Legal 1930. V. 14., p. 81.

flicts of nationality were not avoided, since international law recognized the propriety of both the *ius soli* and the *ius sanguinis* as the basis of the acquisition of nationality at birth. Dual nationality is common. Nor was statelessness avoided, and many individuals were therefore unable to claim the nationality of any state and thus could look to no state for protection against the violent action of any other state.

Lauterpacht, in *An International Bill of the Rights of Man*, properly includes the "right to nationality" in his proposals. He is impressed particularly by the anomaly of statelessness in the international legal order and the resulting hardships of stateless persons. It is true, as he points out, that the stateless person is a *caput lupinum.* "He may be treated according to discretion by the State in which he resides. In cases in which aliens enjoy rights and advantages subject to reciprocity, the stateless person is excluded from such rights and advantages for the reason that he is not a national of any State offering reciprocity. He cannot, as a rule, possess a passport and his freedom of movement is correspondingly impeded. There is no State to which he can be deported, and cases have frequently occurred in which stateless persons have been moved from one frontier to another and were subject to imprisonment by way of punishment for failing to comply with a deportation order." [5] It is also justifiable for Lauterpacht to assert, within the frame of reference of his International Bill of the Rights of Man, that the proper way to eliminate this anomalous condition and to provide some degree of protection for stateless persons is to impose on states an obligation to accord their nationality to all persons born on their territory and not to deprive a person of his nationality by way of punishment or until he has concurrently acquired another nationality. This remedy for statelessness is not inconsistent with the hypothesis on which this book is based; that is, the acceptance of the position that the individual is a subject of international law. It may be true under this hypothesis that the best remedy for the difficulty is that which Lauterpacht suggests; but it is no longer the only solution. If the individual him-

[5] Lauterpacht, *An International Bill of the Rights of Man* (1945), 126. Cf. also Goldschmidt, *Legal Claims Against Germany* (1945), 60; Aufricht, "Personality in International Law," 37 *Am. Pol. Sci. Rev.* (1943), 241; Mansur Guerios, *Condição jurídica do apátrida* (1936).

self has rights, he has them in his own capacity and not derivatively through the state of which he is a national. His possession of international rights thus ceases to be dependent on his possession of a nationality. Procedurally, the vindication of the rights of the individual may be conceived in terms of the development of international organization for the protection of the individual.[6] A violation of a right of a stateless person might be made the concern of an international Commission on Human Rights to which the individual could appeal by right of petition. Another procedural solution under the hypothesis of individual rights could be found in the specific acknowledgment of the rights of the stateless individual against the state of his residence, with duties imposed on all states to provide local or national machinery, open to the stateless person, for the vindication of such rights. In this case, some type of international review or right of appeal might be recognized.

In connection both with nationality and with the rights of the individual irrespective of nationality, the test of residence has utility.[7] It has been a familiar criterion under international law for aiding in the solution of problems of dual nationality. But like other legal concepts, the meaning of the term is by no means clear when it becomes necessary to speak with reference to many different legal systems. The difficulty of defining "residence" is intensified if the term "domicile" is substituted, since, even within the realm of the common law of England and the United States, differences appear in the definition of this term. International law has further complicated the problem by its concept of "belligerent domicile" as a test of rights and status during war.[8] An attempt to meet the terminological difficulty has been made by employing adjectives, as in the term "habitual and principal residence."[9] It will be among the minor problems of the codification of international law to put precise and universally agreed content into one of these terms.

[6] Goldschmidt, loc. cit. See also in general, Lessing, La Obligación internacional de admisión de apátridas (1944).
[7] Cf. 1 Schwarzenberger, International Law (1945), 160.
[8] See 3 Hyde, 2085–89.
[9] The United States Nationality Act of 1940 in sec. 104 defines "residence" for the purposes of certain sections of the act as "the place of general abode." 54 Stat. 1137. See Codification of the Nationality Laws of the United States, House Committee Print, 76th Cong. 1st Sess. (1939), Part I, p. 6.

An insistence on the right to a nationality, regardless of international procedural developments, is a proper insistence so long as the world is organized on the basis of states, since it is only or at least principally through states that an individual has an opportunity for exercising political rights and thus sharing in the privilege and responsibility of government. But while this is true in theory, in reality the fact is that millions of human beings today exercise no political rights. In some instances this situation is due to the primitive political development of the individuals; in other cases it is due to what western nations would call the primitive democracy of the states in which they live. Lauterpacht provides in his International Bill of the Rights of Man that "No State shall deprive its citizens of the effective right to choose their governments and legislators on a footing of equality, in accordance with the law of the State, in free, secret, and periodic elections." In amplifying the clause "in accordance with the law of the State" he makes clear that literacy tests for voters, or even property qualifications, may be defended. The acceptance of his proposal would therefore not require a state to confer the franchise on primitive peoples subject to its rule and treated as wards of the state. In a broader sense Lauterpacht properly argues that unless representative government is established the freedom of the individual, which is the essential objective of the rights of man, is not established. He denies that such a proposal as he makes would mean interference in controlling the activities of all governments or that it negates the right of revolution.[10] It would undoubtedly be true in the world at large, regardless of the acceptance of the principle, that governments would vary widely in the quality and quantity of their democracy. It is a common error in the United States to assume that the American type of democracy is widespread or that it would be congenial to all peoples. It is no more inconsistent with the principle of representative government and equality of political rights to exclude a man from voting on account of his opposition to the government than to exclude him on account of the color of his skin. It is not merely international law and the international system, but also human nature, that must be revolutionized before there will be an end to such violations of political guarantees as those of which the history of the Fifteenth Amendment of the Constitution of the

[10] Lauterpacht, *op. cit., supra* note 5, p. 134 ff.

United States unfortunately affords many examples. If full compliance with such basic guarantees as those contained in that Constitution has not been secured within the United States, one should not anticipate that the formation of a world government would on its vast scale succeed in securing universal local compliance with an International Bill of Rights.

Nevertheless, reasonable anticipation of local violations of an international rule for the protection of the individual should by no means discourage the adoption of the basic guarantees. The way to begin is to begin.

The general international acceptance of the principle of equality of political rights for the individual would have to be subject to reasonable local requirements, which might exclude, for example, the insane and the inmates of prisons from the exercise of the franchise. Again one returns to the procedural difficulties of enforcement and the international supervision of the application of remedies open to the individual. These difficulties, it may be repeated, would exist whether the existing state system continues or whether the world is reorganized on the basis of world government. Under either system there must inevitably be delegation of authority to local units of manageable proportions with gradated units possessing supervisory powers or powers of review.

Similarly, the general international acceptance of the principle that every individual is entitled to a nationality would be pertinent under either the present state system of the world or the various projected forms of world government. Under the latter, however, the significance of nationality would be altered. It would no longer be the *sine qua non* of the availability of international rights, but only the symbol of the allocation of the individual to particular local units of government for purposes of convenient administration and representation in a "world parliament." Such units might vary enormously in size, as the Soviet Union and China now vary in size from Iceland and San Marino, or as Texas and California vary from Rhode Island and Delaware.

Granted that the individual possesses a right to a nationality, it does not follow that he should be free to choose any nationality regardless of reasonable qualifications, such as his identification with a particular community through ties of birthplace, blood, or residence. One may accept also the reasonableness of fairly administered differentials in the exercise of political rights by nationals. Such acceptance would merely continue the existing distinction which is frequently made between nationality, as the tie linking the individual to a governmental unit for international purposes, and citizenship as the quality requisite for the exercise of local political rights. A recent survey indicates that the nationality laws of seventeen states "are based solely on *jus sanguinis*, two equally upon *jus soli* and *jus sanguinis*, twenty-five principally upon *jus sanguinis* but partly upon *jus soli*, and twenty-six principally upon *jus soli* and partly upon *jus sanguinic*." [11] Arguments may be advanced for the choice of either basic system as the one that must be accepted by states to avoid the condition of statelessness, in principle it matters little which one is chosen.

Assuming then that every individual acquired at birth some nationality, two questions remain: first, the question of dual nationality, and secondly the question of changes of nationality.

Dual nationality at birth is the natural and inevitable consequence of the coexistence of the two systems of *ius soli* and *ius sanguinis*. A child born in the United States of French parents has American nationality, *iure soli*, and French nationality, *iure sanguinis*. The United States has for many years insisted that when a person thus born with dual nationality attains his majority, he should be free to elect one or the other of the two national ties,[12] but the statutory law of the United States was not wholly consistent with this claim. Various treaties contain provisions for the termination of such dual nationality by some form of election.[18] International friction has in the past resulted from dual claims to nationality, as was recognized at the First Conference for the Progressive Codification of International Law held at The Hague in 1930. That Conference accordingly drafted conventions to eliminate some of the sources of controversy, e.g. through its Protocol Relating to Military Obligations in Certain

[11] "Harvard Research in International Law, Draft Convention on Nationality," *op. cit., supra* note 3, p. 29.

[12] See 2 Hyde, 1140 ff.

[18] "Harvard Research in International Law, Draft Convention on Nationality," *op. cit., supra* note 3, p. 44. Cf. Flournoy, "Nationality Convention, Protocols and Recommendations Adopted by the First Conference on the Codification of International Law," 24 *Am. J. Int. L.* (1930), 467, 471.

Cases of Double Nationality.[14] The perfection and general acceptance of such agreements would be helpful.

In the Advisory Committee of Jurists which drafted the Statute of
the Permanent Court of International Justice, Professor de Lapradelle
suggested that a person having dual nationality should be enabled to
bring suit against both states in the international court in order to
determine his status, but the committee did not approve the suggestion.[15]

Dual nationality has generally been considered to arise also in
certain cases of changes of nationality after birth, as by naturalization.
The United States, especially following the precept of the Act of
July 27, 1868,[16] long insisted on "the right of expatriation" or the
right of the individual to throw off the nationality acquired at birth
in exchange for the assumption of another nationality through naturalization.[17] This position of the United States was not successfully
maintained and was steadfastly opposed by states which continued to
insist that their nationals could not throw off their allegiance without permission, which would customarily be withheld until the individual had satisfied certain local requirements such as the rendering
of military service. Difficulties were avoided only through the conclusion of bilateral treaties. The basic fallacy of the United States
position was that, under a system of international law which recognized only states as subjects of that law, there was an assertion of the
right of the individual against his state. The United States would
have been on sound theoretical ground had it rather taken the position that international law acknowledges the right of a state to nat-
uralize aliens under certain conditions and that international law
further prescribes that when naturalization is thus accorded its effect
is to terminate the nationality of origin. It is doubtful whether even
this position had achieved such general international acceptance as to
warrant the conclusion that it was supported by international law,
but it would at least have been more logical and theoretically
plausible.

[14] Flournoy, op. cit., supra note 13, p. 480.
[15] P.C.I.J. "Advisory Committee of Jurists, Procès-Verbaux of the Proceedings of the Committee, June 16th–July 24th, 1920" (1920), 210.
[16] 15 Stat. 223.
[17] 2 Hyde, sec. 378.

This long controversy over the "right of expatriation" is deprived of its historical significance if one accepts the hypothesis that the individual does have rights under international law. It then becomes proper to assert, as the Congress of the United States asserted in 1868 and as the United States Delegation declared at The Hague in 1930, that "expatriation is an inherent and natural right of all persons." [18] Thus Lauterpacht cites these and other precedents in support of the provision in his International Bill of the Rights of Man to the effect that "the right of . . . expatriation shall not be denied." Assuming that international law places reasonable restrictions on the requirements for naturalization, such as residence within the naturalizing country, the right of expatriation is an appropriate and a necessary attribute of the free individual.

A right of expatriation is predicated on the principle that the individual has the right to control his nationality, subject to the reasonable requirements of the law of the state involved. Conversely, it might be argued that an individual has a right of retention of his nationality. Actually, the laws of most states contain provisions that enable the state to deprive an individual of his nationality under certain circumstances. Where such provisions take the form of attaching such a legal consequence to the free act of the individual, they do not conflict with proper respect for the rights of individuals. Thus, for example, when the national law provides that nationality shall be lost by naturalization abroad, or by taking an oath of allegiance to or accepting a political office from a foreign power, no exception can properly be taken. It may also be reasonable for a state to assert that if an individual absents himself from the country for a long period of years without retaining his home ties, he shall be deemed to have expatriated himself. In these cases too, the individual acts on notice of the legal consequences of his action. But when loss of nationality is imposed as a penalty for political acts, a different conclusion may be reached. The interest of the state is presumably as well protected by the common type of provision which as a punishment, deprives an individual of the exercise of his political rights, while leaving his nationality unaffected.[19] As already noted, the re-

[18] Hunter Miller, *Acts of the Conference for the Codification of International Law, Meetings of the Committees,* Vol. II Nationality, League, Doc. V. Legal. 1930, V. 15, p. 80.
[19] See Borchard, *Diplomatic Protection of Citizens Abroad* (1915), 687.

duction of cases of statelessness is a desirable international objective, and its attainment would be furthered by prohibiting states from canceling nationality as a penalty.

Following from the same principle of the freedom of the individual to control his nationality is the conclusion that a state should not be free to impose its nationality on an individual against his will. This is the existing rule of international law in cases of forced naturalization.[20] It may be noted, however, that just as the legal consequence of expatriation may properly ensue upon certain voluntary acts of the individual, so there is no reason why a state may not assert that naturalization will automatically result from certain acts. The case of a woman naturalized by marriage to a citizen is a case in point, although attention will be called to the need for eliminating such discriminations because they are based on the sex of the individual. Controversy has been caused by provisions such as that in Mexican laws that the purchase of land by an alien would entail naturalization.[21] It would seem more appropriate in such cases to frame the law in terms of conferring only upon citizens the right to buy land; the individual would then have a choice between becoming a citizen and a landholder, or remaining an alien and not acquiring title to real property.

A form of forced expatriation and sometimes of forced naturalization has been recognized by international law in the case of change of sovereignty of territory. Where, for example, territory is ceded by one state to another, the ceding state is considered to have the power to transfer the allegiance of the inhabitants, and such transfer is deemed an automatic consequence of the cession. Under traditional law, however, the acquiring state was obligated to confer its nationality upon those persons, although not required to give them the political rights of citizens. The growing practice of holding plebiscites to determine whether a transfer of territory is in accord with the will of the majority of the inhabitants should be made the rule in all such cases. Members of the minority who oppose the transfer should be given the right to opt for the old nationality

[20] 1 Hyde, 1066.
[21] *Ibid.*, 1089 note 3. See Feller, *The Mexican Claims Commissions, 1923–1924* (1935), 98–100.

and to transfer to other parts of the territory of the ceding state of which they are nationals.[22]

Change of nationality by voluntary expatriation and naturalization is the result of a free exercise of individual will. Other changes of nationality take place frequently by operation of law. The effect of marriage on the nationality of the woman has been the subject of much international discussion.[23] This discussion is another precedent for the international concern in the status of the individual, and in this instance the concern has been manifested not only from the point of view of the interests of the state, but also from that of the human being, the family. The discrimination against women which was the result of the wide prevalence of laws providing that the nationality of the wife should follow that of the husband led eventually to international action such as, for example, the Inter-American Convention of December 26, 1933 signed at Montevideo providing that "there shall be no distinction based on sex as regards nationality" in the legislation or practice of the contracting states.[24] The provisions of the Charter of the United Nations, beginning with the reference in the Preamble to "the equal rights of men and women" and continuing through the multiple references to the "respect for human rights and for fundamental freedoms for all without distinction as to . . . sex" are confirmatory of the trend.[25] It is reasonable to expect the gradual approach to uniformity in nationality laws, which will remove any discrimination on the basis of sex in regard to nationality. The Nationality Law of 1940 in the United States has effected such equality in the law of this country. The Economic and Social Council of the United Nations through its various com-

[22] See 1 Oppenheim, 434–37.
[23] See Scott, *L'Égalité des deux sexes* (1931). The Supreme Court of the United States rationalized changes of the nationality of a woman effected by marriage to an alien, by asserting that this was an example of "voluntary" expatriation inasmuch as the woman freely contracted the marriage with notice of the consequences; Mackenzie v. Hare, 239 *U.S.* 299 (1915). But the principle of equality of the sexes does not tolerate this explanation so long as only the woman's status is thus affected.
[24] 4 Malloy, *Treaties* (1938), 4813.
[25] Cf. LeFur, "Le Développement historique du droit international" (1932), 41 *Hague recueil des cours* 505, 594; International Labour Office, *The International Labour Code 1939* (1941), Book IV, 176; *Report of the Sub-Commission on the Status of Women to the Commission on Human Rights*, UN Doc. E/38/Rev. 1, 21 May 1946, Appendix I, 14.

missions would appear to have a mandate to maintain and promote such equality in matters of nationality and otherwise.

In regard to minor children, the laws of various states still reveal a lack of uniformity.[26] The naturalization of a parent may include the naturalization of the minor children, and conversely the loss of a parent's nationality may embrace the loss of the nationality of such children. In general such provisions with respect to nationality follow more general provisions of the national law concerning the status of those not yet legally of age. International attention might well be directed to the problem with a view to recommendations for such changes in national laws as might be conducive to the unity of the family, but the problem cannot be considered one which in principle involves the theory of the rights of the individual.

EMIGRATION, IMMIGRATION, AND ASYLUM

A corollary of the right of expatriation is the right of emigration. If the right of the individual to leave the territory of his state is denied, the right of expatriation is effectively denied. Thus in the same year (1868) that the Congress of the United States proclaimed the inherent and natural right of expatriation, the United States concluded a treaty with China whereby the two governments "cordially recognize the inherent and inalienable right of man to change his home and allegiance, and also the mutual advantage of the free migration and emigration of their citizens and subjects respectively from the one country to the other for purposes of curiosity, of trade or as permanent residents. The high contracting parties therefore join in reprobating any other than an entirely voluntary emigration for these purposes." [27]

Lauterpacht thus justifiably couples the right of emigration with the right of expatriation.[28] But he also properly notes that states must be free to impose some limitations upon the right of emigra-

[26] "Harvard Research in International Law, Draft Convention on Nationality," *op cit., supra* note 3, pp. 95, 105.
[27] Article V of the Treaty; 1 Malloy, *Treaties* (1910), 234. Cf. 1 Oppenheim, 515-16. It was alleged at the Paris Peace Conference at the end of World War I that the Treaty of Westphalia in 1648 had recognized the right of emigration; see Bonsal, *Unfinished Business* (1944), 45.
[28] *Op. cit., supra* note 5, pp. 129-31.

tion to prevent the exercise of the right from being utilized as a means for evading the legitimate demands of the state of original nationality. Thus permission to emigrate might be withheld until taxes had been paid or debts discharged. The right can, however, be effectively destroyed by excessive restrictions such as those imposed through exchange controls.[29] Without asserting the accuracy of the account, an item in the *New York Times* for January 2, 1947, may be cited as an example. In a dispatch from The Hague David Anderson asserted that some 2,000,000 Dutch citizens wished to emigrate. "By means of foreign-exchange control the Government maintains a rigid control of emigration. The majority of the persons seeking to leave appear to have sufficient backing in cash or family support; nevertheless they are powerless to convert it into the currency of an adopted land." It is asserted also that a strict system of priorities imposes an equally rigid control over ocean passage on ships. The traditional prohibition of emigration until after the fulfillment of military service should be stripped of its legality. At the same time it would be reasonable for states to limit the right of the expatriate to return to his native country under certain circumstances. The troubles of the United States Government in asserting the right of expatriation were in large measure due to the common practice of individuals coming to the United States to be naturalized and then returning for permanent residence to the country of origin, where the newly acquired nationality would be used as a protection against wholly legitimate demands of the state of origin. The statutory law of the United States was amended in 1907 to take account of this difficulty and to regularize the denial of the protection of the United States to persons who had become naturalized solely or principally for the purpose of evading their native responsibilities and liabilities.[30]

The general denial of the right of emigration would constitute such a limitation on the freedom of the individual as to negate the general acceptance of his international rights. The concept of community interest in international relations could not tolerate a total denial of the right of emigration. It is clear, however, that no simple

[29] Cf. Letter of Philip Cortney to Craven-Ellis in *Commercial and Financial Chronicle*, July 4, 1946.
[30] 2 Hyde, sec. 389.

rule could be self-operating and that international procedures in these as in other instances will be necessary to the realization of individual rights. The difficulties in the way of the necessary international administrative processes can scarcely be exaggerated.

More difficulty is experienced with the right of immigration. Just as the right of expatriation may be nullified by a denial of the right of emigration, so the right of emigration might be nullified by the denial of the right of immigration. There is, however, an important factual difference. A single state, having full physical power over the individual, is in a position to make unreasonable exactions as the price of a permit to emigrate. Theoretically at least, the same individual has sixty-odd choices of states to which to emigrate. The possibility of a conspiracy to deny to a particular individual or group of individuals the right of immigration is thus slight.

Traditional international law has recognized the right of a state to adopt such tests as it wishes for the admission of aliens. This principle was recognized, for example, by the Japanese government at the time when it objected strenuously to the actual exclusion of Japanese nationals from the United States.[31] The United States in that and other instances justified its position on the same theory of reasonable classification that is recognized by its courts in applying the constitutional rule guaranteeing to individuals the "equal protection of the laws." Essentially the protests against the United States immigration laws were based on the assertion of improper discrimination against the nationals of particular countries and especially the countries of East Asia. The protests were answered by the provisions of the Immigration Act of 1924,[32] which provided that only aliens capable of being naturalized in the United States could be admitted as immigrants. (It may be noted in passing that there is general international acceptance of the principle that immigration may be prohibited on the basis of qualifications of health, morals, and the like.) The naturalization law confined the privilege of naturalization to white persons and persons of African descent, thus excluding members of the brown and yellow races. This situation has fortunately been altered by the passage of later laws permitting the naturalization of Chinese, Filipinos, and East Indians and by the allocation of mini-

[31] 1 Hyde, 218.
[32] 43 Stat. 153.

mal immigration quotas to persons of those races.[33] The Australian "white immigration" policy has, however, not been relaxed.

Like other cases of discrimination, the matter is not as simple as some would make out. If all immigration restrictions were removed in certain countries, the effect on their economies might be disastrous. The result would be the termination of those favorable living conditions which attracted the immigrants, with the result that new emigrations to other countries would ensue, the first emigrants being largely drawn from among those native elements of the population which had created the formerly favorable conditions. To carry the example to extremes for purposes of illustration, it might be suggested that if State A has attractive living conditions and draws a mass of immigrants from State B, where living conditions are bad, the ultimate result might be the deterioration of conditions in A and the ultimate improvement of conditions in B, causing the reverse trend in immigration, with the ultimate restoration of the former relative conditions in A and B, thus inducing a further turn in the cycle. In any event, the right of states to set reasonable conditions, whether numerical or in terms of individual qualifications, cannot be denied in any immediate future. Such regulation of immigration is not destructive of an individual right of emigration, even though it limits the choice of destination for the emigrant. Nor is it inconsistent with general freedom of travel, as is shown by the greater latitude in the immigration laws of the United States for various temporary visitors classed under the statute as "non-immigrants" and embracing not only tourists but also business men, seamen, and officials.[34]

Aside from the rankling discrimination against the admission of Asiatic peoples to the metropolitan areas of the western world, the United Nations cannot avoid being concerned with the settlement of colonial areas in which "empty" spaces have been deliberately maintained in the interest of outworn forms of colonial exploitation. It has been well said that "this much is certain—if the peoples of Asia are settled in, and are using the resources of, Borneo and New Guinea in 2000 A.D., they will not make war to take them from the

[33] Act of Dec. 17, 1943, 57 Stat. 600; Act of July 2, 1946, Ch. 534, Public Law 483.
[34] Sec. 3 of the Immigration Act of 1924, *op. cit., supra* note 28.

British, the Dutch, and the Australians, as they well may if the colonial system survives." [35]

There is another side to the question of emigration and immigration which has caused international repercussions in the past. The right of emigration is designed to prevent a state from forbidding the departure of persons from its territory; should a state equally be forbidden to force an individual to leave the country? The right of expulsion has been recognized by international law, although the manner of the exercise of the right has been restricted to avoid undue harshness and hardship.[36] In general the condition of proper solicitude for the interests of the person expelled has been invoked by the state of which he is a national; in other words, it has been applied to the cases of expulsion of aliens. But the expulsion of nationals, or the creation of conditions which force them out of the country, has been considered a matter of concern to the countries to which they may emigrate. Thus President Harrison, commenting on the harsh application of anti-Semitic laws in Russia in 1891, declared that the "banishment, whether by direct decree or by not less certain indirect methods, of so large a number of men and women is not a local question. A decree to leave one country is, in the nature of things, an order to enter another—some other. This consideration, as well as the suggestions of humanity, furnishes ample ground for the remonstrances which we have presented to Russia." [37] In the same connection, Secretary of State Blaine adverted to the question of "asylum" in the countries to which the Jewish émigrés might resort.[38] The right of asylum in international relations, like the right of expatriation, has been talked about as if it were a right of the individual, whereas actually under traditional international law it has referred to the right of a state to afford a safe haven to individuals who sought its protection. The state was privileged, not obligated, to grant asylum.[39] In line with what has been said above about immigration, it must follow that even under a modern law of nations the individual would not have a right of asylum in the sense of a right

[35] Thompson, "Population Growth and Control in Relation to World Peace" (1946), 55 *Yale L. J.*, 1242, 1254.
[36] Borchard, *op. cit., supra* note 19, pp. 48 ff.
[37] *U.S. For. Rel.* 1891, p. xii; 6 *Moore's Digest Int. L.*, 359.
[38] *Ibid.*, 354.
[39] Cf. 1 Oppenheim, 539.

to require any particular state to receive him. But precedent and humanity would suggest that every state should be under an obligation to grant temporary refuge to persons fleeing from persecution. In connection with the clearly distinguishable "right of asylum" in foreign embassies and consulates, the United States has denied the right but has admitted that its foreign missions might give temporary refuge to persons fleeing from a mob in time of unrest or political turmoil.[40] In such cases the United States acknowledged the duty to deliver the refugee to the local authorities, even where it was known that he would be shot for political activities adverse to the government in power. In the cases that we are here considering of refugees from one country to another, there should be no duty to return the individual to the country from which he has fled. The absence of a duty in such cases would be in accord with the well-established practice of providing in extradition treaties that political offenders shall not be surrendered.[41] Exception has been made for assassins, and, in line with the considerations developed in Chapter VII, such an exception might well be retained, subject to the possible establishment of international criminal courts to which the individual could be surrendered for trial. If local persecution reached the extent of the anti-Semitic activities in Russia in 1891 or in Nazi Germany in the 1930's, the view expressed by President Harrison would require that the problem be considered by an appropriate organ of the United Nations, which should decide either to intervene and put an end to the conditions causing the large migration or provide for the resettlement of the refugees.

A special case involving nationality, emigration, and immigration arises in the transfer of territory from one state to another. Attention has already been called to this problem in connection with the forced changes in nationality, and the matter of plebiscites has been touched upon. Where a territorial change has been authorized by a peace conference representing a group of states, by the Concert of Europe purporting to act for the European continent, or by a general or universal international organization acting on behalf of the world community, provision must be made for the future position of

[40] 2 Hyde, 1288.
[41] "Harvard Research in International Law, Draft Convention on Extradition," 29 *Am. J. Int. L. Supp.* (1935), 107.

the individuals affected. In such cases it has been common to allow the inhabitants a right to opt for one country or another. "It is generally admitted," says Kaeckenbeeck,[42] "that the exercise of the right of option in favor of another country entails the obligation to emigrate. Indeed, option made its appearance in Europe in the form of a *jus emigrandi*." Clearly in such cases, if there is a duty of the individual optant to emigrate, there is a duty of the state for which he opts to permit his immigration.

NATIONALITY OF JURISTIC PERSONS

It is generally considered that a corporation or other juristic person has a "nationality" or national character. This attribute is important in determining rights under commercial treaties and in the extension of diplomatic protection. A variety of theoretical arguments have been advanced concerning the proper criteria for determining corporate nationality.[43] In practice, the laws of a majority of states "have accepted the country of domicil (siège, Sitz) as the nationality of the corporation." [44] But differences then arise concerning the identification of the domicile. The matter may lie in the field of Private International Law or Conflict of Laws as Lauterpacht asserts,[45] but it has important consequences in the field of international relations. As noted in Chapter II, the adoption of the concept that the individual is a subject of international law naturally includes the position that a corporate person is also a subject of that law. While it remains true that many aspects of the problem will continue to involve questions of internal law, the juristic person should, under the hypothesis stated, be considered to have rights and duties directly under international law. The acceptance of this concept may facilitate the adoption of international regulations governing cartels and other forms of corporate association. If, for example, through the studies of the Economic and Social Council of the United Nations the conclusion is reached that certain forms of monopolistic inter-

[42] Kaeckenbeeck, *The International Experiment of Upper Silesia* (1942), 183.

[43] See Borchard, *Diplomatic Protection of Citizens Abroad* (1915), sec. 277.

[44] *Loc. cit.*

[45] 1 Oppenheim, 511, note 1.

national combination in restraint of trade should be made illegal under international agreements, a breach of the rule would involve the direct liability of the corporation as under the national laws of the United States. The situation would not be different from that in which an individual or natural person violates a rule of international law. Again the question of enforcement of the penalty for breach of the rule may be delegated to national authorities, or use may be made of various suggestions for international tribunals specially constituted to take jurisdiction of such cases.[46]

NATIONALITY OF SHIPS AND AIRCRAFT

The concept of nationality has also been applied to ships and aircraft, although the term "national character" is preferable. The concept is needed to determine the applicability of national laws to ships on the high seas and in foreign ports and to aircraft over the high seas or territories of states other than the home state. The problems are only in part those of conflict of laws as illustrated in the United States cases of Crapo v. Kelly and Fisher v. Fisher.[47] Public international importance attaches to the identification of the national character of vessels and aircraft in determining the applicability of treaty provisions concerning tonnage taxes, taxes on shipping profits, admissions to ports, and numerous problems which arose under the law of neutrality and of belligerent rights. The fiction of the territoriality of vessels is nothing more than a legalistic explanation of jurisdictional rules and has properly been rejected by the Supreme Court of the United States in a series of recent cases.[48]

Another legal fiction well established in Anglo-American admiralty law personifies the vessel and attributes to it a personalized responsibility in various situations. There is no advantage from the general point of view of a modernized international law in perpetuating or extending such fictions. Desirable results can be secured by straightforward description of factual situations and their legal consequences without resorting to fictional props. No useful purpose

[46] See Chap. VII.
[47] Crapo v. Kelly, 16 Wall. 610 (1872); Fisher v. Fisher, 250 N.Y. 313 (1929).
[48] See Cunard Steamship Co. v. Mellon, 262 U.S. 100, 123 (1923).

would be served by asserting that a ship or aircraft is an international person directly governed by international law. Such a position would constitute the substitution of an inanimate thing for that traditional intermediary between the individual and international law, the state.

SOLUTION OF NATIONALITY CONFLICTS

As already pointed out, questions of conflicts of nationality have frequently provoked international controversy, and they have often engaged the attention of international tribunals, particularly in claims cases. In the case of the Tunis-Morocco Nationality Decrees, the Permanent Court of International Justice pointed out that nationality questions are frequently governed by treaty provisions and in such instances clearly cease to be matters solely of domestic concern. There is no novelty therefore in the suggestion that it should be generally recognized that the administration of international law requires that cognizance be taken of national laws governing nationality and of the situation of individuals where two or more national laws come into conflict. But, as will be pointed out in Chapter V, the abandonment of the fiction that aliens derive their rights to protection and fair treatment only through the states of which they are nationals lessens the importance of the nationality factor in claims cases. It does not wholly obviate that factor, since it may still prove to be convenient from the point of view of procedure to provide for the prosecution of claims through the machinery of national governments. Although the sponsorship of an international body may be utilized in some cases (as for claims of individuals in or from territories under trusteeship, through the Trusteeship Council) it may also be envisaged that special international claims commissions will be established to which individuals may appeal directly for the vindication of their rights against other states. It will also continue to be true that, even where claims are prosecuted on behalf of an individual through the government of a state, it would be undesirable to permit states to prosecute claims of persons other than their own nationals. The danger in allowing a contrary procedure is that certain powerful states might through their power affect the administration of justice.

THE RIGHTS OF MAN

Since the rights of man are placed under international guarantee by the Charter of the United Nations, it would no longer be possible for a state to brush aside international representations concerning a violation of those rights on the ground that the victims were its citizens and that international law leaves a state free to deal with its own as it wills. It should be repeated that the treatment by a state of its citizens is no longer a matter which, under Article 2, paragraph 7 of the Charter, is "essentially within the domestic jurisdiction."[49] For this issue it is immaterial that the Charter language is different from that used in the Dumbarton Oaks text, which excluded from the competence of the international organization "situations or disputes arising out of matters which by international law are solely within the domestic jurisdiction of the state concerned." The elimination of the reference to international law as a test was supported by the argument "that the body of international law on this subject is indefinite and inadequate. To the extent that the matter is dealt with by international practice and by text writers, the conceptions are antiquated and not of a character which ought to be frozen into the new Organization." [50] The development of international law under the auspices of the United Nations has as one of its objectives the filling of such gaps in the law. It is wholly within the competence of the Members of the United Nations to make agreements that will supply in various situations tests which are definite and adequate to determine what matters are "essentially within the domestic jurisdiction."

The General Assembly of the United Nations took on December 8, 1946, action which may prove to be of great importance in this connection. The Government of India complained about the treatment accorded Indians in the Union of South Africa. Replying to the Indian presentation of its case, Field Marshal Smuts for the Union of South Africa "stressed the fact that Article 2, paragraph 7, of the Charter, embodied an over-riding principle, qualifying, subject to one

[49] Cf. 1 Hyde sec. 11c.
[50] *Report to the President on the Results of the San Francisco Conference by the Chairman of the United States Delegation*, Dept. of State Pub. 2349, p. 45. See *ibid.*, 181, for text of the Dumbarton Oaks Proposals.

specific exception, all the provisions of the Charter. That principle recognized that, within the domain of its domestic affairs, a state is not subject to control or interference, and its action could not be called into question by any other State." He recognized that treaty obligations might constitute another exception to the rule of non-interference, but denied that any such obligations were involved in this case. He went on to say that "a third exception to the rule of domestic jurisdiction might be sought in the direction of human rights and fundamental freedoms. . . . Up to the present, however, there did not exist any internationally recognized formulation of such rights, and the Charter itself did not define them. Member States, therefore, did not have any specific obligations under the Charter, whatever other moral obligations might rest upon them." [51] The General Assembly apparently did not share the point of view of Field Marshal Smuts either as to the nonexistence of specific bilateral obligations owed to India by South Africa or as to the nonexistence of legal obligations under the Charter. On December 8, 1946, it adopted a resolution by thirty-two votes to fifteen with seven abstentions, in which it stated that because of the treatment of Indians in South Africa "friendly relations between the two Member States have been impaired, and unless a satisfactory settlement is reached, these relations are likely to be further impaired." [52] This suggests that the jurisdiction of the General Assembly may rest on the impairment of friendly relations, even in cases involving a matter alleged to be within the domestic sphere. But the next paragraph of the resolution recognizes the existence of agreements between the two governments which could be interpreted to mean that the General Assembly found that the case fell within one of the exceptions admitted by Field Marshal Smuts. The resolution further records the opinion that the treatment of Indians in South Africa should also be in conformity with "the relevant provisions" of the Charter, which suggests that the general provisions of the Charter relative to human rights have certain obligatory force even before their explicit formulation.

Even under traditional international law there were examples of obligations which states assumed limiting the general freedom which they possessed in regard to the treatment of their own nationals. The

[51] *Journal of the UN* No. 40, Suppl. Nos. 1 & 6, p. 3, 23 Nov. 1946.
[52] UN Doc. A/205, 2 Dec. 1946.

minorities treaties are the most familiar examples. In 1938 a declaration of the Eighth Conference of American States asserted that "any persecution on account of racial or religious motives which makes it impossible for a group of human beings to live decently, is contrary to the political and juridical systems of America." [53] There is no inherent reason why more definite and inclusive obligations concerning fundamental human rights should not be embodied in a multipartite convention, even though the political difficulties of securing general ratification and the mechanical difficulties of providing appropriate means of enforcement are enormous. It is notable that a Canadian Court has already cited the Preamble and Articles 1 and 55 of the Charter as among the evidences of the public policy of the Dominion which justified the court in holding void a restrictive covenant on land which forbade the sale of land "to Jews or persons of objectionable nationality." [54] A like development in the jurisprudence of the courts of the United States which would invalidate some of the racial discrimination in the United States is by no means impossible.

It has been argued that the attempt to impose international controls on a state's treatment of its nationals tends to increase rather than to lessen both the internal and the external frictions. Viewed in this light, the minorities regime is said to have been detrimental to the achievement of the goal of harmonious relations between a minority group and the state of their residence. It is true that the privileged position of aliens under the former extraterritorial regimes in China and elsewhere tended to provoke hostility to the favored alien group. But the minorities treaties were obnoxious largely because they carried the stigma of imposition upon small states by the great powers, who were unwilling to accept like obligations in their own territories. Xenophobia has not markedly been traceable to the general protective shield which traditional international law has set up for the benefit of the alien. The acceptance by all states of such obligations as are

---

[53] This and other striking examples are noted in *The International Law of the Future* (1944), Comment on Principle 2, 45. To the same effect as the Inter-American resolution of 1938, see Resolution XLI of the Conference of Chapultepec, 1945, *Report of the Delegation of the United States of America to the Inter-American Conference on Problems of War and Peace*, Dept. of State Pub. 2497 (1946), 109.

[54] *Re* Drummond Wren [1945] 4 D.L.R. 674.

contemplated in proposals for an international bill of rights would be nondiscriminatory, and their enforcement would therefore be at least partially free from the element of provocation of local resentment which is the natural concomitant of "foreign" interference in local affairs. Unless such obligations are now generally accepted, the minority clause in paragraph 4 of Article 19 of the Italian Peace Treaty may be open to the objection indicated, since it requires a state to which Italian territory has been transferred to secure to persons *within that territory* the enjoyment of human rights and fundamental freedoms.[55] The implication is that it has no such duty in other parts of its territory. Article 15 of the same treaty [56] imposes upon Italy the general obligation to "take all measures necessary to secure to all persons under Italian jurisdiction, without distinction as to race, sex, language or religion, the enjoyment of human rights and of the fundamental freedoms, including freedom of expression, of press and publication, of religious worship, of political opinion and of public meeting." It is to be hoped that this article is designed to subject Italy as a nonmember of the United Nations only to the same obligations that members have under the Charter.   ·

If, in the early stages of the international development of the protection of human rights, enforcement is left to the national state, subject to review by an international authority, one may gradually approach a situation analogous to that in the federal system of the United States, where constitutional rights may be first considered by state courts and ultimately reviewed by federal courts. As the experience in the United States also teaches, it is of primary importance that flexible administrative procedures be developed and that the system be not left entirely in the more rigid hands of strictly judicial tribunals.

It is inherent in the concept of fundamental rights of man that those rights inhere in the individual and are not derived from the state.[57] This philosophy is as old as the struggle for human rights and human dignity. "The doctrine of inherent rights as expressed in the American Declaration of Independence, in the first American consti-

---

[55] *New York Times,* Jan. 18, 1947, p. 25.

[56] Similar provisions are in Article 2 of the Hungarian and Bulgarian treaties and Article 3 of the Rumanian treaty.

[57] The question whether special rights should be accorded individuals in their position as "aliens" is considered in the following chapter.

tutions, and in the French Declaration of the Rights of Man was not
an original invention. It put to revolutionary use the accumulated
power of what had been for a long time the backbone of the doctrine
of the law of nature on which James Otis, Samuel Adams, Jefferson,
and the other Fathers of the Revolution leaned so heavily." [58] It is
also true that among the jurists who developed the system of international law, those who took the natural law point of view were
influential. Yet the more recent period, notably in the nineteenth
and twentieth centuries, and particularly perhaps in the United States,
has seen the dominance of the positivist position. As the Fathers of
the American Revolution put to revolutionary use theoretical doctrine, the opportunity now exists for similar revolutionary application of that same theoretical doctrine as the foundation of a modernized law of nations. The confirmed positivist need have no quarrel
with such a position. The quarrel of the positivist is with those international lawyers who look backward rather than forward and who
then read into the past and into existing law the ideals they would
like to see achieved. Since this book is written *de lege ferenda*, the
attempt is made throughout to distinguish between the existing law
and the future goals of the law. It is already the law, at least for
Members of the United Nations, that respect for human dignity and
fundamental human right is obligatory. The duty is imposed by the
Charter, a treaty to which they are parties. The expansion of this
duty, its translation into specific rules, requires further steps of a
legislative character. It is immaterial to this discussion whether such
international legislation takes the form of additional treaties entered
into by the Members of the United Nations as states, or whether, as
is urged by many advocates of "world government," it takes the
form of real legislation enacted by a world parliament composed of
representatives not of states but of peoples. As already pointed out,
what many advocates of world government fail to take into consideration is the necessity, in view of the existing composition of the
world community, of action by states to create any new international
parliamentary body. Governments may be moved by men and
women, but organization of some sort is essential to governmental
development, whether on a national or an international scale. When
the unit is as large and as diverse in composition as the world, it is

[58] See Lauterpacht, *op. cit., supra* note 5, p. 31 and generally Part I.

advantageous if not essential to progress through the governments of existing states.

No attempt is made here to draft an international Bill of the Rights of Man. Effective spadework has already been done, and the task is in the hands of the United Nations Commission on Human Rights.[59] The human rights to be defined and protected must be considered not in a vacuum of theory, but in terms of the constitutions and laws and practices of more than seventy states of the world. Not every personal guarantee which is congenial to the constitution of the United States of America is necessarily well adapted to other civilizations. In the relatively simple question of adopting fair procedures for the Nürnberg Tribunal for the trial of the major German war criminals, American lawyers had to reconcile their views, their traditions, and their prejudices to the different views, traditions, and prejudices of European lawyers. It may be true that jury trials are necessary to the well-being of every tribe in Africa; but they are not utilized in every western country, and it may be that they should not be used. Throughout its work the Commission on Human Rights will be tossed from substantive problems to the procedures for their enforcement. It would do well to avoid seeking to impose as universal concepts those which are historically local phenomena. When the United States assumed the government of the Philippine Islands the Commission sent out to undertake the task was instructed by President McKinley, in terms drafted by Secretary of War Root, that they

[59] Among the official documents on this subject attention may be drawn to the Draft Declaration of the International Rights and Duties of Man and Accompanying Report, formulated by the Inter-American Juridical Committee and published by Pan American Union in March 1946; various proposals considered at San Francisco are summarized in the Statement of the Uruguayan Delegation on Committee I/1, Doc. 995, I 1/41, June 15, 1945, UNIO, *United Nations Conference on International Organization, San Francisco, 1945* (1945), 627; *Statement of Essential Human Rights by the Delegation of Panama*, UN Doc. E/HR/3, 26 Apl. 1946; *Cuban Proposal*, UN Doc. E/HR/1; 22 Apl. 1946; *Chilean Proposal*, UN Doc. E/CN, 4/2, 8 Jan. 1947; *Report of the Commission on Human Rights to the Second Session of the Economic and Social Council*, UN Doc. E/38/Rev. 1, 21 May 1946. Among the unofficial discussions, see Lauterpacht, *An International Bill of the Rights of Man* (1945); Robinson, *Human Rights and Fundamental Freedoms in the Charter of the United Nations* (1946); "Essential Human Rights," *Annals of the American Academy of Political and Social Science* (1946); "Commission to Study the Organization of Peace, Bill of Human Rights," *Int. Conciliation* (1946) No. 426; *American Federation of Labor Proposal*, UN Doc. E/CT. 2/2, 20 Aug. 1946.

"should bear in mind that the government which they are establishing is designed, not for our satisfaction or for the expression of our theoretical views, but for the happiness, peace and prosperity of the Philippine Islands, and the measures adopted should be made to conform to their customs, their habits, and even their prejudices, to the fullest extent consistent with the accomplishment of the indispensable requisites of just and effective government." [60]

The United Nations Commission on Human Rights might well be inspired by a like philosophy.[61] Its work might well proceed in stages. There might be a Declaration of Human Rights to serve as a standard and a goal. There might also be specific proposals designed to meet the most pressing needs of the people of the world through viable procedures. The philosopher may aid in drafting the Declaration; the practical statesman will have to devise the procedures.

[60] Jessup, 1 *Elihu Root* (1938), 356.
[61] Its Report of May 21, 1946, to the Economic and Social Council, already cited *supra* note 59, is a most encouraging indication of the wisdom with which it has envisaged its task.

CHAPTER V

THE RESPONSIBILITY OF STATES FOR INJURIES TO INDIVIDUALS

THE INTERNATIONAL LAW governing the responsibility of states for injuries to aliens is one of the most highly developed branches of that law.[1] The practice which has become so frequent in the course of the last century and a half of setting up mixed claims commissions for the adjudication of claims presented by states for injuries to their nationals in other states has provided an abundant body of the "case law" which appeals so strongly to the lawyer trained in the common law. Masses of briefs and of dissenting opinions are also available for study, and these frequently constitute useful guides to the diplomatic correspondence in which governments have set forth their views as to the applicable rules of international law. As on other subjects also, the preparatory documentation for the Hague Codification Conference of 1930, which constitutes the most fruitful work of that whole endeavor of the League of Nations, yields much evidence of governmental viewpoints on the law of responsibility.[2] The subject has also attracted the attention of numerous writers who have canvassed the subject from both the theoretical and practical points of view in general treatises and in monographs. Although frequently represented as a weapon of the strong against the weak states, in recent times the

---

[1] The author wishes to acknowledge his debt to the discussions at a meeting convened by the Division of International Law of the Carnegie Endowment for International Peace at the Council on Foreign Relations, New York City, on January 18, 1941. The following participated in the discussions. Prof James W. Angell, Prof. Percy W. Bidwell, Dr. Chao Ting Chi, Prof. Percy E. Corbett, Prof. Frederick S. Dunn, Dr. Ernst Feilchenfeld, Prof. A. Feller, Mr. George A. Finch, Judge Manley O. Hudson, Mr. William L. Lockwood, Prof. Charles F. Remer, Dr. William Sanders, Prof. James T. Shotwell, Mr. Frank A. Southard, Mr. Lionel M. Summers, Prof. Frank Tannenbaum, Mr. Edgar Turlington, Dr. Bryce Wood, Mr. Oliver J. Lissitzyn. The discussion covered broadly the field of foreign investments and the development of international law relative thereto.

[2] League Doc., C. 196. M. 70. 1927. V.; League Doc. C. P. D. 1. 95 (2), 1927.

subject affords perhaps the most striking example of the effectiveness of international law as the protector of weak. More claims by aliens inevitably arise in countries which have not yet attained their full economic development or in which there have been recurrences of violent political turmoil, but the United States and Great Britain have satisfactorily utilized mixed claims commissions for the disposition of their reciprocal claims. Judge Hudson counts some sixty mixed claims commissions which have functioned during the past one hundred years. "The United States has had twenty-six of these tribunals with other States . . . and three with Great Britain; nine of these tribunals were created by Great Britain with eight Latin American States, and three with two European States; Venezuela was a party before fourteen tribunals; Mexico before eight; France before seven; Colombia before five; Italy and Chile each before four; Belgium, Germany, Panama, and Spain, each before three; and Netherlands and Sweden each before two tribunals." [3] The dockets of many of these commissions were large; Hudson notes that the 1868 American-Mexican Claims Commission had 2015 claims before it and that of 1923, 3617 claims. The British claims alone before the commission established with the United States after the Civil War totaled $96,000,000. Considerable case material of value on the subject resulted from the operation of the Mixed Arbitral Tribunals established by the peace treaties at the end of World War I; Hudson mentions 30,000 claims before the German-Polish tribunal, 20,000 before the French-German tribunal, and 13,000 before the American-German Claims Commission set up in 1922.[4] In addition to the mixed claims commissions, other international tribunals, including the Permanent Court of International Justice, have dealt with particular claims and thus have had to rule on questions of the law of responsibility.

The history of this branch of international law during the nineteenth and twentieth centuries exemplifies the way in which a body of customary law develops in response to the need for adjustment of clashing interests. It was inevitable that the states which had achieved a large measure of local industrial and financial development should seek outlets for the investment of surplus funds and for the energies of their ranchers, bankers, mining engineers, railroad builders, con-

[3] Hudson, *International Tribunals Past and Future* (1944), 196.
[4] *Ibid.*, 9.

structors of ports, and other trained personnel. In many instances those energies found an outlet in colonies. In other instances colonial outlets were few and attention was turned to those independent countries which were on the threshold of their economic development. In the background as a driving force was the desire of governments for political influence in certain countries, the scramble for markets and for sources of rew materials which induced organized state support for the export of capital and industrial skill. The history of the development of the international law on the responsibility of states for injuries to aliens is thus an aspect of the history of "imperialism," or "dollar diplomacy." [5] It is remarkable that in this struggle which so generally involved the relations between the strong and the weak, international law, for all its primitiveness, developed as a balance for conflicting interests. The fact that several strong states found themselves simultaneously interested in the welfare of their nationals in states which were "exploited" may have assisted the legal development. Frederick S. Dunn, in the most imaginative and penetrating analysis of the problem which has been published, suggests that governments of even the most powerful states "are normally well disposed toward settling their differences on matters of protection [of their nationals abroad] by appeal to existing law" because "the interests involved in individual cases are not usually very extensive." [6] Considering the thousands of individual claims which demand a government's attention, this is probably true despite the recurrence of major disputes such as that attending the nationalization program in Mexico. Long-range policies of economic expansion can never be carried through without utilizing the inevitable bureaucratic techniques that permanent officials in foreign offices perfect and cling to as the means for handling routine appeals. Blanks, questionnaires, and printed forms are the inevitable human devices for disposing of individual cases when the scale becomes too vast to permit each case to be handled on a personalized basis, whether in government, business, or educational and philanthropic organizations.[7]

[5] The connection between expansionist state policy and foreign investments has been graphically recorded in Feis, *Europe the World's Banker* (1930). See Moon, *Imperialism and World Politics* (1930), c. IV.

[6] Dunn, *The Protection of Nationals* (1932), 1.

[7] See *ibid.*, 98 *et seq.* Although procedural details are not discussed in this Chapter, attention should be drawn to the practice of securing lump sum pay-

Dunn notes that the problem of the international law governing the protection of nationals abroad—which is the converse way of labeling the subject of the responsibility of states for injuries to aliens —"is ultimately concerned with the possibility of maintaining a unified economic and social order for the conduct of international trade and intercourse among independent political units of diverse cultures and stages of civilization, different legal and economic systems, and varying degrees of physical power and prestige." [8] That problem would remain unchanged in its substantive essentials if there should be developed a world government; that is, if the present emphasis on the separateness, independence, and sovereignty of the individual states were minimized. It is notable that among current proposals in the United States by advocates of world government, there is a tendency to confine the first efforts to achieve "world law" to the problem of the use of force, with considerable emphasis on the retention of economic autonomy. [9] Even in the federal system of the United States the right of business interests (corporations) from one state to do business in other states has required federal regulation and no small amount of judicial legislation. [10]

The embodiment in international law of the principle of the duty to respect the rights of man suggests new complications. The topic formerly known in international law as "the responsibility of states for injuries to *aliens*" might be transformed into "the responsibility of states for injuries to *individuals*." As already pointed out, the term "alien" connotes one of the relationships between individuals and states, in this instance the relationship of noncitizenship. Cases of statelessness being left aside, the assumption is that the "alien" is at the same time a citizen or national of another state. The state of which he is a national is interested in protecting him against the state to

---

ments to cover a large number of claims, the distribution to individual claimants being determined by an *ad hoc* domestic tribunal. See McKernan, "Special Mexican Claims," 32 *Am. J. Int. L.* (1938), 457.

[8] *Ibid.*, 1.

[9] "Dublin Manifesto," *N. Y. Times,* Oct. 17, 1945, p. 4, col. 4; "Rollins College Manifesto," *N. Y. Times,* Mar. 17, 1946, p. 5, col. 1. Cf. Reves, *Anatomy of Peace* (1945), pt. 2.

[10] See Henderson, *The Position of Foreign Corporations in American Constitutional Law* (1918), especially c. VII; Ribble, *State and National Power Over Commerce* (1937); cf. Wechsler, "Stone and the Constitution" (1946), 46 *Col. L. Rev.,* 764.

which he is an alien. This state interest has been asserted even in opposition to the will of the individual, and it is independent of the individual's interest. There are numerous grandiloquent statements about the "duty" of a state to protect its nationals abroad, but actually no such duty is imposed either by international law or, so far as appears, by national law. In the United States and in most states the extension of diplomatic protection and the prosecution of claims is a matter of discretion with the Secretary of State or the Foreign Secretary.[11] Protection was accorded, for example, over the opposition of American missionaries who have notified the Department of State that they did not wish to present any claim. The Department of State has insisted that it must bear in mind the general welfare of all American citizens abroad and that it must exercise its own judgment as to whether neglect of an injury to one citizen may inure to the damage of other citizens and to the general prestige of the United States. The action of the person damaged may be taken into account, but only if the government concerned wishes.[12] As Dunn has pointed out, the denial of international status to the individual has caused government officials in claims cases to "gravely [overemphasize] the importance of the political relations of states at the expense of the activities of men as human beings." [13] Instances in which the Department of State has declined to press diplomatic representations on behalf of importunate claimants are frequent and have often been due, not to the demerits of the claims, but to some overriding policy of fostering friendly relations. The Foreign Offices of small states may hesitate to antagonize a powerful neighbor by pressing against it the claim of one of its nationals.[14] On the other hand Brierly has argued effectively that the recognition of the international position of the individual in

[11] 2 Hyde, sec. 273; 1 Whiteman, *Damages in International Law* (1937), 275; McNair, *The Law of Treaties* (1938), 333.

[12] 1 Whiteman, *op. cit., supra* note 11, 184; Feller, *The Mexican Claims Commission 1923–1934* (1935), 90; see opinion dealing with Germany's Obligation and the Jurisdiction of this Commission as Determined by the Nationality of Claims and Administrative Decision No. V (1923–1925) Mixed Claims Commission U. S. and Germany, Administrative Decisions and Opinions 144, 190.

[13] Dunn, "The International Rights of Individuals," 1941 *Am. Soc. Int. L. Proc.*, 14, 16, 17.

[14] Cf. Scott, *The Hague Peace Conferences of 1899 and 1907* (1900), 487, 488; see Borchard, "The Access of Individuals to International Courts" (1930), 24 *Am. J. Int. L.*, 359, 362.

such cases would promote international peace, since the difficulties of the individual would not automatically be raised to the diplomatic level where they become entwined in "that mysterious but potent abstraction, 'national honor.' " Such recognition would also tend to check the grave menace of the promotion by states of private economic interests with which they identify national interests.[15] Under existing law, in at least some situations, such as disputes over administration of mandated areas, the state must not only espouse a claim but also make it the subject of an insoluble diplomatic controversy before the matter can be submitted to an international tribunal.[16]

Under traditional international law a state may not make diplomatic representations to another state on behalf of an individual who is not its national.[17] Rules have developed concerning the nationality of claims which are generally said to require not only that the claim must be national in origin, but also that it must remain continuously national up to the time of presentation or even of adjudication by an international tribunal.[18] Where states have made representations on behalf of oppressed groups of peoples they have been justified by identifying the representation either as a friendly gesture not based on claim of legal right, or by basing it on a treaty relationship be-

[15] Brierly, "Le Fondement du caractère obligatoire du droit internationale" (1928), 23 Recueil de cours, 467, 531.

[16] Cf. the reasoning of Judge Moore, dissenting in "Case of the Mavrommatis Palestine Concessions," P.C.I.J., Ser. A, No. 2, 54, 61 (1924).

[17] According to the Permanent Court of International Justice. ". . . the rule of international law . . . is that in taking up the case of one of its nationals . . . a State is in reality asserting its own right, the right to ensure in the person of its nationals respect for the rules of international law. This right is necessarily limited to intervention on behalf of its own nationals because, in the absence of a special agreement, it is the bond of nationality between the State and the individual which alone confers upon the State the right of diplomatic protection, and it is as a part of the function of diplomatic protection that the right to take up a claim and to ensure respect for the rules of international law must be envisaged. Where the injury was done to the national of some other state no claim to which such injury may give rise falls within the scope of the diplomatic protection which a State is entitled to afford nor can it give rise to a claim which that State is entitled to espouse." Case of the Panevezys-Saldutiskis Ry., P.C.I.J., Series A/B, No. 76, 16 (1939).

[18] See Hurst, "Nationality of Claims," 1926 Brit. Y. B. Int. L., 163. Members of the Institut de Droit International in 1932 questioned the rules on the nationality of claims on the ground that they reflected the basic artificiality of the law governing the diplomatic protection of citizens abroad; 1932 Annuaire de l'Institut de droit international, 479 ff.

tween the two states or on broad grounds of humanitarian appeal.[19] In cases of dual nationality there has been confusion because some judicial decisions have suggested that there are tests provided by international law for establishing the priority of one nationality claim over another.[20] Actually the cases establish that one state may not assert a claim of one of its nationals against another state of which he is also a national, on the ground that the second state is free under international law to treat its own national as it pleases, despite the fact that he has also the nationality of another state. In other words, the right of a state to deal unhampered with its own nationals has been considered a right superior to its duty to deal fairly with the nationals of another state.[21]

As noted in the preceding chapter, a stateless person cannot have a claim pressed on his behalf, because under the traditional view "A State . . . does not commit an international delinquency in inflicting an injury upon an individual lacking nationality, and consequently, no State is empowered to intervene or complain on his behalf either before or after the injury." [22]

Assuming the acceptance of the hypothesis that the right to fair treatment is a right of the individual and not merely the right of a state with which he is connected, the cases of dual nationality offer an illuminating picture of the change that would take place in international law. If X is a national of both States A and B and is mistreated in B, A could make legal representations on his behalf and B could not offer as a defense that X was at the same time its national, since B would owe a duty to X, not as a national of A, but as an

[19] See Jessup, "The Defense of Oppressed Peoples" (1938), 32 *Am. J. Int. L.*, 116.

[20] Lavigni and Bister claim, Spain-United States Claims Commission of 1871, 3 *Moore's International Arbitrations* (1898), 2454; Maninat claim, France-Venezuela Claims Commission of 1903, Ralston, *Venezuelan Arbitrations of 1903* (1904), Sen. Doc. No. 316, 58th Cong., 2d Sess. (1906), 44.

[21] "A State does not incur international responsibility from the fact that a subject of the claimant State suffers damages as a corollary or result of an injury which the defendant State has inflicted upon one of its own nationals or upon an individual of a nationality other than that of the claimant country, with whom the claimant is united by ties of relationship." The United States of America on behalf of Dickson Car Wheel Company *v.* The United Mexican States (1930-31), General Claims Commission United States and Mexico 175, 191 (1931), and cf. *ibid.*, 188.

[22] *Ibid.*

individual. Granted appropriate procedural developments in international relations, such as the establishment of special claims commissions to which the individual would have the right of direct access, X himself could present his claim and the question of nationality would clearly become irrelevant and immaterial. It might still be true, however, that international law would embody two sets of norms; one, those based on an international bill of rights and therefore appertaining to any individual, and another, those based on special additional rights accorded aliens. The justification for the existence of the second set of norms might be found in further attempts to solve the problem that Dunn states as the basis for the existing law on the protection of nationals, namely the orderly promotion of international trade and intercourse. The interests of the world community may require that additional safeguards be provided for the individual who as laborer, engineer, banker, or contractor goes into a strange country at its request or with its consent for the rendering of what are considered to be useful services. The issue is now acute with reference to the resettlement of displaced persons. Such a stranger or alien would not have the familiarity with local law, language, and custom that would be possessed by the native and would not have the opportunity for the exercise of political rights that appertain to the citizen. Under the traditional international law it has been said that "the individual in his capacity as alien enjoys a larger measure of protection by international law than in his character as the citizen of his own State." [23] The balance needs to be redressed, but the pendulum should not swing to the other extreme.

Latin-American jurists and governments have long asserted that the test for appropriate treatment of aliens should be equality with the nationals of the country in which they come to reside. This position has been countered, especially by the United States, with the assertion that there exists such a thing as an international standard for the administration of justice and the protection of the individual. If, in a particular state, the international standard is not maintained, the alien is entitled to the protection of his government. Secretary of State Cordell Hull sought to state a *reductio ad absurdum* in paraphrasing the Mexican Government's defense of the expropriation of agrarian properties, by declaring that it was the Mexican contention

[23] Lauterpacht, *An International Bill of the Rights of Man* (1945), 48.

"that it is wholly justifiable to deprive an individual of his rights if all other persons are equally deprived, and if no victim is allowed to escape." [24] There was something illogical in the traditional assertion of the international standard against the background of the conception of state interest and the denial of the existence of the individual as a subject of international law. In appearance, the international standard might be deemed the equivalent of the adoption of an international bill of rights; actually it did not envisage the existence of an international duty of a state with respect to its own nationals.[25] It thus was descriptive of a special duty with respect to aliens imposed on states by international law. Equality of treatment with nationals under this hypothesis was never really a defense against an international claim, even where the local standard was the same as the international standard. The defense was that the treatment of *aliens* was in accordance with the international standard; it was irrelevant whether nationals were treated in accordance with the same standard. If all states accepted an international bill of rights and if a denial of such rights constituted a breach of international law, the subsequent differences between the new and the old system might be merely procedural. International law might still permit the state of which the injured individual was a national to interpose on his behalf, to be his agent for securing the vindication of his rights. In such instances the protecting state would no longer be seeking to vindicate the traditional right of the state, which was said to be injured by the injury to its national. International law might likewise empower some international agency such as the United Nations Commission on Human Rights to take steps on behalf of the individual, at his request or on its own initiative.[26] Action by such an

[24] Dept. of State Pub. 1288, Communication to the Mexican Ambassador at Washington of Aug. 22, 1938 (1938); 2 Hyde, *op. cit., supra* note 12, 877. In a case arising under the terms of a special treaty between England and Russia the law officers of the Crown held that Russia was entitled to discriminate against British Jews provided she applied the same discriminatory treatment to her own Jewish nationals, although the language of the treaty favored the equal treatment of all British nationals. Report of the Law Officers of the Crown to Earl Granville dated November 5, 1881, McNair, *The Law of Treaties* (1938), 193.

[25] Hyde, "Confiscatory Expropriation" (1938), 32 *Am. J. Int. L.*, 759, 763.

[26] See the interesting suggestion for the establishment of an international body without power to adjudicate but charged with investigating and reporting on claims in Turlington, *A New Technique in International Reclamations* (1943), 37 *Am. J. Int. L.*, 291. Cf. Cowles, *The Hannevig Case* (1938), 32; *ibid.*, 142.

international body would under these circumstances take no account of the nationality of the injured individual.

Many suggestions are currently being made concerning the possible content of an international bill of rights.[27] At this point it is pertinent to consider whether a modernized international law would have need of an additional set of rules designed for the particular protection of a special class of individuals, identifiable by the label "aliens." In addition, emphasis on the acceptance of the concept of the individual as a subject of international law, and therefore as a direct beneficiary of the rights which it confers, should not blind the eye to the possible need for international legal rules designed for the protection of groups of individuals associated together in what we call a state. Such a need might exist even when the significance of the state has been diminished through reduction of the importance of the concept of absolute sovereignty and through the acceptance of the concept of community interest. As in other matters, it is convenient to explore this subject by further examination of the relevant traditional international law, in this instance the law determining the responsibility of states for injuries to aliens.

Two rules are generally accepted as starting points in the approach to the determination of a state's responsibility for an injury to an alien. The first of these is that the alien, by entering a foreign country, subjects himself to the local law.[28] The second rule is that the state is not an insurer of the safety and lives of aliens.[29] Offsetting the first rule is the concept of the international standard which qualifies the supremacy of the local law, including law administration, by asserting that the local law is not the last resort if it falls below the standard, in general or in its application to the particular case. Thus a Mexican citizen residing in Texas subjects himself to the law of that state and of the United States, but the United States has been held liable when the trial of an American citizen who injured the Mexican was characterized by excessive delays amounting to maladministration.[30] The second rule is qualified by a set of sub-

[27] See Chap. IV *supra*.
[28] Borchard, *Diplomatic Protection of Citizens Abroad* (1915), 179.
[29] *Ibid.*
[30] The United Mexican States on behalf of Salomé Lerma Vda. de Galván *v.* United States (1926-27) General Claims Commission, United States and Mexico 408 (1927).

sidiary rules stating the conditions under which the state is liable for an injury to an alien. In general, liability is predicated on fault (*culpa*). Thus if a British national residing in the United States is run over by a bus or if his wallet is stolen by a pickpocket in the subway, the United States is not liable. But if his fishing boat is run down by a negligently operated naval vessel, or if after warning of an impending mob attack complacent police officials decline to take preventive action, or if agencies of the federal government take his property without paying proper compensation, the United States is liable.[81]

The responsibility of the state for an injury to an alien may be predicated on a sin of omission or on one of commission. If the state fails under certain circumstances to use the means at its disposal to ward off a threatened injury of which it has advance notice or if it fails to provide appropriate remedial processes through its courts, it may be liable.[82] If its soldiers, in line of duty, shoot an alien without justification, responsibility has attached.[83] A simple breach of contract between a state and an alien is a violation of local law, not of international law; if it is accompanied by forcible seizure or destruction of property amounting to what is called tortious or confiscatory breach of contract, the state's responsibility will be engaged.[84]

As a corollary to the rule that the alien subjects himself to the local law, there is a well established but inadequately defined rule that the alien must exhaust his local remedies before a diplomatic claim is made. The assumption is that if the alien resorts to the local courts, justice will be done. The line of reasoning then leads to the formulation of the rule that the state is liable for a denial of justice. This would be a satisfactory test if there were agreement on the meaning of the term, but there is not, and, as Lissitzyn has

[81] In the Matter of the Lindisfarne (1913), *Am. J. Int. L.*, 875; Case of the Confidence, 1855, 3 *Moore's International Arbitrations* (1898), 3063, commented on in Borchard, *op. cit., supra* note 28, p. 188. Cf. "The I'm Alone," Dept. of State Arbitration Ser. No. 2 (1) (1931); cf. the Norwegian Ships case (1922), 17 *Am. J. Int. L.*, 362 (Permanent Court of Arbitration), commented on in 2 Hyde, 936.

[82] Borchard, *op. cit., supra* note 28, p. 224; 2 Hyde, 917 *et seq.*

[83] Borchard, *op. cit., supra* note 28, p. 193.

[84] 3 Whiteman, *op. cit., supra* note 11, p. 1555; 2 Hyde, 988.

shown, the variety in the definitions of the term has robbed it of utility.[35]

The conclusion must be reached that while there is abundant precedent and general statement of principle to enable international tribunals to make or to refuse awards in any particular claim, the lack of precision in the law leaves to the tribunal wide latitude and inevitably results in a very large measure of subjectivity in these judicial decisions. Since few jurists still cling to the old view that the role of the judge is merely mechanical, requiring him to identify the law of the case and to turn out the judgment as if he were tapping keys and pulling levers on an adding machine, this characteristic of the law of responsibility of states does not imply that it is encumbered by more defects than many branches of national law. It does suggest, as Dunn has amply demonstrated, that there is room for creative reappraisal of the function of the law in such cases in order that the judge's choice may be guided by accepted standards and principles.

The function of the law of responsibility of states for injuries to aliens, in terms of the modernization of international law, is to provide, in the general world interest, adequate protection for the stranger, to the end that travel, trade, and intercourse may be facilitated. The law must take into account the fact that in States A and B peaceful habits, a minimum of violence, and well-developed law administration prevail, whereas in States C and D conditions of turmoil, violence, and imperfect or slovenly law administration are characteristic. One trouble has been that statesmen, writers and judges on international tribunals have all too often set up in their minds an ideal condition which rarely exists and have tended to assert a perfect international standard which does not reflect actual conditions in the most orderly states. Municipal graft and corruption, packed juries, and delays in law administration have existed in the United States while it has sought to hold others to a nonexistent perfection.[36] And yet the general standard of law administration in the

[35] Lissitzyn, "The Meaning of the Term Denial of Justice in International Law," 30 *Am. J. Int. L.* (1936), 632, 645, 646; 2 Hyde, p. 911.

[36] In his annual message to Congress on December 6, 1904, President Theodore Roosevelt declared: "We have plenty of sins of our own to war against, and under ordinary circumstances we can do more for the general uplifting of humanity by striving with heart and soul to put a stop to civil corruption, to brutal lawlessness and violent race prejudices here at home than by passing reso-

United States has undoubtedly been higher than that in some other states.

Attempts have been made to invoke the doctrine of the equality of states as a bar to considering factual inequalities in these respects. But any reasonable application of the doctrine of equality before the law requires merely that the same objective tests be applied to the conduct of all states. A state unable or unwilling in general or in particular cases to order its own affairs in such a way as to facilitate the promotion of the interests of the world community must be made to pay the penalty. Granted adequate international tribunals staffed by judges unswayed by prejudices, responsibility can be fairly assessed. By and large the experience with the existing system of law, despite its defects, has been satisfactory.[87]

The conception of territorial sovereignty has also been invoked to justify unreviewable exercises of state will within the national territory. If the concept of absolute sovereignty yields to the concept of community interest, as this study assumes by way of hypothesis, this logical difficulty that pervades international law in many if not all of its branches loses its importance.

Dunn has suggested a satisfactory basis for the development of this branch of international law:

> "It seems that a workable test can only be arrived at by giving consideration to the general purpose of the notion of international responsibility in connection with the injuries to foreigners. As already suggested, that purpose seems to be to preserve the minimum conditions which are regarded as necessary for the continuance of international trade and intercourse on its present basis. That purpose does not require that

___

lutions about wrong doing elsewhere. Nevertheless there are occasional crimes committed on so vast a scale and of such peculiar horror as to make us doubt whether it is not our manifest duty to endeavor at least to show our disapproval of the deed and our sympathy with those who have suffered by it. The cases must be extreme in which such a course is justifiable. There must be no effort made to remove the mote from our brother's eye if we refuse to remove the beam from our own." *For. Rel.,* U. S. 1904, xlii.

[87] The term "satisfactory" is used here with reference to the criterion of monetary compensation to injured individuals. Before the term could be used to suggest that the law has adequately discharged the function of facilitating international trade and intercourse, more detailed studies than are yet available would

a state be made to answer for every injurious act of every one of its many officials and employees. At the same time, it does require that the state be held responsible for certain types of misuse of governmental power.

"Here one can have recourse to the notion of risk allocation (as developed in Anglo-Saxon law in recent years) in place of the old notion of fault as the determinant of responsibility. It is obvious that normal business and social relations can still be carried on although there is a certain percentage of abuses of governmental power by individual officials and employees. The existing system takes account of the fact that a certain proportion of these is inevitable, and makes allowances for them without expecting compensation from the state. Normal business and social relationships, in other words, are capable of taking a certain degree of risk in this matter. There is a point, however, where derelictions and errors on the part of government officials (regardless of rank) might become so numerous as to make the usual course of social and economic life difficult, if not impossible, to carry on. In other words, these relationships are not able to absorb the entire risk of such derelictions. From this point on, the state should take over the risk of injuries from misuses of the governmental power. Failures beyond this point are occasionally bound to occur, regardless of the care exercised in the selection of personnel or the amount of supervision used, but the state can and should assume the risk of these failures; otherwise it would not be fulfilling the primary purpose of political organization, which is to maintain conditions under which social life is possible." [38]

Dunn continues to show that his test is applicable even in those instances where the legal jargon talks in terms of the responsibility of the state for the acts of individuals, since in these cases responsibility

---

[38] Dunn, *op. cit., supra* note 6, p. 133. Dunn's discussion of the quantum of derelictions and errors perhaps glosses over situations in which unique acts of maladministration of justice in a well-ordered state subject an individual to injury for which he should equitably be entitled to compensation. If the law of responsibility be considered, like criminal law penalties, in the light of a deterrent to further improper acts of government officials, other elements such as the individual liability of the official to punishment for an "international crime" would need to be weighed; see Chap. VII.

is ultimately predicated on the action or inaction of officials. The question of denial of justice also resolves itself into a consideration of the propriety of the acts of the judicial branch of the government. In all cases therefore it is possible to return to the theory of risk allocation. Dunn admits that his test does not eliminate all vagueness, but he demonstrates that it is easier of application than the traditional tests, which often rested on fictions and forms of words devoid of real meaning.

The test of risk allocation may itself be tested by problems which arise in connection with contractual claims.[89] Two typical situations may be analyzed. Specific states may be used for purposes of illustration. The first situation is that of a Delaware corporation which contracts with the Government of Iran to construct a railway from point A to point B in Iran. The contract provides that the corporation shall complete X miles of roadbed within six months and the entire job within twelve months. The Government agrees to pay the contractor Y dollars per mile of finished roadbed, the sums to be paid in two installments, one at the end of each six-month period. The Government further agrees to allow the free importation of all necessary materials, machinery, and supplies and the free entry of all necessary personnel. The corporation begins work, bringing in goods and engineers and supervisory personnel. In the course of the first six months a revolution occurs in Iran. Fighting continues for two months after which the revolution is suppressed. In the course of the fighting, revolutionists seize a quantity of food and other supplies belonging to the corporation, and an officer of the government forces requisitions the services of a number of the men working on the railway to build fortifications. The result is that

[89] A complete test of the theory obviously requires a much wider sampling of various types of claims. It is not derogatory to assert that Dunn's book is itself only an introduction to the subject. Further detailed studies will be required before one can be dogmatic in asserting that the theory of risk allocation meets all needs even of the traditional system of international law. Its utility in new situations that may develop under present and future conditions is a challenging topic, which this chapter does not seek to exhaust. For interesting examples of the application of the theory of risk allocation in cases involving currency and foreign exchange restrictions see Domke, "La Législation allemande sur les devises en droit international privé," 64 *Journal du droit international* (1937), 226, 243; "Nouveaux aspects des restrictions de transfert en droit international privé," *ibid.*, 990; "International Loans and the Conflict of Laws," 1937 *Trans. of the Grotius Society.* 47.

work on the railway is interrupted and the scheduled mileage is not completed until three months after the first six-month period. The corporation demands the payment of the sum stipulated for the first installment, which the Government declines to pay on the ground that the contractor has not fulfilled his contract. The corporation thereupon abandons work on the railway and seeks to remove its supplies. The government prevents the removal. The corporation appeals to the United States Department of State for assistance.[40]

A number of rules of international law enter into the picture. Ordinarily the Government of the United States will not interpose diplomatically in contract claims, but it will on occasion do so in case of "tortious interference" with the performance of contracts. A simple breach of contract, as already mentioned, constitutes a violation of local but not of international law. In the next place, the Government of Iran would undoubtedly reply to any diplomatic representation that the courts of Iran are open to the corporation and that they will adjudicate upon the rights under the contract according to the Iranian law. It may be assumed that under Iranian law contractual suits against the government may be entertained by the Iranian courts. It is a further rule of international law, frequently applied by international tribunals, that a state is not liable for the acts of unsuccessful revolutionists, but is liable for the acts of its own military officers in the performance of their duty. If the corporation resorts to the Iranian courts and if, after prolonged litigation with appeals to the highest courts, the judgment is adverse to its claims, it will undoubtedly allege that there has been a "denial of justice." At this point the governments of the United States and Iran might agree to submit the claim to an arbitral tribunal. Granted the establishment of appropriate international procedures, the corporation might itself invoke the international jurisdiction.

If such a tribunal were applying an international law based on the theory of risk allocation, what judgment would be rendered? It would be reasonable to assert that under such circumstances the corporate contractor, while assuming the normal risks of weather,

[40] Analogous factual situations can be found in various claims cases before international tribunals, e.g., The North and South American Construction Co. claim, United States and Chile, 1892, 3 *Moore's Arbitrations* (1898), 2318; Martini case, France and Venezuela, Ralston (1904), *op. cit., supra* note 11, p. 819; French Company of Venezuelan R. R. case, *idem*, 367.

terrain, and the like, should not be expected to assume the risk of revolutionary disturbance; that latter risk should be borne by the government. This result is diametrically opposite to that obtained under the existing law based on fault, but it may be noted that there are precedents for a state's assumption of an obligation to make compensation for injuries suffered by aliens during periods of revolutionary disturbance. The most notable case is that of Mexico in 1923, which concluded agreements with six states whereby it was agreed that claims commissions should determine the amounts of such claims and that they should be paid by Mexico *ex gratia* and without reference to their basis in the international law of responsibility.[41] The 1903 arbitration protocols with Venezuela contained an admission of liability to pay for certain types of claims. Umpire Duffield in the German-Venezuelan Commission construed the language as including liability to pay for damages inflicted by revolutionary forces. Umpire Ralston in the Italian-Venezuelan Commission reached the opposite result in the Sambiaggio claim, which has become a leading case for the proposition that no liability attaches for such damages.[42] It would also be reasonable to assert that such a contract made in Iran and to be performed in Iran is governed by Iranian law. That law may provide that breach of contract by one party does not justify breach by the other. The corporation by entering into the contract took the risks of the local law. The conclusion would be that Iran, having the benefit of the completed mileage, was obligated to pay the stipulated sum for that amount of finished roadbed;[43] that it was obligated to reimburse the company for the value of the supplies confiscated by the revolutionists. On the other hand the corporation would not be justified in its refusal to continue the work, and the loss of machinery, supplies, and materials due to its abandonment of the work must be borne by it.

Let it be assumed that the contract also embodied a "Calvo Clause"; that is, a clause providing that the corporation should in all matters connected with the contract be deemed an Iranian national and should not under any circumstances seek the diplomatic protec-

[41] Feller, *The Mexican Claims Commissions 1923–1934* (1935), 157–58.

[42] Borchard, *op. cit., supra* note 28, pp. 229, 231, n. 7.

[43] The international law on state succession has taken into account the principle of unjust enrichment. Kaeckenbeeck, "The Protection of Vested Rights in International Law," 16 *Brit. Y. B. Int. L.* (1936), 1, 10, 11, 15, 16.

tion of its government.[44] The long controversy over the Calvo Clause in which the United States has been the chief protagonist of the opposition and the Latin-American countries the chief defenders has focused on the traditional precept of international law that only states are subjects of that law. Therefore all of the law having to do with the responsibility of states for injuries to aliens is law conferring rights on states, which are said to be injured by injuries to their nationals. Accordingly the United States has consistently maintained that the individual could not waive a right which was not his, but was the right of his state. Under the hypothesis that it is the individual himself who has rights under international law, this basic objection loses all logical force. The rights which appertain to the individual may be waived by the individual. But the *raison d'être* of the Calvo Clause also disappears with the acceptance of this hypothesis. Under the traditional law the individual himself could not vindicate his rights, but must act through his government. If, as already envisaged, there are established international claims commissions to which the individual has direct right of access, the corporation in our illustrative case would not need to proceed through the Department of State, but might take its case direct to the international tribunal. This situation illustrates the utility of retaining in a modernized international law the rule of exhaustion of local remedies. Claimants should be required to resort first to the local courts in order to avoid overburdening the international tribunals.[45] A Calvo Clause may be nothing more than a promise to use local remedies and thus be unnecessary but harmless. International tribunals should be called on to act only after the use of the local remedies has failed to yield satisfaction. In this connection it should be the rule that if the international tribunal finds that the local courts acted through prejudice or corruption, the costs of the litigation should be collectible as part of the judgment in favor of the claimant.

Under the new hypothesis, would the signature of a Calvo Clause be effective if the contractor agreed to waive not only the right to appeal to his own government but also the right to appeal direct

[44] See 2 Hyde, 994.

[45] Cf. Coudert and Lans, "Direct Foreign Investment in Undeveloped Countries: Some Practical Problems," 11 *Law and Contemporary Problems* (1946), 741.

to an international tribunal which otherwise would have jurisdiction? The answer should be that in the general interest an individual should not be free to oust the international jurisdiction unless an adequate substitute is utilized. The case would be comparable to one under the law of the United States in which the contracting parties seek to oust the jurisdiction of the courts.[46] Such provisions are held to be unenforceable on the ground of public interest, although the rigid earlier attitude of the courts, applying this notion even to the exclusion of agreements to submit disputes to private arbitration, has been modified.[47] It should be possible for the private contractor and the state to agree on an alternate method of impartial adjudication in case of an allegation of denial of justice. This would be in line with the arbitration clauses which are becoming common in international private commercial contracts, and on the other hand would be comparable to the option reserved by some states when accepting the compulsory jurisdiction of the International Court of Justice, to submit a dispute to settlement by some other tribunal. International public policy should ban only such clauses as would prevent impartial review by some tribunal freely chosen by the parties. It may be argued that if the parties freely choose in advance to accept as final the decision of the local courts, this agreement should be sustained. In the typical concession contract there may be sufficient equality of bargaining power between the foreign corporation and the contracting state to warrant such a conclusion.

The second typical hypothetical situation which may be considered is that in which private bankers in one state extend a loan to the government of another state. A somewhat extreme case may be taken from history for purposes of illustration. The first foreign loan negotiated by the Mexican government after the establishment of its independence was negotiated with the British house of Goldschmidt in 1824. The face value of the 5 per cent bonds issued was 16,000,000 pesos, of which 8,000,000 pesos were placed at the disposal of the Mexican government, but 2,000,000 pesos were first deducted for interest, sinking fund, and commissions, netting Mexico 6,000,000

[46] 2 Williston, *Contracts* (2d ed. 1938), sec. 1919, cf. Doleman & Sons *v.* Osset Corporation, [1912], 3 *K. B.* 257 (C. A.).

[47] 2 Williston, *Contracts* (2d ed. 1938), sec. 1920; Nussbaum, "The 'Separability Doctrine' in American and Foreign Arbitration" (1940), 17 *N. Y. Univ. L. Q. Rev.*, 609.

pesos. Goldschmidt sold the bonds to the public at 58, grossing a quarter of a million pounds plus subsequent commissions.[48] Default on this loan did not lead to intervention by the British Government, but nonpayment of 100 per cent of the loan placed by Mexico in 1859 with the Swiss-French banking firm of J. B. Jecker and Company—when Mexico borrowed at a cost of about 90 per cent—was one of the justifications advanced by the French government for its intervention in 1862 leading to the establishment of the Maximilian "empire."[49] Venezuela's nonpayment of loans and of other foreign claims led in 1902 to the celebrated action of three European powers, Great Britain, Germany, and Italy, which first established a pacific blockade and later a belligerent blockade. These events led the Argentine Foreign Minister Drago to send his famous note to the United States proposing an international agreement prohibiting the use of force for the collection of such debts. Drago supported his views by arguing that a loan contract was of a special nature, contracted by the bankers with the realization that it was not enforceable in any court and therefore rested on the good faith of the borrowing government.[50] Thanks to the support of Secretary of State Root the Pan-American Conference in 1906 endorsed the Drago Doctrine, and under the leadership of the United States the so-called Porter Convention was signed at the Second Hague Peace Conference in 1907. This convention prohibited the use of force for the collection of any contract debts, but left a loophole through which a fleet of warships could sail; the undertaking was not applicable "when the debtor state refuses or neglects to reply to an offer of arbitration, or, after accepting the offer, prevents any *compromis* from being agreed on, or, after the arbitration, fails to submit to the award." [51] Drago and other Latin-American spokesmen at the Hague pointed out that this agreement in effect legalized the use of force in certain contingencies. That their fears were justified is illustrated by a subsequent incident. In 1912 there was a discussion in the Department of State between a banking representative acting as agent for the Honduran government and Department officials concerning a proposed loan to Honduras. It

[48] Turlington, *Mexico and Her Foreign Creditors* (1930), 35.

[49] *Ibid.*, 141.

[50] Drago, "State Loans in Their Relation to International Policy" (1907), 1 *Am. J. Int. L.*, 692.

[51] See 2 Jessup, *Elihu Root* (1938), 74.

was proposed to include in the loan contract a provision for arbitration in case of difficulty. The bankers' representative doubted the efficacy of this provision, whereupon one of the officials told him about the provisions of the Porter Convention, adding that the inference was "clear that this [United States] Government would have the right, should any of these exceptions arise [regarding the agreement to arbitrate or the carrying out of the award], to use force in behalf of the Americans making the loan." The representative of the bankers "seemed very pleased upon learning of this Hague Convention, and seemed to think that it afforded a satisfactory guaranty." [52] The dissatisfaction with the Porter Convention persists and at the Chapultepec Conference of 1945 the Mexican Delegation suggested that it be abrogated.[53] In view of the provisions of the Charter of the United Nations restricting the use of force, the Porter Convention may now be deemed supplemented by that greater treaty which, according to its Article 103, prevails over any conflicting international agreement.

States have in the past interposed not only at the request of the bankers, but also on behalf of bondholders. There may be no inequity in this practice where there is a submission to an international tribunal as in the case of the French-Serbian and French-Brazilian submissions to the Permanent Court of International Justice to determine the proper interpretation of the terms of the loan contract concerning the form of payment.[54] But in other instances the bondholders may be individual speculators who have bought the bonds at a large discount on the open market in the hope that their government will collect a profit for them.[55] In such cases governments have sometimes refused to press the claims.[56]

Whether the claimant be the bankers or the individual bondholders, the case seems to be a clear one for the assumption of the risk of default by the lender and not by the borrower. Banking practice calculates the risk, discounts it in advance, and sets the price of the issue and the interest rate in terms of the appreciation of the risk. It is obviously inequitable to permit a situation in which they may

[52] *For. Rel.*, U. S. 1911, 616.
[53] Carneiro, *O Direito internacional e a democracia* (1945), 139.
[54] P.C.I.J., Series A/B No. 10/4.
[55] Cf. the dissenting opinion of Judge Pessoa, *ibid.*, 64.
[56] 3 Whiteman, *op. cit.*, *supra* note 11, p. 1584 ff.

eat their cake and have it too in the sense that default will bring to bear the military power of their state to exact 100 per cent compliance, perhaps through the seizure of customs houses or other revenue-producing assets. If the use of force for the collection of the loan were lawful, the bonds should be issued on terms reflecting not the financial and political hazards of the borrowing state, but the superior military power of the state of the lender.

The whole subject of international loan contracts was studied by a League of Nations Committee whose report was published just before the outbreak of World War II.[57] The Committee recommended the creation of an International Loans Tribunal with power to adjudicate upon the terms of loan contracts.

Such a Tribunal would be useful even under the newer practices in international financing. Where loans are extended by one government to another the problem is at once set upon a different plane and some of the bases of Drago's arguments are eliminated. But such intergovernmental loans may still be used as the basis for pressure by a strong state against a weak. That difficulty will not be overcome until international loans are contracted under international auspices. The League of Nations loans to Bulgaria, Danzig, Estonia, Greece, and Hungary are precedents which will presumably be built up by the activities of the new International Bank for Reconstruction and Development which should be in a position to guard against the old practice of forcing excessive loans on borrowers and to assure the floating of loans on equitable terms.[58] Granted that the loans are floated on an equitable basis, that the use of force for the collection of the loan is banned in case of default, that an International Loans Tribunal is established to settle questions of interpretation of the contract, the whole field may be taken out of the realm of diplomatic interposition and intervention. If the borrower defaults, the loss will fall on the investor as has long been true in the case of loans of some

---

[57] Report of the Committee for International Loan Contracts, League Doc. C. 145. M. 93. 1939. II. A; League Doc. II Economic and Financial 1939. II. A. 10.

[58] See address by the U. S. Secretary of the Treasury at the closing plenary session of the Bretton Woods Conference, Dept. of State Pub. 2187, United Nations Monetary and Financial Conference (1944), 7; ibid., Articles of Agreement of the International Bank for Reconstruction and Development, Art. I, 68.

of the states of the United States.[59] Refunding operations or other measures to put the debtor back on its financial feet would again be the concern of such international agencies as the International Bank, the Monetary Fund, and perhaps the Economic and Social Council. The bondholders' equities would not be ignored, but the procedures for satisfying them would be brought under international legal control. The history of international loans and their use as an instrument of imperialism demonstrate that this is a field to which the concept of community interest should apply.[60] The recognition of the individual as a subject of international law and the possibility envisaged by the League Committee that groups of bondholders might resort to an international tribunal without the interposition of their governments would further remove this subject from its unsavory record as a producer of international conflict.

A modernized international law of responsibility of states for injuries to individuals would, in the manner sketched, provide two sets of rights for individuals, one *qua* individual and one *qua* alien. There remains for discussion the question whether the traditional monopolizer of such international rights—the state—should retain any rights under this branch of international law.

It follows from what has already been said that the old Vattelian fiction of the injury to the state through the injury to its national should, in the ordinary claims case, be abandoned. It is not inconsistent with such abandonment to agree that the state retains the right to represent its national, to be what has already been referred to as his agent for collective bargaining. Just as the individual worker is at a bargaining disadvantage in dealing with a great corporation, so the individual traveler or business man or resident alien

[59] See Randolph, "Foreign Bondholders and the Repudiated Debts of the Southern States" (1931), 25 *Am. J. Int. L.*, 63, 77; the Florida Bonds case, (U. S.-Great Britain Commission 1853), *Hudson's Cases on International Law* (2d ed. 1936), 1104, 1105.

[60] It should be observed that in this as in other respects the hypothesis of the acceptance of the concept of community interest presupposes the development of an effective and viable international organization. But even if such an organization is thought of in terms of a "world government," there will be, at least in the transitional stage, inevitable delegation of rights and powers to the several states of the world. Effective international organization therefore does not preclude the continued use of the state as an agent of the individual in his international contacts.

worker is at a disadvantage in dealing with a foreign government. The disadvantage of the individual in dealing with his own state for recognition of his rights under an international bill of rights may be met, as indicated in the preceding chapter, by provision for international procedures of petition to an international authority. Where the individual seeks vindication of his rights as an alien, similar international procedures should be available, but these should be supplementary to the traditional procedure of diplomatic interposition. If the state declines to interpose, the individual is free to resort to the international procedures. Under the contemplated changes in the law, diplomatic interposition could not be extended without the concurrence of the individual, since it is his right that is being protected and not the right of his state. Such a situation would justify those decisions of international tribunals which have held that the claim must be dismissed where the individual has already reached a settlement with the foreign government [61] or where he refuses to sign the memorial or otherwise approve the claim.[62]

It might still be true that the old practice of diplomatic interposition could be used as a device for securing economic or political domination or supremacy in the life of another state, but any such tendency should be checked by other rules controlling state action. Economic imperialism is not consistent with the modern concepts on which the United Nations is built and should function. Article IV of the Atlantic Charter asserts the purpose "to further the enjoyment by all states, great and small, victor and vanquished, of access on equal terms to the trade and to the raw materials of the world which are needed for their economic prosperity." Chapter IX of the Charter of the United Nations contains a pledged program for the development of international trade on the basis of economic co-operation rather than economic cutthroat competition. The Economic and Social Council, the Food and Agriculture Organization, the ILO, the International Monetary Fund, the International Bank for Reconstruction and Development, and probably other agencies to be established under the United Nations have a joint task of supervision of the economic development of the world through the

[61] The Tattler, U. S.-Great Britain Claims Commission (1926), *Hudson's Cases on International Law* (2d ed. 1936), 1183.
[62] Feller, *op. cit., supra* note 41, § 103.

co-operative interrelationships contemplated by the Charter, as Herman Finer has shown.[63] One may note as a precedent in the new direction the establishment of the European Coal Organization in 1946 by the United States, Great Britain, Turkey, France, and six other European states. According to Article 4 of the constitutive agreement the "purpose of the Organization is to promote the supply and equitable distribution of coal and scarce items of coal-mining supplies and equipment while safeguarding, as far as possible, the interests of both producers and consumers." By Article 6 the principle of generalization of such an agreement is recognized by the provision that the Organization shall communicate with the Economic and Social Council of the United Nations (which had not been established when this agreement was concluded) to determine the relationships which should exist "and, in particular, whether its functions can and should be taken over by the Council." [64] In future, under such a co-operative international system, the legitimate commercial rights and interests of states are to be sought through international media [65] rather than through the traditional individualistic espousal and protection of separate national interests by strong states against their weaker comembers of the international community. The special provisions of the Charter in Chapter XI regarding nonself-governing territories, and in Chapters XII and XIII concerning the Trusteeship system, envisage particularly the development of international standards and procedures for colonial areas, which have in the past been such fruitful sources of international rivalry and of economic exploitation.

Nevertheless, various situations in the history of international claims reveal that in addition to the rights of its nationals a state has, in its relations with other states, certain rights which appertain to it in its collective or corporate capacity. The typical cases are those in which injury is done to an official of the state, particularly a consular

[63] Finer, *The United Nations Economic and Social Council* (1946), Chap. II.

[64] *Treaties and Other International Acts Ser. 1508* (Dept. of State, 1946), 4.

[65] Cf. Dept. of State Pub. 1598, *Suggested Charter for an International Trade Organization of the United Nations* (1946). In pointing to these trends in international commerce and finance, it is not intended to suggest that statism on an international scale is likely to supersede at once all forms of individual enterprise.

or diplomatic official. The recognition accorded their special status in traditional international law is extended because of their representative character and not because of their status as individuals, although a supplementary claim may lie for the injury to the individual as such. The fact that in the past states have taken advantage of such situations to exact punitive damages from the state inflicting the injury should not cloud the real equity of the state in seeking proper satisfaction for injury to its official. In 1924 Robert Imbrie, a Vice Consul of the United States in Persia, was murdered by a mob in Teheran. The United States demanded and Persia accorded expressions of "deepest regret"; Persia paid the cost of $110,000 to have Imbrie's body transported to the United States on an American warship; appropriate honors and salutes were rendered as the body left Persia. In addition Persia paid an indemnity of $60,000 for the benefit of the widow.[66] But in other cases of injuries to consular officers the state has not made a claim on its own behalf, and mixed claims commissions have made awards solely for the benefit of the individual, recognizing at the same time that the defendant state was responsible for not extending adequate protection to such officials.[67] On the other hand, the assassination of the British Governor General of the Sudan, Sir Lee Stack, at Cairo in November 1924 resulted in a British claim for £500,000 as a financial indemnity and also a demand for an apology and Egyptian evacuation of the Sudan.[68] Similarly the death of the German Ambassador in China and the siege of the Legation Quarter in Pekin during the Boxer Rebellion in 1900 contributed to the allied demands for an excessive indemnity and political concessions.[69] The murder of the Italian General Tellini and members of his suite at Janina in 1923, where they were engaged in the delimitation of the Greco-Albanian frontier, resulted in Italian demands for an official apology, a formal memorial service, honors to the Italian flag, an inquiry by the Greek authorities within five days, capital punishment of the murderers, 50,000,000 lire indemnity

[66] 1 Whiteman, *op. cit., supra* note 11, p. 136 ff.
[67] United States on behalf of William E. Chapman *v.* United Mexican States, 1930 (1930–1931) General Claims Commission United States and Mexico, 121; The United Mexican States on behalf of Francisco Mallén *v.* United States (1927) General Claims Commission United States and Mexico, 254.
[68] 19 *Am. J. Int. L.* (1925), 384.
[69] 5 *Moore's Digest of Int. L.* (1906), secs. 809–810.

to be paid within five days, military honors to the victims, and a reply within twenty-four hours. When these demands were not met within the time fixed in the ultimatum, Italian forces bombarded and occupied the Greek island of Corfu.[70]

International tribunals have frequently distinguished between a general injury to a state and specific damage. Thus in the case of the S.S. *Wimbledon*, the Permanent Court of International Justice acknowledged the legal interest of Great Britain, Italy, and Japan as parties to the peace treaty granting free passage through the Kiel Canal, to join with France in submitting a case against Germany for the denial of passage to a French ship, but the judgment was for money damages to be paid to the French Government alone for the losses sustained by the vessel.[71] In the *I'm Alone* arbitration between the United States and Canada, the award, which held that the sinking of the Canadian vessel by an American Coast Guard Cutter was illegal, provided money damages for the losses suffered by the captain and crew and also called for an apology by the United States to Canada plus the payment of $25,000 "as a material amend in respect of the wrong."[72] In the Trail Smelter Arbitration between the United States and Canada, damage from smelter fumes had been suffered by properties located in the United States across the border from the Canadian plant. Some of these properties were owned by private persons and some were United States Government lands. The Tribunal made an award of $350,000 for the injury to the private property but noted that the United States had explicitly withdrawn any claim for injury to its own lands.[73]

It should be one of the tasks in the codification of international law to catalogue the types of direct injuries to states for which the state would be privileged to require another state to pay such indemnity as might be determined by an international tribunal to be appropriate to the case. Among these types, in addition to those which have been illustrated by the cases just cited, should be those resulting from direct injury to a state instrumentality engaged in the conduct of commercial and other business activities. The modern practice of

[70] 1 Whiteman, *op. cit., supra* note 11, pp. 714–15.
[71] Case of the S. S. Wimbledon, *P.C.I.J.*, Ser. A, No. 1 (1923).
[72] "The *I'm Alone*," Dept. of State Arbitration Ser. No. 2 (7), p. 4 (1935).
[73] Trail Smelter Arbitration between United States and Canada, Dept. of State Arbitration Ser. No. 8 (1941). Cf. 25 *Am J. Int. L.* (1931), 540.

states in organizing state corporations for the management of business affairs such as shipping, railways, state monopolies, and the like has caused confusion in the application of the traditional rules of sovereign immunity in national courts.[74] Where state activities are completely socialized as in the Soviet Union, the number of state claims arising from the transactions of such governmental organs is increased, but the principle is the same as that applicable to the United States Emergency Fleet Corporation operating during and after World War I, or such enterprises as the United States Rubber Development Corporation in the Amazon Valley during World War II. On the procedural side it may be found useful to provide special international tribunals to hear such cases if satisfaction is not obtained in national courts. It seems clear that in the development of these aspects of the law of responsibility a difference should be made between cases of injuries to such officials as diplomats and consuls and those suffered by the managers of state commercial enterprises.

International law will also need to be developed in such a way as to define the rights and duties of international agencies and their officials and personnel, particularly when a local development project or the mining of uranium by an international authority is involved. It is quite conceivable that, just as the financing of international development projects is being assumed by the International Bank for Reconstruction and Development instead of by private bankers or individual state loans, so such projects as that of the building of a railroad in Iran, which was taken as an illustrative case above, might be handled by an international agency.[75] Such an agency might let sub-contracts to a private contractor, but might also employ its own personnel and in any case would have direct contractual relations with the Iranian Government. So far, international law has felt the need to regulate the privileges and immunities of international officials by analogy with the traditional rights of diplomatic officials. The Charter and the Constitutions of the various new United Nations agencies contain provisions to this effect.[76] When such inter-

[74] See *Harvard Research in International Law, Draft Convention on Competence of Courts in Regard to Foreign States* (1932), 597.

[75] Finer, "The T.V.A.: Lessons for International Application" (1944), *I. L. O., Studies and Reports,* ser. B, no. 37.

[76] The United Nations Charter only provides for "necessary" privileges and immunities. *Charter of the United Nations,* Art. 105; compare *Statute of the*

national agencies take on the administration and performance of actual engineering and similar projects within states, it will be necessary to develop new rules, just as the traditional international law is in course of modification to meet the new situations presented by the activities of the national state as trader, ship-owner, and general business man in the international field.

International Court of Justice, Art. 19. For a full discussion of the problem see Dept. of State Pub. 2349, Conference Series 71, *Report to the President on the Results of the San Francisco Conference, 1945*, 158 *et seq.*; see Preuss, "The International Organizations Immunities Act," 40 *Am. J. Int. L.* (1946), 332.

CHAPTER VI

THE LAW OF CONTRACTUAL AGREEMENTS

DIPLOMACY HAS DEVELOPED a large amount of formalistic ritual, much of which is reflected in international law. The titles and ranking of diplomats are the most striking example. Curiously enough, this tendency is not wholly reflected in the modern law and practice of treaty making. It is of no legal consequence, for example, whether an agreement between or among states is called a treaty, a convention, a statute, an agreement, a protocol, or a covenant or charter.[1] Certain labels, such as *"modus vivendi"* and "exchange of notes," are used with a degree of consistency to signify the informal or temporary character of an agreement, while others, such as "covenant" and "charter," have been utilized to suggest the basic and overall importance of the instrument. The labels do not, however, indicate whether the agreement registers a boundary settlement, the conclusion of a peace, a political and military alliance, or provisions for the extradition of fugitive criminals, arrangements for the distribution of radio frequencies, adjustment of double taxation, respect for copyrights, or facilities for traveling salesmen. The applicable substantive law similarly fails to distinguish among such diverse subjects and covers them all with the same rules concerning conclusion, interpretation, and termination. Such uniformity is convenient for the student, the statesman, and the judge, but in some important respects which will be discussed in this chapter it is not responsive to the needs of the international community.

Agreements between and among states also reveal other important basic differences. To use the analogous terminology of private or national law, some agreements are essentially contracts, as, for example, agreements for the sale of surplus war supplies, loan agree-

[1] "Harvard Research in International Law, Draft Convention on the Law of Treaties," 29 *Am. J. Int. L. Supp.* (1935), Introductory Comment, 667.

123

ments, and agreements for the maintenance of national monuments or memorials. In a sense all international agreements are contractual in that they derive their validity from the agreement of the parties, but Judge Hudson has properly emphasized (as Lord Salisbury suggested in 1897)[2] the fact that many such agreements are more closely analogous to legislation, despite the nonexistence of any international legislature.[3] This is true of many of the great multipartite instruments which are becoming more and more characteristic of the international legal order, such as those setting up permanent machinery and procedures for managing the world's affairs in matters of communications, health, morals, and the like. Still other instruments are of a quasi-constitutional nature, as the Covenant of the League of Nations and the Charter of the United Nations.

The traditional discussions in the books about treaties are usually concerned only with agreements to which states are parties. This is the natural consequence of the accepted doctrine that only states are subjects of international law. The acceptance of the hypothesis that individuals are also subjects of international law necessitates consideration here of agreements between states and individuals.[4] The rapid development of international organizations with far-flung interests and activities, and with relationships to states and to each other as well as perhaps to individuals, requires consideration as well of all types of agreements concluded by and with such international agencies; and in this connection it will be recalled that colonies and other political dependencies have already been accorded membership in international unions.

It is a common lay error to draw a sharp distinction between treaties and international law in general. Many who are not aware of the operation of the international legal process are wont to assert that "there isn't any international law," but that treaties are something different. Some advocates of world government who maintain that there can be no international law until international government is established proceed, perhaps subconsciously, to suggest that states should agree by treaty to establish such a government. This reasoning overlooks the fact that no agreement has legal significance except

---

[2] 1 Westlake, *International Law* (2d ed. 1910), 322.
[3] 1 Hudson, *International Legislation* (1931), xiii.
[4] Only some aspects of the law of treaties, selected with a view to illustrating modern problems, are treated here.

against the background of a system of law which attaches legal consequences to the contractual act. In international law, some jurists have
maintained that the basic rule or principle of that law is the maxim
pacta sunt servanda.[5] But this primary duty to observe the obligations assumed in agreements would be difficult of operation if the law
did not also indicate when an agreement becomes binding, how it is
to be interpreted during its effective life, and how it may be terminated. The confusion in the lay mind has not been dissipated by the
common practice in the United States of referring to international
law as embracing only customary law, which, to be sure, includes
the law of treaties but not the treaties themselves. Thus it is frequently said that international conduct is regulated by international
law and treaties.[6] The European practice of distinguishing between
customary and contractual international law and including both
types when the term "international law" is used alone is more helpful. Similarly clarifying is the European practice of referring to
"general" or universal international law, partly customary and binding the international community as a whole, and "particular international law," which binds only certain members of the international
community.

THE CONCLUSION OF INTERNATIONAL AGREEMENTS

It is common practice to conclude treaties subject to ratification
by the contracting parties. Ratification is "the formal confirmation
and approval of the written instrument."[7] Such confirmation and
approval is given in accordance with the constitutional processes
and requirements of each state. In the United States, for example,
ratification of treaties is an executive function; the Senate "advises
and consents" to ratification where the agreement takes the formal
treaty character.[8] The popular assertion that the Senate "ratifies"

[5] See Briggs, *The Law of Nations* (1938), 24, Kunz, "The Meaning and the
Range of the Norm Pacta Sunt Servanda," 39 *Am. J. Int. L.* (1945), 180.
[6] The title of an able article by Prof. Quincy Wright illustrates the usual use
of the term· "Conflicts Between International Law and Treaties," 11 *Am. J. Int.
L.* (1917), 566.
[7] 2 Hyde, 1429.
[8] For discussion of various methods that may constitutionally be utilized by
the United States in order to conclude an international agreement, see Mc-
Dougal and Lans, "Treaties and Congressional-Executive or Presidential Agreements: Interchangeable Instruments of National Policy," 54 *Yale L. J.* (1945),
181, 534.

treaties may be ascribed to the fact that, particularly in the newspapers, the longer constitutional phrase is found too awkward for general use.

Ratification is not the final step requisite to bringing a treaty into force. The final step is the reciprocal communication of the fact of ratification, generally termed the "exchange of ratifications," or, as is common in the case of multipartite instruments, the deposit of ratifications with an agreed depositary, which may be the chancellery of a single state or an international official such as the Secretary-General of the United Nations.

Although it is usual to conclude agreements subject to ratification, this is not the universal practice, and international law interposes no obstacle to bringing an agreement into force on signature by a duly authorized agent of the state.[9] It is a matter of the constitutional law of the state whether any particular international agreement or type of agreement may be thus concluded.

No change in the existing law regarding the ratification of agreements or the exchange or deposit of ratifications seems to be necessary in connection with agreements to which all the parties are states. It may be pertinent to note, however, the provisions of Article 102 of the Charter of the United Nations, which reads as follows:

> 1. Every treaty and every international agreement entered into by any member of the United Nations after the present Charter comes into force shall as soon as possible be registered with the Secretariat and published by it.
>
> 2. No party to any such treaty or international agreement which has not been registered in accordance with the provisions of paragraph 1 of this Article may invoke that treaty or agreement before any organ of the United Nations.

At the San Francisco Conference the above phraseology was preferred to that found in Article 18 of the Covenant of the League of Nations, which declared that unregistered treaties should not be binding. The exact legal effect of that provision had not been made clear in practice, and the Charter text avoids making registration a

---

[9] See J. Mervyn Jones, "International Agreements Other than 'Interstate Treaties': Modern Developments," 21 *Brit. Y. B. Int. L.* (1944), 111.

prerequisite to the coming into force of the agreement. [10] It may be noted that Article 102 of the Charter applies to "every international agreement entered into by any Member of the United Nations"; it does not specify that both or all parties to the agreement shall be states. It is doubtful whether the drafters paid particular attention to agreements between a state on the one hand and an individual on the other, or to agreements to which an international agency is a party, but the language would cover such cases if one party were a Member, assuming that the agreement in question could properly be considered to fall within the term "international agreement." The case considered at San Francisco was one in which a treaty or agreement was concluded between a Member and a non-Member; in such a case the Member is under an obligation to register. The same rule should be applied in the case of international agreements between a Member and an individual or an international organization.

The text of an agreement between a state and an international organization might provide that it shall be subject to ratification by the state and to "approval" by some designated body in the international organization. Under Article 43 of the Charter of the United Nations all Members are required to conclude agreements with the Security Council relative to the armed forces, assistance, and facilities which the Member will supply when required. According to paragraph 3 of that Article such agreements "shall be concluded between the Security Council and Members or between the Security Council and groups of Members and shall be subject to ratification by the signatory states in accordance with their respective constitutional processes." Article 79 provides that Trusteeship Agreements shall be concluded among "the states directly concerned," and under Articles 83 and 85 the agreements shall be "approved" by the General Assembly or by the Security Council, depending on designation in the agreement of a strategic area.

The Working Draft of an agreement between the United Nations and the United States relative to the arrangements for the site of the

[10] See *Report to the President on the Results of the San Francisco Conference by the Chairman of the United States Delegation*, Dept. of State Pub. 2349 (1945), 154. On Art. 18 of the Covenant, see Hudson in 19 *Am. J. Int. L.* (1925), 273, and 28 *ibid.* (1934), 546; 2 Oppenheim, 721 ff. See also claim of Pablo Nájera, French-Mexican Mixed Claims Commission, *An. Dig.* (1927-28), Case. No. 271.

United Nations headquarters is in typical treaty form and provides in Section 42 that the convention (or agreement) "shall be brought into force by an exchange of notes between the Secretary-General, duly authorized by a resolution of the General Assembly of the United Nations, and the United States of America." [11] UNRRA concluded agreements with various states regarding the distribution of relief supplies. I have seen the text of one of these agreements which was to take effect on signature by a Deputy Director-General of UNRRA and by a cabinet minister of the government concerned; no ratification was required. The *modus vivendi* of September 18, 1926 concerning diplomatic immunities of League of Nations officials was agreed to by the Swiss Federal Government, the Secretary-General of the League, and the Director of the International Labour Office; it was taken note of by the League Council, but was not subject to ratification.[12] Agreements between two or more international organizations are contemplated by recent instruments. According to Article 63 of the Charter the Economic and Social Council "may enter into agreements" with the various specialized agencies. These agreements are "subject to approval by the General Assembly." Under Article XII of the Constitution of the Food and Agriculture Organization agreements may be made with other public international organizations to define distribution of responsibilities and methods of co-operation. The agreements are to be made by the Conference, which is the general assembly of the FAO, with "the competent authorities" of the other organization. Subject to control by a decision of the Conference, the Director-General of FAO may "enter into agreements with other public international organizations for the maintenance of common services, for common arrangements in regard to recruitment, training, conditions of service, and other related matters, and for interchanges of staff." The FAO constitution was drafted before the United Nations came into existence, but Article XIII contemplates that a relationship will be established between the two organizations. In this connection the Article speaks not of "agreements" but of "arrangements"; these are subject to approval by the Conference.[13] The World Health Organization may enter into agreements with the United Nations or other intergov-

[11] UN Doc. A/67, 1 Sept. 1946.
[12] 1 Hudson, *op. cit., supra* note 3, p. 224.
[13] *Food and Agriculture Organization, Report of the First Session of the Conference* (1946), 87.

ernmental organizations; according to Articles 69 and 70 of the Constitution, such agreements are subject to approval by a two-thirds vote of the Health Assembly. Presumably the agreement would be negotiated and signed by the Secretary-General. Under Article 71 "The Organization may, on matters within its competence, make suitable arrangements for consultation and co-operation with nongovernmental international organizations and, with the consent of the government concerned, with national organizations, governmental or non-governmental." There is no indication of the procedure for concluding such "arrangements." [14] UNESCO's Constitution in Article XI similarly provides for agreements with other organizations; the Director-General makes the agreement subject to the approval of the Executive Board. "Arrangements" may also be made with nongovernmental international organizations.[15] The Suggested Charter for an International Trade Organization of the United Nations in Article 71 contains similar provisions; the agreement on relationship to the UN "shall be concluded by the Director-General and approved by the Conference." Relations with other international organizations may be established by the Director-General, and "Formal arrangements for cooperation" may be entered into by the Executive Board. If the Conference and the competent authorities of another organization believe that the ITO should absorb functions of the other body, "the Director-General, subject to the approval of the Conference, may enter into mutually acceptable arrangements." [16] Under Article 64 of the Convention creating the International Civil Aviation Organization, "the Organization" may enter into appropriate arrangements with the UN "by vote of the Assembly." Article 65 reads: "The Council, on behalf of the Organization, may enter into agreements with other international bodies for the maintenance of common services and for common arrangements concerning personnel and, with the approval of the Assembly, may enter into such other arrangements as may facilitate the work of the Organization." [17]

[14] "Acts of the International Health Conference" (1946), UN Doc. E/155, p. 29.
[15] "The Defenses of Peace"—*Documents Relating to UNESCO*, Part I, Dept. of State Pub. 2457 (1946), 20.
[16] *Suggested Charter for an International Trade Organization of the United Nations*, Dept. of State Pub. 2598 (1946), 43.
[17] *International Civil Aviation Conference, Chicago, 1944, Final Act and Related Documents*, Dept. of State Pub. 2282 (1945), 78.

It is evident that when an organization enters into an agreement it will be necessary for the other contracting party to examine the constitutional basis of the agreement-making power. It could not properly be asserted, as it has been with reference to interstate agreements, that the Director-General or Secretary-General had "apparent authority" to conclude the agreement and that the organization was accordingly bound by his act, though the constitution might require ratification or approval by one of the other organs. It would be convenient to develop a practice of reciprocal confirmation that approval has been given—the equivalent of the exchange of ratifications. It might be appropriate to provide generally in such agreements that notice of approval should be deposited with the Secretary-General of the United Nations and should take effect on his receipt of the last required notice of approval. As Professor Finer has pointed out, collaboration between international agencies will be of great importance, and it is to be anticipated that there will be a considerable volume of agreements among them.[18]

The Regulations for the registration of treaties under Article 102 of the Charter, as adopted by the General Assembly on December 14, 1946, take account of the developments relative to the conclusion of international agreements by international organizations. Treaties and international agreements are to be registered only when a state is a party to the agreement, and under Article 4 of the Regulations one of the cases in which such a document is to be "registered *ex officio* by the United Nations" is that in which "the United Nations is a party to the treaty or agreement." Such a treaty or international agreement may be registered with the Secretariat by a specialized agency in the following cases:

(a) Where the constituent instrument of the specialized agency provides for such registration;

(b) Where the treaty or agreement has been registered with the specialized agency pursuant to the terms of its constituent instrument;

(c) Where the specialized agency has been authorized by the treaty or agreement to effect registration.

[18] Finer, *The United Nations Economic and Social Council* (1946).

Article 10 of the Regulations provides a special procedure for treaties or international agreements entered into by the United Nations or by one or more of the specialized agencies where a Member of the United Nations is not a party; the Secretariat "shall file and record" such documents. Both the registered treaties and those filed and recorded are to be published in a single series.[19]

International agreements between states and individuals may take a variety of forms and cover a variety of subjects. As will be explained later, such agreements may be contracted with reference to international law or to national law. Agreements made by the great chartered companies with native chiefs and princes have been recognized as important international documents even though not treaties in the traditional sense.[20] An individual or a private group such as a corporation may enter into an agreement with a state on a highly important political question. Thus in 1940 an agreement was entered into by the Dominican Government and the Dominican Republic Settlement Association, Inc., a New York corporation, relative to the settlement of refugees in Santo Domingo.[21] At the time the agreement was concluded the corporation had no individual status under international law, and it must be assumed that the agreement was a contract concluded under Dominican law. With the acceptance of the hypothesis that an individual (or corporation) is a subject of international law, such an agreement could, if the parties so desired, be an international law agreement. The agreement or contract actually provided in Article VI that it should be ratified by a resolution of the Board of Directors of the Association and approved by the Congress of the Dominican Republic. The signatures were affixed by the President and Vice-President of the Association and by two ministers of the Dominican Republic. It might be more convenient in such cases to determine in advance the authority of the negotiators, let us say the cabinet minister and the president or general counsel of the company, and to provide that the agreement should come into force on signature. The agents presumably would not

[19] UN Doc. A/266, 13 Dec. 1946.
[20] See the opinion of Judge Huber, sole arbitrator in the Island of Palmas Case, The Netherlands v. The United States (1928), Scott, *The Hague Court Reports* (2d. ser., 1932), 83, 115.
[21] See "Refugee Settlement in the Dominican Republic," *A Survey Conducted Under the Auspices of the Brookings Institution* (1942).

affix their signatures until they had consulted their superiors in case of necessity.

Agreements may also be made between international organizations and individuals, again including groups such as corporations within the term "individuals." An obvious case would be that of an employment contract between the United Nations and a member of the Secretariat.[22] Such contracts might be made with reference to the law of a particular state, such as that of the state in which the headquarters of the United Nations is located. It would seem more appropriate, given the acceptance of the position of the individual as a subject of international law, to conclude such agreements under international law and make that law applicable to disputes concerning interpretation and the like. On the procedural side it is to be presumed that special tribunals will be established for the solution of such controversies, but the law to be applied and developed by such special tribunals should be a branch of international law, not of some national law. Similarly the World Health Organization might enter into an agreement with the Rockefeller Foundation concerning some joint enterprise. In all such cases there may be developed formulae and procedures for bringing the agreement into force on signature or on reciprocal confirmation of approval by designated authorities.

THIRD PARTY BENEFICIARIES

Under existing international law a treaty is a source of rights and obligations only for the parties to it; *pacta tertiis nec nocent nec prosunt*.[23] However, as the Permanent Court of International Justice suggested in the Free Zones case,[24] it is legally possible for contracting states to create a right in favor of a third state not a party to the treaty. The practice is so unusual that such a result or the intention to achieve such a result "cannot be lightly presumed." Professor Hyde cites an excellent example in the case of the Hay-Pauncefote treaty of 1901 between the United States and Great Britain, stipulating that the Panama Canal "shall be free and open to the vessels of commerce

---

[22] Cf. Hudson, *International Tribunals, Past and Future* (1944), 220–22, Schwarzenberger, 1 *International Law* (1945), 477.

[23] 2 Hyde, sec. 529 A, and 1 Oppenheim, sec. 522, and authorities there cited.

and war of all nations observing these Rules, on terms of entire equality, so that there shall be no discrimination against any such nation, or its citizens or subjects, in respect of the conditions or charges of traffic or otherwise." In 1921 Secretary of State Hughes wrote that "other nations . . . not being parties to the treaty have no rights under it." [25] In other words, the obligation of the United States was an obligation to Great Britain only, and those two states remained at all times free to change their agreement so as to eliminate the clause in question. But the whole question of the rights of third parties under treaties establishing the status of international waterways is by no means free from controversy under international law.[26] Usually, when two or more contracting states desire to make the rights or privileges of a treaty available to other states, they include a provision for the adhesion or accession of other states, whereby they may become parties to the treaty and thus share its rights and obligations. This type of subject matter illustrates the utility of the adoption in a modern law of nations of the doctrine of community interest.

There is a growing tendency in international practice to acknowledge the existence of "law-making treaties." In terms of the traditional view the term is misleading, since in general it is used to suggest merely the stipulation of general rules of conduct for the parties to the treaty, but the trend in the use of the term supports the view that in this respect there is a growing acknowledgment of a basic community interest which contrasts with the traditional strict bilateralism of law. Article 17 of the Covenant of the League of Nations suggested something of an innovation. It provided that in case of a dispute between a member and a nonmember the latter should be

[25] See 2 Hyde, 1467, n. 9. Senator Root had taken the same position in 1914, 5 Hackworth, *Digest Int. L.*, sec. 492.

[26] Cf. Diena, "Der Plan eines neuen interozeanischen Kanals in Nicaragua," 15 *Zeitschrift für internationales Recht* (1915), 19. The Convention of October 29, 1888, between nine powers specified the freedom of the Suez Canal (79 *British and Foreign State Papers*, 18) but the United States was unwilling to take the position that it derived rights or duties from the convention; Secretary of State Day to Ambassador Hay, July 14, 1898, 3 *Moore's Dig.* (1906), 267. Cf. such treaties as that between Bolivia and Brazil, August 12, 1910, 7 Martens *Nouveau recueil général*, 3d Ser. (1913), 632, for the free navigation of the Paraguay River; the Argentine-Chilean treaty of July 23, 1881, relative to the Straits of Magellan, 3 *Moore's Dig.*, 268, and the Treaty of London of March 13, 1871, on the Black Sea, 61 *British and Foreign State Papers*, 7.

invited to accept the obligations of membership for the purpose of the dispute. In case of refusal, Article 16, providing for sanctions, might become applicable. Some writers have thought to find here a juridical novelty and conclude that the Covenant imposes a legal obligation on nonmembers, while others reconcile the provision with the traditional law by asserting that Article 17 represents merely a political program of the League.[27] In practice, thanks largely to the political fact of the nonmembership of the United States, no attempt was made to develop the idea that nonmembers were bound by the Covenant. Nevertheless the principle behind Article 17 was different from that behind some of the older "law-making" treaties, such as the great maritime conventions. These agreements may be said to have created law in the sense that they laid down rules found acceptable to the majority of states—rules which, as a matter of practice, became embodied in the customary law of nations.[28] A combination of arguments has been used to support the view that the Briand-Kellogg Pact of 1928 for the Renunciation of War as an Instrument of National Policy created general law binding on signatories and nonsignatories alike.[29]

[27] See Hoijer, *Le Pacte de la Société des nations: Commentaire théorique et pratique* (1926), 319 ff.; Schwarzenberger, *The League of Nations and World Order* (1936), Chap. VI; Anzilotti, *Corso di diritto internazionale* (3d ed. 1928), 380; Schücking and Wehberg, 1 *Die Satzung des Völkerbundes* (3d ed. 1931), 245 ff.; "Harvard Research in International Law, Draft Convention on the Law of Treaties," 29 *Am. J. Int. L. Supp.* (1935), 921. German criticism of any League claim to universality of legal power is expressed by Von Freytagh-Loringhoven, *Die Satzung des Völkerbundes* (1926), 16–17, and 201 ff., and Von Bülow, *Der Versailler Volkerbund* (1923), 183 ff. (The restrictive view is supported by citing the opinion of the Permanent Court of International Justice in the Eastern Carelia case. *P.C.I.J.*, Ser. B, No. 5.)

[28] Cf. 2 Hyde, 1466, and see the reasoning of the Supreme Court of the United States in The Scotia, 14 *Wall.* 170 (1871), and of the Mixed Tribunal of Port Said in Crichton v. Samos Navigation Co. and Others, *Ann. Dig.* (1925–26), Case No. 1.

[29] "This pact altered the legal status of a war of aggression." "Opening Statement for the United States of America," by Mr. Justice Jackson, *The Case Against the Nazi War Criminals* (1946), 75. See Wright, "The Meaning of the Pact of Paris," 27 *Am. J. Int. L.* (1933), 39. See also Schwarzenberger, *op. cit.*, *supra* note 27; note from the Minister for Foreign Affairs of Egypt to the Secretary-General of the League of Nations, League of Nations *Off. J. Spec. Supp* 150 (1936), 328; "Budapest Articles of Interpretation," 38 *Rep. Int. L. Assn* (1935), 66, and comments thereon by Lauterpacht in 20 *Trans. Grotius Soc.* (1934), 178, and in "Harvard Research in International Law, Draft Convention on Rights and Duties of States in Case of Aggression," 33 *Am. J. Int. L. Supp.* (1939), 826.

Paragraph 6 of Article 2 of the Charter of the United Nations is the most recent basic statement of the kind illustrated by Article 17 of the Covenant. It provides: "The Organization shall ensure that states which are not members of the United Nations act in accordance with these Principles so far as may be necessary for the maintenance of international peace and security." It is to be noted that the language employed does not suggest that non-Member states are under obligation to comply with the Charter, but rather indicates a warning to non-Members that under certain circumstances the Organization will use the combined power of its Members to exact compliance with the Charter in the interest of the world community as a whole. Surely the Members intend to assert their legal right to take such measures, but to admit also that the right flows from their assumption of the role of guardian of the world's peace rather than from any theory of an obligation on non-Members derived from a treaty to which they are not parties. In a sense, therefore, the United Nations assumes a legislative role; but the frank assertion of the fact must wait on the creation of an actual world legislature.[80]

The instances in which states have agreed to be bound by majority decisions in which they do not participate, or which they oppose, suggests no change in the traditional rule that only parties to a treaty derive rights or obligations from it.[81] The legal theory of the binding force of a majority decision of an international body is that the parties to the treaty have agreed in advance to be bound by certain decisions even if at the time they do not acquiesce in them.

The acceptance of the hypothesis of community interest would pave the way to the development of an actual system of international legislation under which an international body would have the legal authority to prescribe rules binding the community as a whole. Presumably the system would be created by an exercise of the will of states in becoming parties to some basic agreement; but if such a development takes place, it would not be long, as time is measured in the lives of nations, before the original basis of mutual consent would be submerged in the exercise of what was originally a delegated authority. Law-making by the Congress of the United States

[80] See Kelsen, "Membership in the United Nations," 46 *Col. L. Rev.* (1946), 391, 394.

[81] See Riches, *Majority Rule in International Organization* (1940).

is theoretically based on the consent of the governed, because the members of the Congress are elected by the free franchise of the people, but in the experience of daily life the citizen thinks of the law as laid down by a superior authority and not as flowing from an exercise of his will or as being binding on him by his consent.

It is perhaps somewhat easier to contemplate the development of the law of nations so as to assure to individuals, or to groups of individuals not constituting states, rights and duties under agreements to which they are not parties. Despite the traditional concept that individuals are not subjects of international law, there has been acknowledgment of their rights under treaties.[32] The result is illogical and has been advanced as evidence of the unsoundness of the basic concept of international law as a law solely between states. Thus in its Advisory Opinion concerning the Jurisdiction of the Courts of Danzig, the Permanent Court of International Justice said that ". . . it cannot be disputed that the very object of an international agreement, according to the intention of the contracting Parties, may be the adoption by the Parties of some definite rules creating individual rights and obligations and enforceable by the national courts."[33] In the case of Steiner and Gross v. Polish State, the Upper Silesian Arbitral Tribunal in 1928 held that a citizen of Czechoslovakia, which was not a party to the treaty establishing the tribunal, could bring an action there against one of the parties to the treaty.[34]

As has been noted in Chapter II, the acceptance of the hypothesis that individuals are also subjects of international law would not require the extension of the doctrine of equality of states so as to give parity of legal rights to individuals. It is thus possible to take the position that, while in general international law will not recognize the notion that duties may be imposed on third states by parties to a treaty and that beneficiary rights of third states will not lightly be presumed, the law will be receptive to rights and duties of individuals created through agreements concluded by states or through deci-

---

[32] See Kaufmann, *Die Rechtskraft des internationalen Rechtes und das Verhältnis des Staatsgesetzgebungen und der Staatsorgane zu demselben* (1899), 23-7.

[33] P.C.I.J., Ser. B. No. 15, p. 17, and see Lauterpacht, *The Development of International Law by the Permanent Court of International Justice* (1934), 50 ff. But cf. 1 Schwarzenberger. *International Law* (1045). 60.

sions of international organizations. It should at the outset be agreed that the Charter of the United Nations creates rights for individuals, rights which are stated in the basic instrument in general terms and which are to be defined more precisely in an International Bill of Rights. Similarly, nonself-governing territories and dependent peoples placed under trusteeships should be considered to possess rights under the Charter and under the trusteeship agreements which are to be concluded. At this writing it seems that an International Atomic Energy Authority may be given power to establish rules binding on individuals. The precedent of the war criminal trials in Germany and Japan suggests that new international law relative to the use of force in violation of the Charter or in violation of the rules of an Atomic Energy Commission will be clearly stated in terms of the duties of individuals.[85]

With the acknowledgment of the individual as a person of international law, it will no longer be necessary to speak solely in terms of rights of states when dealing with privileges and rights conferred by commercial treaties and other treaties dealing with economic and social rights. States may still conclude treaties on behalf of their nationals; they may be, so to speak, convenient instruments for collective bargaining. The state may retain its own right to proceed against another state in case of a treaty breach, but the individual citizen may likewise have his own procedures for vindication of his own rights. Thus the infringement of a trademark or patent under the protection of an international convention may be the basis for a cause of action in an appropriate forum by the individual possessor of the right, which he would derive immediately from the convention and not mediately through some national law passed for the implementation of the treaty. Procedurally speaking, it may prove advantageous to have suits instituted first in national courts, but there might be subsequent review by an international tribunal, as already discussed in claims cases.[86] Likewise the individual, black or white, would have a cause of action in case he or she were the victim of a breach of an international slavery convention. More prosaically, the individual business man, airline, or steamship company would not have to wait on the slow wheels of diplomacy to secure damages for

[85] See Chap. VII.
[86] See Chap. V.

a violation of rights under a bipartite treaty of commerce or a multi-partite convention concerning commerce and navigation. It would still be true, however, that, subject to respect for fundamental provisions of the International Bill of Rights, a state might by national law restrict the freedom of the individual in the national interest, just as the world community may restrict the freedom of states in the international interest. The international interest may require that states shall not interpose any obstacles to the filing of petitions by a national in a nonself-governing territory, a territory under trusteeship, or a territory to which minority treaties apply. So far, the United Nations Charter provides for the hearing of individual petitions only in the case of territories under trusteeship.[87] But the international interest might not require a state to refrain from ordering its nationals to follow a designated procedure, such as notice to the foreign office, in pressing a claim against another state. A state might equally be free to insist that the national interest takes precedence over the individual interest and that in certain situations of international tension no national shall press a claim without prior permission from his government.

INTERPRETATION OF AGREEMENTS

The international law relative to the interpretation of treaties is an example of the evils of excessive formalism. So-called "canons of construction" have been utilized by foreign offices and international and national courts. Professor Hyde has rendered a distinguished service to international law in his outstanding contributions to the clarification of this subject. He has pointed out that the function of interpretation is to ascertain the design of the parties, always bearing in mind that they are free to employ words in any sense they choose.[88] A large amount of controversy, mainly based on the fundamental lack of appreciation of the simple basic principles to which Professor Hyde draws attention, has revolved around the question of the propriety of using preliminary materials, *travaux préparatoires*, to aid in the task of interpretation. The difficulty may derive in large

---

[87] See Art. 87 of the Charter and (on right of petition of private persons) Lauterpacht, "An International Bill of the Rights of Man" (1945), 199 ff.
[88] See, in general, 1 Hyde, Title E., 1468 ff.

part from a lawyerlike obsession with more familiar norms of domestic law that have been developed for reasons which may have been historically sound in the circumstances that led to their formulation. Thus the familiar rule of the common law that extraneous data may not be invoked to vary the terms of a written instrument may be quite necessary to guard the character of a negotiable instrument, but wholly inappropriate to a political treaty. Treaty law is a good example of the point that international law was originally developed largely by jurists trained in the civil law, and some civil law concepts which seem strange to the lawyer trained in the common law have been incorporated into international law. At this time the international community has had enough experience of its own to justify the development of the law on the basis of its own needs and not with reference to some system of domestic law.

It may be asked whether there should be different rules of interpretation for those agreements which are essentially of the nature of bilateral contracts and those which have been called international legislation. In national law there are familiar distinctions between the interpretation of contracts and the construction of statutes. Except that the relevant evidence to be marshaled may differ in character, there is no reason why two sets of rules and principles should be utilized in international law with this distinction in mind.

CHOICE OF LAW

When the term "international agreement" is used, as here, to embrace not only agreements between states but also agreements between states and individuals, between states or individuals and international organizations, and between two international organizations, it is important to ascertain what law governs the agreement, since such agreements may be governed by international law or by national law.[39] No general rule determines the choice of law by the parties in such cases. State A, entering into a concession contract with Corporation X from State B, may specify in the text of the document that the contract is to be governed by the law of A. It may, on the

[39] Cf. the excellent article by Mann, "The Law Governing State Contracts," 21 *Brit. Y. B. Int. L.* (1944), 11. See also Feilchenfeld in *Am. Soc. Int. L., Proc.* (1932), 175.

other hand, specify that the contract shall be governed by international law. The importance of the point may be illustrated by suggesting a case in which, after the contract has been concluded, certain fundamental conditions undergo a change not contemplated by the parties when they signed the agreement. Under such circumstances the law of State A may provide an equitable procedure for the reformation of the contract by the court, but may declare that the court cannot pronounce the contract at an end. On the other hand, it may be assumed, for the purpose of argument, that international law contains no such procedure for the reformation of the contract, but that under the doctrine of *rebus sic stantibus* a court of competent jurisdiction may declare the obligations of the contract terminated.

If the parties did not explicitly state which law was to govern, the court would need to decide this point. In the field of national law such decision would be reached by the application of private international law or conflict of laws. The rules of private international law are essentially part of the law of the state whose courts apply them; they have no force derived from any external authority.[40] The reluctance in the past to consider private international law as part of or similar to public international law was due, at least in large measure, to the fact that private international law dealt principally with the rights and duties of individuals and not of states. In the federal system of the United States it is now undersood that a large part of what was formerly considered conflict of laws is in reality part of constitutional law. In other words, the conflicts rules derive their validity from a constitutional norm.[41] Likewise in the international field, many states have become parties to multipartite conventions which lay down rules of private international law and thus transform them into, or make the duty to observe them, an obligation of public international law. Such are the several Hague Conventions concluded by numbers of European states at a series of conferences ranging from 1893 to 1928, the Montevideo Convention of 1899

[40] Cf. the Serbian and Brazilian loans cases, *P.C.I.J.*, Ser. A. No. 20/21 (1929), 41. See also Lepaulle, "Nature et méthode du droit international privé," 63 *Journal du droit international* (1936), 284; Sauser-Hall, "Les Règles générales des conflits de lois," 43 *Die Friedens-Warte* (1943), 35.

[41] See Cheatham, "Sources of Rules for Conflict of Laws," 89 *U. Pa. L. Rev.* (1941), 430, 437-39.

among the South American States, the Bustamante Code adopted at Havana in 1928, and the Montevideo treaty of 1940.[42]

The rapid growth of commercial arbitration, with the establishment of many private arbitration tribunals which have already achieved widespread international recognition and authority, suggests the procedural line that may be followed in dealing with agreements between individuals and states. The conclusion of international conventions whereby states have agreed to recognize the binding force of such arbitral awards is further evidence of their increasing international stature.[43] The special case of loan contracts between states and private parties has received much attention, with varying suggestions regarding an appropriate forum for the determination of applicable law and the solution of controversies.[44] Since states, as parties to agreements with alien individuals, are reluctant to submit disputes to the courts of the alien's country, and since the alien contractor may be unwilling to leave adjudication to the courts of the contracting state, some international forum is clearly requisite. Original submission to private arbitration in some form or to a special international loans tribunal with the possibility of appeal to the International Court of Justice on general questions, might well afford a satisfactory solution and tend to develop rather rapidly a most useful body of jurisprudence.

It would be useful for the future to reach agreement that private international law is a part of public international law. The result might be achieved through the wide signature of a general convention embodying at least a minimum of agreed principles on the subjects which would most frequently be involved in cases involving some public international interest. Principles determining the choice of law in the absence of explicit agreement by the parties might be placed in this category.

[42] On Inter-American developments in this field, see Carneiro, *O Direito internacional e a democracia* (1945), 381 ff.

[43] For a concise summary of the development, see Sir Lynden Macassey "International Commercial Arbitration: Its Origin, Development and Importance," 24 *Trans. Grotius Soc.* (1938), 179. See also "Report of the French Sub-Committee on Commercial Arbitration," *Int. Law Association, 40th Report* (1938), 275; Rundstein, "L'Arbitrage international en matière privée," 23 *Haegi recueil des cours* (1928), 331.

[44] See Hudson, *op. cit., supra* note 22, pp. 204 ff.; *supra*, Chap. V, note 57.

When an agreement has been concluded between two or more states on a subject traditionally recognized as a proper subject for a treaty, a court would be justified, in the absence of other evidence, in assuming that the parties intended to contract with reference to international law. On the other hand, if an agreement between two states regarding the lease of embassy property is couched in the language and form of a contract under the law of the state where the property is situated, that fact would be some evidence that the parties intended to contract with reference to that law. If therefore the law of the situs required any contract relating to real property to be sealed or notarized or registered as a prerequisite to its validity, the omission of the necessary formality would be held to invalidate the contract, and neither party would be heard to argue that under international law such formalities are not required.[45]

To give another example, it may be recalled that the international tribunal in the North Atlantic Coast Fisheries Arbitration rejected the contention of the United States that an international servitude had been constituted over the British territory. This conclusion was reached partly on the ground that the British and American negotiators in 1818 were apparently not conversant with the doctrine of international servitudes and partly through an analysis of the nature of an international servitude. If two states, or a state and an individual, or a state and an international organization such as an International Atomic Energy Commission, chose to contract with reference to the law of the state of the situs, and if that state had a clearly developed law concerning servitudes, the problem before a tribunal in case of a disputed interpretation would be simplified.

An agreement between two or more international organizations would in most instances be concluded with reference to international law, since neither of the contracting parties would have a national law of its own. But nothing would prevent one organization from leasing office space to another organization through an instrument intended to be governed by the law of the situs.

AMENDMENT AND TERMINATION OF AGREEMENTS

In considering the amendment of agreements it may be advantageous to approach the subject from the procedural point of view.

[45] See Feilchenfeld, op cit., supra note 39, p. 177.

Two procedures for change need to be contemplated, the one by vote of the properly authorized organ of some international agency, and the other by judicial decision. The ordinary process of amendment by negotiation of the parties and the special problem of reservations, particularly to multipartite treaties, are not included in this discussion.

Generally speaking, any amendment to an agreement creates a new or different obligation to which the consent of the parties must be obtained in the same way as their original consent. It has, however, been the practice for a considerable period for the parties to an agreement establishing some international agency or organization as a continuing instrument of their purpose, to agree that some designated organ of the agency may adopt specified types of changes by majority vote and that decisions so reached shall be binding on all the parties to the treaty. Such decisions may result in actual modifications of the original treaty, or they may take the form of new rules supplementary to the treaty. Authorization for this type of legislative process in international affairs has generally been confined to technical details.

A striking development in ideas and national attitudes is to be found in the provisions for the amendment of the Covenant of the League of Nations and the Charter of the United Nations. According to Article 26 of the Covenant, amendments were to take effect when ratified by the states represented in the Council and by a majority of the states represented in the Assembly. If, however, a state signified its dissent from the amendment, it would not be bound, but it would cease to be a Member of the League. This system imposed strong pressure on states to accept the will of the majority but fundamentally retained the traditional rule that a state could not be bound without its consent. At the same time it marked a departure from the rule that a treaty could not be amended without the consent of all the parties; states Members of the League had no vested right to block a change in the treaty. The exception to this last proposition is found in the special position accorded the states members of the Council. Nonpermanent members had, as it were, a transitory right to block amendments, a right which would be lost when their terms of office expired. Permanent members of the Council, on the other hand, always enjoyed this additional feature of the recognition of their special position as great powers.

This special position of the great powers received in the Covenant a legal recognition which actually merely put the stamp of general acquiescence on a practice long familiar. As Tobin showed in tracing the history of the great treaties of Vienna and of subsequent European conferences of major political consequence, the supposed rule that treaties could not be amended without the consent of all parties was honored more in the breach than in the observance.[46] Under the system of the Covenant, the great powers were no longer free to make changes on their own initiative and responsibility, but they retained what became the exceptional power to block any change of which they disapproved.

The issue was sharply drawn at the San Francisco Conference in the drafting of the Charter of the United Nations. To the United States Delegation the problem appeared in the following light:

> Those who seek to develop procedures for the peaceful settlement of international disputes always confront the hard task of striking a balance between the necessity of assuring stability and security on the one hand and of providing room for growth and adaptation on the other. This difficulty was present at San Francisco. If the possibility of Charter amendment was to be one method of satisfying those who feared lest the status quo be permanently frozen, how make sure that the rights and duties of Members would not, in the process of amendment, be brought into a different balance from that which members had originally accepted? This was of serious concern to the powers which were preparing to undertake primary responsibility for the maintenance of peace and security, even, if need be, by force of arms. It was also of concern to all states whose constitutions require that amendments to any treaty must secure parliamentary ratification. In a third category of interested states were those which feared that amendments might change the original relationship set up among the great powers, or between them and the smaller powers, and that such a change might adversely affect their own interests.[47]

[46] Tobin, *The Termination of Multipartite Treaties* (1933); cf. Stephens, *Revisions of the Treaty of Versailles* (1939).
[47] *Report to the President, op. cit.*, supra note 10, p. 166.

The outcome of the long negotiations was the adoption of the text of Article 108 of the Charter, which provides:

> Amendments to the present Charter shall come into force for all Members of the United Nations when they have been adopted by a vote of two-thirds of the members of the General Assembly and ratified in accordance with their respective constitutional processes by two-thirds of the Members of the United Nations, including all the permanent members of the Security Council.

Article 109 was also adopted as part of the compromise solution; it gives assurance to the states not permanent members of the Security Council that those great powers cannot block the consideration of amendments to the Charter if they are favored by a two-thirds majority of the members of the General Assembly and by any seven members of the Security Council.

No provision for the withdrawal or termination of the membership of a state opposing an amendment was inserted in the Charter, but the Conference adopted a Committee report that included the following paragraph:

> Nor would a Member be bound to remain in the Organization if its rights and obligations as such were changed by Charter amendment in which it has not concurred and which it finds itself unable to accept, or if an amendment duly accepted by the necessary majority in the Assembly or in a general conference fails to secure the ratification necessary to bring such amendment into effect.[48]

It would therefore appear to be the view of the Members of the United Nations that they cannot be bound by an amendment in which they have not concurred, although, as in the League system, the penalty for dissent is termination of membership in the United Nations. Again the great powers, which have permanent seats on the Security Council, enjoy a privileged position in that any one of them may exercise the veto power to prevent the adoption of an

[48] UNIO, 7 *Documents of the United Nations Conference on International Organization, San Francisco, 1945* (1945), 267. Cf. *Report to the President, op. cit., supra* note 10, p. 49.

amendment. The progress marked by Article 26 of the Covenant in terminating the system whereunder the great powers could as a matter of political reality bring about changes in multipartite treaties without securing the consent of the lesser powers is preserved by the Charter text.

Notwithstanding these formal provisions concerning amendments, it is true under the United Nations Charter, as under the League Covenant, that interpretative resolutions adopted by a majority vote of the General Assembly may have or come to have such compelling force as to constitute in effect changes which will bind all members. Compliance may be secured by political considerations, and the interpretative "changes" may find legal justification in the contention that they merely clarify the nature of the obligations which states have already assumed by ratifying the Charter.[49] The entire development is of interest in relation to the progress toward a system of international legislation by majority rule. When such a system is sufficiently familiar and has sufficiently justified itself in practice the old obstacle of absolute sovereignty, which is at the basis of the traditional rule that a treaty may not be modified without the consent of all the original parties, may gradually disappear.

Another aspect of this same development of a legislative process in international affairs is to be traced in connection with decisions of an international organization such as the United Nations that affect states not Members. During the League of Nations period, the political importance of the non-membership of the United States prevented such a process from attaining great significance. As the United Nations approaches universality of membership there may well be a growing tendency for the Organization to assert its right to speak on behalf of the world community and to exact the compliance of non-Members with its decisions. Some aspects of this problem have already been noted in this Chapter in discussing the question of the rights of third parties. The issue was raised at San Francisco in considering the Statute of the International Court of Justice. There was much sentiment in favor of continuing the Permanent Court of International Justice, but there was general acknowledgment of the need for making certain changes in its Statute to bring the Court into gear with the other organs of the

[49] Cf. Lauterpacht's note 3 in 1 Oppenheim, 311; *supra*, Chap. III, note 11.

United Nations. Sixteen states, parties to the old Statute, were not represented at San Francisco. It was believed that enemy states' approval of changes in the Statute could be secured through the peace treaties,[50] but such a solution would have left unsolved the situation of the neutral states. Had the Conference decided to "legislate" changes in the old Statute, the practical result would probably have been that the amended Statute would have been freely accepted by all the states parties to the old Statute. For various reasons such a procedure did not appear to be advantageous, and accordingly a new Statute was drawn up.[51]

The same practical considerations did not prevent the Members of the United Nations from terminating the existence of the Permanent Court of International Justice. This is technically what has occurred, although "the chain of continuity with the past" has not been broken and the International Court of Justice is in a very real sense the continuation of the Permanent Court of International Justice. Nevertheless the case illustrates a technical legal termination of, and therefore change in, the Protocol of Signature of 1920 to which the old Statute was annexed, without the participation of all states that were parties to that agreement.

The termination of the existence of the League of Nations did not require any such legislative step. The states which were Members of the League and are also Members of the United Nations formed a link between the two organizations. The matter was handled as a negotiation between the United Nations and the League regarding the transfer of assets and functions.[52] The actual dissolution of the League will take place in accordance with a resolution of the special League Assembly held in Geneva in April 1946.[53]

Again in solving the difficult problem of the "assumption" by

[50] Art. 39 of the Peace Treaty with Italy as published in the *New York Times*, January 18, 1947, provides as follows: "Italy undertakes to accept any arrangements which have been or may be agreed for the liquidation of the League of Nations, the Permanent Court of International Justice and also the International Financial Commission in Greece."

[51] See *Report to the President, op. cit., supra* note 10, pp. 140–41.

[52] See Reiff, "Transition from League of Nations to United Nations," 14 Dept. of State *Bulletin* (1946), 691, 739; *The League Hands Over*, Series of League of Nations Publications, General, 1946, 1.

[53] *The League Hands Over, op. cit., supra* note 52, p. 97; League Doc. A. 32 (1). 1946. X, 12.

the United Nations or its appropriate organs of various functions attributed to the League and its organs by a variety of treaties, no attempt was made to legislate on behalf of states not Members of the United Nations. The Report of the League of Nations Committee to the General Assembly of the United Nations [54] includes the following paragraphs, which reveal the principle utilized:

> Under various treaties and international conventions, agreements and other instruments, the League of Nations and its organs exercise, or may be requested to exercise, numerous functions or powers for the continuance of which, after the dissolution of the League, it is, or may be, desirable that the United Nations should provide. . . .

> The General Assembly records that those Members of the United Nations which are parties to the instruments referred to above assent by this resolution to the steps contemplated below and express their resolve to use their good offices to secure the co-operation of the other parties to the instruments so far as this may be necessary.

It may well prove, as this process is followed, that some state or states, not Members of the United Nations, may decline to acquiesce in the substitution of the United Nations for the League of Nations in one or more of the international agreements involved. In this event it is to be anticipated that the rest of the states which are also parties to such agreements will proceed to act under the revised or amended instruments, regardless of the dissents. Dissenting states would be justified in thereupon declaring that they were no longer bound by such amended agreements, but the practical fact of amendment would have taken place without their participation, thus affording another example of what may properly be styled legislative action by the United Nations in the interest of the world community as a whole.

The Sixth (Legal) Committee of the General Assembly considered this general problem in connection with the proposals for the transfer to the United Nations of powers exercised by the

[54] UN Doc. A/28, 4 Feb. 1946, *Journal of the General Assembly*, No. 30, 526–27; No. 34, 706–9.

League of Nations under the six agreements, conventions, or protocols providing for the international control of narcotic drugs. A protocol containing provisions for the necessary amendments was reviewed by the Sixth Committee in order to determine the legal position of those parties to the original instruments which do not become parties to the new protocol. The proposals submitted to the General Assembly specifically provided that Spain, a party to the earlier agreements, should not be invited to become a party to the protocol; other states not Members of the United Nations had no voice in the proposed changes. The Sixth Committee concluded that any group of states parties to the earlier agreements could clearly make amendments which would be binding as between themselves. As to other states not becoming parties to the new protocol, the Committee concluded that they would remain bound by various obligations in the original instruments, although the actual machinery for international control set up by the original instruments "will be altogether dissolved" and the corresponding parts of those instruments "will thus be a dead letter." [55] The effect of these actions and interpretations is that, while the states in the United Nations have not asserted the right to impose new obligations on states not freely accepting the new agreement, they have asserted the right to make important changes in multipartite agreements without the consent of all the parties and with the consequence of materially altering the nature of the obligations by which those other states remain bound.

The second procedure for change which has been suggested is that which takes place by judicial decision. Here the difficulties which confront the development of a modern law of nations are far greater, since states are still reluctant to confide broad powers to international courts. The factual difficulty to be solved is the existence of a situation in which a state, party to a treaty, feels that its noncompliance with the treaty obligation is justified for one or another reason. Under the traditional international system there was no established court of general jurisdiction competent to pass on such pleas justificatory of nonfulfillment of an obligation. On the contrary, each sovereign state would assert for itself the legal right

[55] UN Doc. A/194, 15 Nov. 1946; *Journal of the UN*, No. 38, 21. Nov. 1946, *Supp.* A-A/P. V./49, 328.

on which it relied, and the other party to the treaty could merely fall back upon procedures registering displeasure, which ranged all the way from a note of protest, through the rupture of diplomatic relations and retaliation, to war itself. True, the states might agree to arbitration, and during the interwar period a large number of states vested compulsory jurisdiction in the Permanent Court of International Justice. The difficulty, as Lauterpacht has pointed out, was in large measure procedural; the international community had not attained that ripeness of legal development which would enable national systems of law to entrust greater authority to courts. "The rule that compacts must be kept," writes Lauterpacht, "is certainly one of the bases of the legal relations between the members of any community. But at the same time the notion that in certain cases the law will refuse to continue to give effect to originally valid contracts is common to all systems of jurisprudence." [56] He proceeds to cite the rule *ad impossibilia nemo tenetur* in Roman law, the doctrines of frustration and impossibility of performance in English law, and comparable provisions in a number of European civil codes and the jurisprudence of France and Germany.

In international law the doctrine *rebus sic stantibus* is the equivalent exception to the maxim *pacta sunt servanda*. The doctrine constitutes an attempt to formulate a legal principle which would justify nonperformance of a treaty obligation if the conditions with relation to which the parties contracted have changed so materially and so unexpectedly as to create a situation in which the exaction of performance would be unreasonable. Invoked unilaterally without the opportunity for impartial review, the doctrine is anarchic; in some form it is an essential part of any well-developed legal system.

The doctrine *rebus sic stantibus* illustrates, perhaps better than any other part of the law of treaties, the need for adopting distinctions between different types of treaties. For political treaties and for the invocation of political changes in the balance of power, the doctrine is pernicious. In such situations it would amount to the proposition that no peace treaty accepted by a defeated state remains valid after that state recovers sufficiently or the victors weaker

[56] Lauterpacht, *The Function of Law in the International Community* (1933), 273.

sufficiently to make it politically possible for the defeated state to throw off the burden without danger of another defeat. No more unsettling legal principle could be imagined; but it would in fact, if accepted, reflect what has frequently occurred. For this very reason the doctrine *rebus sic stantibus* has been discredited. On the other hand, suppose a commercial treaty in which special privileges in the use of valuable port facilities are reciprocally exchanged by States A and B; assume that in State B there is only one important port, and that this port is later ceded by B to State C. It would be unreasonable to require State A to continue to accord the treaty privileges to B after it became impossible for B to perform its reciprocal obligation.[57] In an organized world society any question of the revision of a peace treaty should be resolved by the political wisdom of a body such as the Security Council or the General Assembly. Article 19 of the Covenant was a recognition of this fact, as are the vaguer provisions of the Charter such as those in Articles 11, 14, and 34. It is not the type of question that should be resolved by a court. On the other hand, a case such as that suggested, involving reciprocal use of port facilities, might properly be weighed and decided by the International Court of Justice.[58] If in the gradual evolution of the law of nations it is necessary to make haste slowly, it may be suggested that a first step might be agreement on a rule of law that could be applied by an international court so as to relieve a state from a continuing obligation to perform the duties imposed by a treaty under certain defined circumstances, with the consequence that the other party to the treaty would be simultaneously freed. The result would be a judicial declaration that the treaty was no longer binding on either party to it. This step would be far short of one which would entrust to international tribunals the power of equitable reformation of a contract so as to require the performance by a state of some obligation different from that originally assumed.

The suggested principle could be applied without great difficulty

[57] Cf. the case of Bremen v. Prussia, *Ann. Dig.* (1925–1926), Case No. 266, cited by Lauterpacht, *op. cit.*, *supra* note 56, p. 277–78; cf. also the distinction made by 2 Hyde, sec. 544A.

[58] See Sir John Fischer Williams, "The Permanence of Treaties," 22 *Am. J Int. L.* (1928), 89, 103, and Potter, "Article XIX of the Covenant of the League of Nations," 12 *Geneva Studies* No. 2, 1941.

to international agreements between states and individuals, as for
example in the case of a concession contract concluded by the parties
as an international law agreement. In such a case the judgment of
an international court might appropriately assess the financial recom-
pense to be paid by one or the other party to avoid unjust enrichment, in addition to declaring the contract terminated.

Another principle of traditional international law justifies a state
in denouncing a treaty in the event of a material breach by the other
party.[59] But the Harvard Research in International Law pertinently
points out in the Comment to Article 27 of its Draft Convention on
the Law of Treaties that unilateral determination of what constitutes
a material breach makes for lawless conduct.[60] In such cases it is
highly suitable for an international tribunal to pass judgment on the
merits of the claim of the state which seeks to free itself from its
obligation. Again it is suggested that a distinction should be drawn
between political and other types of treaties, because the breach of
a political treaty so frequently involves considerations affecting the
peace of the world. In this respect the Charter fully recognizes the
idea of community interest, inasmuch as any state or the Secretary-
General may bring such a situation to the attention of the General
Assembly or of the Security Council under Article 11, 35, or 99.

Another principle of international law susceptible of application
by an international court is that which relates to the effect of war on
treaties. There has been dispute whether war terminates or merely
suspends the operation of treaties, but the basis for judicial decision
is clearly available.[61] Professor Hyde and Sir Cecil Hurst have
properly pointed out that in many instances the problem is merely
one of treaty interpretation, which is essentially a judicial function.[62]
In a well-organized world system operating under a modernized law
of nations, war in its old sense will no longer escape legal regulation,
and the consequences of war upon treaties as well as upon other
legal relationships would stand in need of redefinition. But force

[59] See 1 Hyde, sec. 546.
[60] *Op. cit., supra* note 27, p. 1077.
[61] Cf. Judge Cardozo in Techt *v.* Hughes, 229 N.Y: 222 (1920).
[62] 2 Hyde, sec. 547; Hurst, "The Effect of War on Treaties," 2 *Brit. Y. B.
Int. L.* (1921-1922), 37, 39-40. This approach seems to have been adopted by the
Circuit Court of Appeals, Ninth Circuit, in Allen *v.* Markham, 156 F. (2d) 653
(1946).

may still be used in case of necessity on behalf of the international community, and the legal consequences of the use of force will need to be determined.[63] For example, under Article 41 of the Charter of the United Nations the Security Council may call upon the Members to apply such measures as complete or partial interruption of economic relations and of international communications, and the Members are under a duty to comply. It cannot be doubted that action taken by a Member in compliance with such directions of the Security Council would constitute justification for any incidental breach of a treaty obligation calling for freedom of commercial intercourse or of communications. This would be true not only vis-à-vis the state against which the measures are taken, but also vis-à-vis any third state, whether Member of the United Nations or not, which might because of its geographical position be incidentally affected. Such a result might ensue, for example, from the imposition of a blockade that, to be effective, required limitation on free access to a state bordering on the state against which the measure was applied.

The need for some development of international law in such cases is indicated by the conservative position which the Secretary-General of the League of Nations felt obliged to take in his Report in 1927 concerning the legal positions arising from the application of sanctions. He concluded that the Covenant could not be interpreted "as imposing on the Members of the League an obligation to violate the rights" of a non-Member state.[64] He used the language of hope in regard to the possible acquiescence of third states, which would be conscious that the Members of the League were acting on behalf of the peace of the world; further he was not prepared to go. The view was sound under the existing international law. A modernized law of nations should provide, not an obligation on Members of the United Nations to violate the "rights" of non-Members, but the right of the Organization to take action under the Charter in the interest of world peace, and the *duty* of non-Members to acquiesce. In other words, the old principle which the

[63] See Chaps. VII, VIII.
[64] League Doc. A. 14. 1927. V., V Legal, 1927, V. 14., p. 86. See also the circular letter of the Secretary-General of June 14, 1933, concerning measures proposed relative to the non-recognition of "Manchukuo," League of Nations *Off. J. Spec. Supp.* (1933), No. 113, p. 10.

Secretary-General of the League of Nations felt obliged to cite, *pacta tertiis neque nocent neque prosunt,* needs revision.

COMMUNITY INTEREST AND BREACHES OF AGREEMENTS

The acceptance of the hypothesis of community interest would require an acknowledgment of the right of any state to take cognizance of a breach of a treaty even if not directly affected by the breach. This is probably true under existing international law with reference to a multipartite treaty, any party to which would be justified in protesting against a breach of the agreement, because of its interest in the maintenance of the system which the treaty establishes. This would be clearly true in regard to a breach of the Charter and would be equally so in regard to a breach of an international sanitary convention, a postal convention, a convention on radio, or particularly a treaty codifying some part of international law. If the party directly affected should submit the case to the International Court of Justice, any other party to the treaty might appropriately apply to the Court under Article 62 of the Statute for permission to intervene on the ground that "it has an interest of a legal nature which may be affected by the decision in the case." If the state directly affected should take no step to vindicate its rights, another party to the treaty might itself apply to the Court or might bring the matter to the attention of the General Assembly or the Security Council with a view to inducing one of those bodies to make a request to the Court for an advisory opinion.

More broadly, the acceptance of the hypothesis of community interest should be considered to vest in all members of the international community a legal interest in respect for treaties.[65] Despite the development of general international law, it is to be anticipated that much of the world's affairs will continue to be governed by agreements concluded by two or more states. Respect for the maxim *pacta sunt servanda* and the development of treaty law will be matters of concern to all states, and an infringement of the law will affect the interests of all.

A modernized law of nations would also accord enlarged recog-

[65] Cf. Wright, "Collective Rights and Duties for the Enforcement of Treaty Obligations," *Am. Soc. Int. L., Proc.* (1932), 101.

nition of the right of international organizations to take legal steps in any case in which the constitution of the organization or any convention concluded under its auspices is breached. This principle is already in part recognized in the Charter through the provisions in Article 96 which authorize the General Assembly or the Security Council to request an advisory opinion from the Court. At San Francisco attempts were made to accord a like privilege to other international organizations such as the International Labour Office. The Conference was not prepared to go so far, but the point was met by the second paragraph of Article 96, which states: "Other organs of the United Nations and specialized agencies, which may at any time be so authorized by the General Assembly, may also request advisory opinions of the Court on legal questions arising within the scope of their activities." [66] As part of the same discussion in the Conference, there were included in Article 34 of the Statute of the International Court of Justice the following two paragraphs, which follow the statement that "Only states may be parties in cases before the Court":

2. The Court, subject to and in conformity with its rules, may request of public international organizations information relevant to cases before it, and shall receive such information presented by such organizations on their own initiative.

3. Whenever the construction of the constituent instrument of a public international organization or of an international convention adopted thereunder is in question in a case before the Court, the Registrar shall so notify the public international organization concerned and shall communicate to it copies of all the written proceedings.

It should not be long before the personality of international organizations is fully recognized and they are accorded, through an amendment to the Statute, the full right to be parties in cases before the Court.[67]

The acceptance of the hypothesis that individuals are also

[66] Under the authority of Art. 96 of the Charter the General Assembly on December 11, 1946, adopted a resolution authorizing the Economic and Social Council to request advisory opinions. UN Doc. A/201. See also *supra* Chap. II, note 43.

[67] See Chap. II.

subjects of international law would not necessarily involve according the right to individuals to appear as parties before the International Court of Justice. As already suggested, it will become necessary to limit the types of cases which will be taken to that high tribunal, at least in the first instance, and other tribunals will be needed for the handling of cases in which one of the parties is an individual. In treaty cases such international tribunals will be needed, since under the hypothesis, as stated earlier in this chapter, individuals themselves may have rights under treaties, and in the event of breach of such rights an individual should not be left to find satisfaction only in the courts of the state which would be the other party to the litigation. The same considerations would apply to cases involving agreements between individuals and states or between individuals and international organizations.

CHAPTER VII

THE LEGAL REGULATION OF THE USE OF FORCE

THE MOST DRAMATIC WEAKNESS of traditional international law has been its admission that a state may use force to compel compliance with its will.[1] This weakness has been the inevitable consequence of two factors: (1) the concept of absolute sovereignty, and (2) the lack of a well-developed international organization with competent powers.[2] Both are in course of losing their old significance. The United Nations as an organization for the maintenance of peace reveals progress over the League of Nations. As is pointed out in the introductory chapter, the concept of absolute sovereignty is under vigorous attack and has already lost much of its magic. The adoption of the two hypotheses on which this book is based will be utilized to examine ways in which the law of nations may develop in order to place legal limitation on the use of force.

It sometimes appears strange that traditional international law, while leaving untouched the ultimate right to resort to war, achieved some regulation of use of force short of war. But this apparent paradox should not cause surprise; it is illustrative of the manner in which international law has developed over the centuries in a world of sovereign states. The regulation of the resort to war itself constitutes the ultimate problem toward the solution of which the world has been groping. Along the way it has been possible to secure a measure of agreement on lesser problems. The resort to war was difficult to control because states have not in modern times made war for frivolous reasons, but only when a conviction of some large interest to be served seemed to afford a justification, at least in their own eyes. The interest might be and usually was purely selfish,

---

[1] See 3 Hyde, 1686.
[2] Cf. 2 Oppenheim, 145.

but in the eyes of the warmaker it was not insignificant. If the interest involved was not sufficiently great to justify, from a domestic or from an international point of view, actual resort to war, it was of a degree of magnitude susceptible of legal regulation. Local feeling or general Pan-American policy might induce the United States to avoid making war on Nicaragua but would not preclude the sending of a cruiser and the landing of marines. National justifications for the lesser uses of force have been generally couched in legal terms— self-defense, defense of national lives and property, reprisals, retaliation—and the customary law developed tests of the propriety of such conduct. National justifications for war itself have more frequently been placed on moral grounds or high political aspirations and ideals, and the customary law has at best characterized war as un-legal—neither legal nor illegal.[3] Utilizing humanitarian sentiment and, more effectively, the notions of military utility and anticipation of retaliation, international law developed rules for the conduct of warfare, as in the prohibition of explosive bullets and the poisoning of wells and the regulations for the treatment of prisoners of war.[4] Because of the coexistence of clashing interests which needed to be reconciled and which, by and large, represented sufficient elements of balance of power to bring about reconciliation, the law of neutral rights and duties grew into a body of highly developed jural doctrine, aided by the functioning of prize courts, which built up a large body of case law.[5]

The Charter of the United Nations is the latest milestone on the road to the legal regulation of war and, in general, of the use of force in international relations. According to the fourth paragraph of Article 2: "All Members shall refrain in their international relations from the threat or use of force against the territorial integrity or political independence of any state, or in any other manner inconsistent with the Purposes of the United Nations." This statement derives added significance from its context. The first principle stated in this same article is "the principle of the sovereign

---

[3] See "Harvard Research in International Law, Draft Convention on Rights and Duties of States in Case of Aggression," 33 *Am. J. Int. L. Supp.* (1939), 857; cf. 2 Oppenheim, 145.

[4] See Royse, *Aerial Bombardment and the International Regulation of Warfare* (1928), Chaps. I, IV.

[5] See *Neutrality, Its History, Economics and Law,* 4 vols. (1935-36).

equality" of all the members of the Organization, which is "based" on that principle. From the coexistence of these two principles it is to be deduced that the regulation of the threat or use of force is not inconsistent with the principle of sovereign equality. A resort to war can, therefore, no longer be justified by an invocation of the old concept of absolute sovereignty, which in the last analysis left every state the final judge in its own cause. In the next place, the third principle is that "All Members shall settle their disputes by peaceful means in such a manner that international peace and security, and justice, are not endangered." The coexistence of this third and the fourth principle require the conclusion that there are alternatives to war and that these alternatives are peaceful ones. The fifth principle states the obligation of all Members to co-operate in measures taken by the United Nations to preserve the peace, measures already indicated in the first stated Purpose of the Organization in Article 1. The significance of this principle, together with the others, is that the alternatives to war are not merely those pacific methods of a state's own choosing, but also the "police" action of the international community marshaled in the common interest to preserve the peace.

Of equal if not of greater importance from the standpoint of the progress of the world toward a basis of organized peace are those provisions of the Charter designed to make effective the second and third Purposes stated in Article 1. These purposes are:

> 2. To develop friendly relations among nations based on respect for the principle of equal rights and self-determination of peoples, and to take other appropriate measures to strengthen universal peace;
>
> 3. To achieve international cooperation in solving international problems of an economic, social, cultural, or humanitarian character, and in promoting and encouraging respect for human rights and for fundamental freedoms for all without distinction as to race, sex, language or religion.

Obviously law must be developed for the regulation of human activities in all of these fields as a part of the process of establishing and maintaining peace, but such fields of legal regulation do not form part of the subject of this chapter, and many of them are beyond the scope of this introduction to a modern law of nations. It is necessary to observe that peace will never be secure if progress is confined to putting an international lid on a national boiling pot. When there is a strong national feeling of injustice, resentment will eventually produce conflict unless there is some assurance that there is a peaceful substitute for resort to violence. This is the perennial problem of "peaceful change," which has so far defied all the efforts devoted to its solution.[6]

With respect to the central problem of war itself, the United Nations has already taken an important step to supplement the provisions of the Charter. On December 13, 1946 the General Assembly unanimously adopted a resolution in which it affirmed "the principles of international law recognized by the Charter of the Nürnberg Tribunal and the judgment of the Tribunal."[7] That Charter, in Article 6, declared that certain acts are "crimes coming within the jurisdiction of the Tribunal for which there shall be individual responsibility":

> (a) Crimes against peace: Namely, planning, preparation, initiation or waging of a war of aggression, or a war in violation of international treaties, agreements or assurances, or participation in a common plan or conspiracy for the accomplishment of any of the foregoing. . . .[8]

The General Assembly took note of the fact that "similar principles have been adopted in the Charter of the International Military Tribunal for the trial of the major war criminals in the Far East. . . ." The comparable Article 5 of that Charter employs a slightly different phraseology:

> (a) *Crimes against Peace:* Namely, the planning, preparation, initiation or waging of a declared or undeclared war of aggression, or a war in violation of international law, treaties, agreements or assurances, or participation in a common plan

[6] See Dunn, *Peaceful Change* (1937); Dulles, *War, Peace and Change* (1939); Wood, *Peaceful Change and the Colonial Problem* (1940); Manning (ed.), *Peaceful Change, an International Problem* (1937); "International Studies Conference, Peaceful Change," *Tenth Int. Stud. Conf., Proc.* (1937).

[7] *Journal of the General Assembly,* No. 58, Supp. A–A/P. V./55, p. 485.

[8] *Trial of War Criminals,* Dept. of State Pub. 2420 (1945), 16.

or conspiracy for the accomplishment of any of the fore-going.[9]

The General Assembly went on to direct the Committee on the Codification of International Law "to treat as a matter of primary importance plans for the formulation, in the context of a general codification of offenses against the peace and security of mankind, or of an International Criminal Code, of the principles" so recognized. Although this affirmation does not have the binding force of a treaty, it has the legal importance already discussed in Chapter III with reference to resolutions of such a representative international body.

It is true to say that the trial of the war criminals and the resolution of the General Assembly affirming the bases of those trials involves the rejection of the theory that the state itself is guilty and can be punished for waging aggressive war. Reparation payments are being considered more as compensatory damages in a civil suit than as fines in a criminal action.[10] The net result of the war trials, however, particularly in the light of the discussions attending them, must lead to the conclusion that the waging of aggressive war is considered an international crime regardless of whether the anthropomorphic fiction of the state or the flesh-and-blood cabinet or military officer is held liable to punishment. Under the traditional law the full acceptance of the illegality of war would have led to the conclusion that the state which waged war would be guilty of an illegal act; under the current development it is the individual who is held to have committed an internationally criminal act. The traditional system would have put the burden on the state to restrain the individual, whereas the precedent of the war trials suggests that pressure in the form of fear of punishment would be put on

[9] *Trial of Japanese War Criminals*, Dept. of State Pub. 2613 (1946), 40.
[10] The Potsdam Agreement declared: "In accordance with the Crimea Decision that Germany be compelled to compensate to the greatest possible extent for the loss and suffering that she has caused to the United Nations and for which the German people cannot escape responsibility, the following agreement on reparations was reached. . . ." 13 Dept. of State *Bulletin* (1945), 157. In contrast, Art. 231 of the Treaty of Versailles contains the "war-guilt" clause whereby the Allies affirmed and Germany accepted responsibility for the damage suffered as a consequence of the war imposed by the aggression of Germany and her allies.

individuals to restrain the state. As international organization develops and is perfected, it may be assumed that collective force will be used in case of necessity to restrain states or other groups in advance, but that punishment after the event will be visited on individuals and not on the group.

In relatively minor cases of the illegal use of force, provision might be made for the imposition of a pecuniary penalty on the offending state. Although the terminology differed, this was in effect the outcome of the excessive use of force by a United States Coast Guard Cutter against the Canadian rum-smuggling vessel *I'm Alone*. The Commissioners to whom the issue was referred concluded that the United States should apologize to the Canadian Government and "that as a material amend in respect of the wrong the United States should pay the sum of $25,000 to His Majesty's Canadian Government." This amount was in addition to the sums to be paid for the benefit of the captain and crew.[11]

It will also be desirable, within a new framework, to build on the theory of the Stimson nonrecognition doctrine, which was thought of as a deterrent to the use of aggression, especially in the conquest of territory. Because of the weakness of world organization the doctrine was not effective, but it should be utilized in the future as a sanction that denies to an aggressor the fruits of aggression. It seems unnecessary to describe here in detail a doctrine so generally familiar,[12] and it is referred to merely as an indication of a precedent which may be inspired with reality in a more adequately organized international community.

Returning to the terms of the Charter of the United Nations, it may be noted that Article 2, paragraph 4, is not an absolute prohibition of the use of force. If force can be used in a manner which does not threaten the territorial integrity or political independence of a state, it escapes the restriction of the first clause. But it must then be established that it is not "in any other manner inconsistent with the

[11] *"I'm Alone" Case, Joint Final Report of the Commissioners*, Dept. of State Pub. 711 (1935), 4.
[12] The basic documents illustrating the historic developments of the nonrecognition doctrine are collected in the "Harvard Research in International Law, Draft Convention on the Rights and Duties of States in Case of Aggression," *op. cit., supra* note 3, 889. An excellent comprehensive study will be found in Langer, *Seizure of Territory* (1947).

Purposes of the United Nations." It seems clear at once that the use of force under direction of the Security Council and its Military Staff Committee, as provided for in Chapter VII of the Charter, is free of such inconsistency. Does there remain any other area in which the threat or use of force is legal? The answer to that question may be sought through a re-examination of the traditional practices of forceful action as they are listed in nearly every treatise on international law.

SELF-DEFENSE

International law recognizes the right of a state to resort to force in self-defense. Where the use of force has this justification, the incidental or consequent infringement of the rights of another state is excused, although the other state may be legally privileged to resist.[13] A forcible act of self-defense may amount to or may result in war, but it may frequently be a single incident of short duration, especially when the two states involved are of unequal strength. Self-defense has also been a commonly invoked political justification on moral grounds for resort to war.

When, in 1928, states renounced war as an instrument of national policy and agreed that they would not seek to settle their disputes by other than peaceful means, the right of self-defense was expressly reserved. Thus the United States note of June 23, 1928 declared that the proposed treaty did not in any way restrict or impair the right of self-defense. "That right is inherent in every sovereign state and is implicit in every treaty. Every nation is free at all times and regardless of treaty provisions to defend its territory from attack or invasion and it alone is competent to decide whether circumstances require recourse to war in self-defense." [14] Such a statement suggests that the right of self-defense by its very nature must escape legal regulation. In one sense this is true. Secretary of State Daniel Webster, in the course of discussions with the British Government concerning the celebrated affair of the *Caroline*, stated in 1842 that action in self-defense was justified only when the necessity for action is "instant, overwhelming, and leaving no choice of means,

[13] See 1 Oppenheim, 242 ff., and 1 Hyde, 237 ff.
[14] *Treaty for the Renunciation of War*, Dept. of State Pub. 468 (1933), 57.

and no moment for deliberation." [15] This definition is obviously drawn from consideration of the right of self-defense in domestic law; the cases are rare indeed in which it would exactly fit an international situation. It is an accurate definition for international law, however, in the sense that the exceptional right of self-defense can be exercised only if the end cannot be otherwise obtained. In 1926, when League of Nations experts were studying the problems which would result from the application of sanctions under Article 16 of the Covenant, a Belgian jurist noted that "Legitimate defense implies the adoption of measures proportionate to the seriousness of the attack and justified by the imminence of the danger." [16] When an individual is set upon by an armed thug who threatens his life, instantaneous action is clearly requisite and it can be said that there is "no moment for deliberation." When a state anticipates a threatened injury from another state or from a lawless band, there is usually opportunity for deliberation in a chancellery or war office, and an officer on the spot does not act until he has received instructions from a higher command. Telegraphic or radio communication between the officer and his superiors can be taken as a counterpart of the impulses in the nervous system of the individual whose brain instructs his arm to strike.

Granted the necessary degree of immediacy and urgency, it is of course true, as Lauterpacht has pointed out, that every state must be the judge in its own cause, since it would be impossible to await the decision of an international authority and since, if such decision were secured, the act of the state would constitute the execution of the decision rather than an act of self-defense.[17]

The provisions of the Charter of the United Nations are in accord with this reasoning. According to Article 51:

> Nothing in the present Charter shall impair the inherent right of individual or collective self-defense if an armed attack occurs against a Member of the United Nations, *until*

[15] 2 *Moore's Digest of Int. L.,* 412.
[16] M. Louis de Brouckère, Rapporteur, *Reports and Resolutions on the Subject of Article 16 of the Covenant,* League of Nations Doc. A. 14. 1927 V. V. Legal 1927. V. 14, pp. 60, 69. In general see Reitzer, *La Réparation comme conséquence de l'acte illicite en droit international* (1938), 91 ff.
[17] Lauterpacht, *The Function of Law in the International Community* (1933), 179.

the Security Council has taken the measures necessary to maintain international peace and security. Measures taken by Members in the exercise of this right of self-defense shall be immediately reported to the Security Council and shall not in any way affect the authority and responsibility of the Security Council under the present Charter to take at any time such action as it deems necessary in order to maintain or restore international peace and security.

The italicized words and the following sentence bring out the point at which the law regulates the act of self-defense. The actor invokes the right at his peril, and his conduct is subject to subsequent review. As the Nürnberg Tribunal asserted: ". . . whether action taken under the claim of self-defense was in fact aggressive or defensive must ultimately be subject to investigation and adjudication if international law is ever to be enforced." [18] Should the Security Council decide that the act was not justified, it might impose its measures of forcible restraint on the state that had claimed to act in self-defense instead of on the state alleged to be the aggressor.

The reference in Article 51 to "collective self-defense" was designed to safeguard the inter-American system of mutual defense as outlined in the Declaration of Lima in 1938, the Act of Havana of 1940, and the Act of Chapultepec of 1945.[19] Such regional collective measures are also subordinated to the world authority vested in the Security Council. The Charter and the Organization of the United Nations thus supply the mechanics for international review that were missing from the system of the Briand-Kellogg Pact, the absence of which constituted its chief weakness. It was indeed the weakness of the entire international policy of the United States throughout the League of Nations period.

Article 51 of the Charter suggests a further limitation on the right of self-defense: it may be exercised only "if an armed attack occurs." The classical case of the seizure of the Danish fleet in

---

[18] See Fite, "The Nürnberg Judgment: A Summary," 16 Dept. of State *Bulletin* (1947), 9, 10.

[19] See *Report to the President on the Results of the San Francisco Conference by the Chairman of the United States Delegation,* Dept. of State Pub. 2349 (1945), 107.

Copenhagen by the British in 1807 because of fear that the Danes would be coerced into surrendering the fleet to the French would not be the type of case justified by Article 51. Neither would the case of Amelia Island in 1817, wherein President Monroe ordered a United States vessel of war to wipe out a nest of marauders established on that island, which was then in Spanish territory.[20] The case of the *Caroline* in 1837 and that of the pursuit of Villa by United States Army forces in 1916 might come within the permitted cases,[21] but it would seem that Article 51 has rather in mind such a position as that of China when Japan attacked Manchuria in 1931; Japan's allegation that it acted in self-defense could not be supported under traditional law or under Article 51[22] This restriction in Article 51 very definitely narrows the freedom of action which states had under traditional law. A case could be made out for self-defense under the traditional law where the injury was threatened but no attack had yet taken place. Under the Charter, alarming military preparations by a neighboring state would justify a resort to the Security Council, but would not justify resort to anticipatory force by the state which believed itself threatened.

The documentary record of the discussions at San Francisco does not afford conclusive evidence that the suggested interpretation of the words "armed attack" in Article 51 is correct, but the general tenor of the discussions, as well as the careful choice of words throughout Chapters VI and VII of the Charter relative to various stages of aggravation of dangers to the peace, support the view stated. The interpretation is, moreover, supported by the views of the United States with respect to proposals for control of atomic warfare. In United States Memorandum No. 3, of July 12, 1946, after quoting the text of Article 51 of the Charter, the following significant statement is made:

> Interpreting its provisions with respect to atomic energy matters, it is clear that if atomic weapons were employed as part of an "armed attack," the rights reserved by the nations to themselves under article 51 would be applicable. It is

[20] See 1 Oppenheim, 245–6.
[21] See 1 Hyde, secs. 66, 67.
[22] 1 Oppenheim, 248. In general reference to Art. 51, see Goodrich and Hambro, *Charter of the United Nations* (1946), 174–81.

equally clear that an "armed attack" is now something entirely different from what it was prior to the discovery of atomic weapons. It would therefore seem to be both important and appropriate under present conditions that the treaty define "armed attack" in a manner appropriate to atomic weapons and include in the definition not simply the actual dropping of an atomic bomb, but also certain steps in themselves preliminary to such action.[23]

The "treaty" referred to in this passage is the proposed agreement relative to the control of atomic warfare and the functions and powers of an Atomic Development Authority. If Article 51 justified the use of force in self-defense in anticipation of an armed attack but before such an attack had actually been made, the suggested clarification would not be necessary. The First Report of the Atomic Energy Commission to the Security Council of December 30, 1946 is less conclusive and suggests the possibility that in connection with atomic warfare something short of armed attack might justify resort to measures of self-defense under Article 51. In Part III of the Report it is said: "In consideration of the problem of violation of the terms of the treaty or convention, it should also be borne in mind that a violation might be of so grave a character as to give rise to the inherent right of self-defense recognized in Article 51 of the Charter of the United Nations." [24] The point may well become one of utmost importance, but the view may be hazarded that, because of the political difficulties involved, no forthright interpretation or clarification will be achieved in the course of the negotiations. It is to be hoped that the occasion will not arise for individual states to resort to their individual interpretations in some great crisis.

Article 51 is also restricted to defining the rights of Members of the United Nations and does not seek to lay down a general principle, since it refers only to "an armed attack . . . against a Member of the United Nations." A non-Member state would accordingly still look to general international law for a definition of

[23] *International Control of Atomic Energy: Growth of a Policy*, Dept. of State Pub. 2702 (1946), 164.
[24] 16 Dept. of State *Bulletin* (1947), 112.

its right of self-defense. It is not to be assumed, however, that the United Nations, particularly as it approaches closer to universality, would tolerate a resort to force in self-defense by a non-Member against a Member, or by one non-Member against another under circumstances wherein the act would be a violation of Article 51 of the Charter if performed by a Member. Any such use of force is in one sense a "breach of the peace" within the meaning of Chapter VII of the Charter, even where it is a justifiable breach. The language used throughout Chapter VII indicates an assertion of the right of the Security Council to take or require action even against a non-Member; such steps would be in accord with the sixth Principle stated in Article 2: "*The Organization* shall ensure that states which are not Members of the United Nations act in accordance with these principles so far as may be necessary for the maintenance of international peace and security." Under traditional international law, such treaty provisions do not bind a third state, but a third state would be politically alive to the possible consequences of action in defiance of the United Nations. The acceptance of the hypothesis of community interest would unite the practical and formally legal points of view and expand the rule of self-defense stated in the Charter to a rule of general application.

An armed attack on a state which would justify that state in using force in self-defense would clearly itself be an illegal act. Accepting the hypothesis that individuals are directly bound by international law would result in the conclusion that the individual or individuals responsible for such an attack would themselves be liable to punishment under international law. Thus if such acts as the pursuit of Villa and the destruction of the *Caroline* were justifiable acts of self-defense, Villa in the one case and the American sympathizers with the Canadian insurgents in the other case would themselves be liable to such trial and punishment. This conclusion leaves open the answer to the procedural question of the proper forum, national or international, in which such offenders should be tried. It may be suggested that, in cases such as that here discussed, international law should recognize the competence of the jurisdiction of any state, as it does today in trials for piracy. If an International Criminal Court were established, that Court might have jurisdiction, and procedures akin to extradition might be established to bring about the delivery of the offenders to the custody of the Court.

DEFENSE OF NATIONAL LIVES AND PROPERTY

Traditional international law has recognized the right of a state to employ its armed forces for the protection of the lives and property of its nationals abroad in situations where the state of their residence, because of revolutionary disturbances or other reasons, is unable or unwilling to grant them the protection to which they are entitled. Such action by a protecting state is not properly classified as self-defense, and it may fall short of intervention as that term is narrowly defined.[25] The United States has taken such protective action on a large number of occasions, which have been listed in a publication of the Department of State.[26]

Since such use of force for the protection of nationals may be free of an interventional attempt to impair the political independence or territorial integrity of another state, it may escape the prohibition of the first clause of Article 2 of the Charter. Is it, however, "inconsistent with the Purposes of the United Nations"? The answer must be yes. The first Purpose of the Organization as stated in Article 1 is "To maintain international peace and security, and to that end: to take effective *collective* measures for the prevention and removal of threats to the peace, and for the suppression of acts of aggression or other breaches of the peace, and to bring about by peaceful means, and in conformity with the principles of justice and international law, adjustment or settlement of international disputes or situations which might lead to a breach of the peace." The landing of armed forces of one state in another state is a "breach of the peace" or "threat to the peace" even though under traditional international law it is a lawful act. It is a measure of forcible self-help, legalized by international law because there has been no international organization competent to act in an emergency. The organizational defect has now been at least partially remedied

[25] See 1 Hyde, sec. 69.
[26] Clark, *Right to Protect Citizens in Foreign Countries by Landing Forces* (1929, 2d rev. ed.), Dept. of State.

through the adoption of the Charter, and a modernized law of nations should insist that the collective measures envisaged by Article 1 of the Charter shall supplant the individual measures approved by traditional international law. Typical cases of the use of force for the protection of nationals may be examined to test the new procedure.

In 1900 there occurred the incidents of the Boxer Rebellion in China, which led to the joint use of armed forces by a group of states whose diplomatic representatives were threatened by the seige of the Legation Quarter in Peking.[27] This was a case of "collective" measures undertaken before the existence of a competent international organization. Under comparable circumstances today, the necessary action should be undertaken by the direction of the Security Council utilizing the national contingents to be placed at its disposal.

In 1926–27 there was civil war in Nicaragua. United States armed forces were landed. "As a means of insuring the maintenance of communications between the Legation and the Legation guard at Managua and the seacoast, United States naval forces declared neutral the zone along the Pacific Railway, including the cities through which the railway passed, and prohibited fighting in that zone. . . . After an attack by unknown parties on the American Consular Agent at Matagalpa, that city was declared a neutral zone and American marines stationed there. By March 15 a total of 2,000 naval and military forces had been landed in Nicaragua to maintain the neutral zones and protect American and other foreign lives and property." [28] Under comparable circumstances today, any necessary action should be undertaken by the direction of the Security Council, and not on the unilateral decision of any one Member of the Organization.

It would seem that the only possible argument against the substitution of collective measures under the Security Council for individual measures by a single state would be the inability of the international organization to act with the speed requisite to preserve life. It may take some time before the Security Council, with its

[27] 5 Moore's Digest of Int. L., 476 ff.
[28] The United States and Nicaragua: A Survey of the Relations from 1909 to 1932, Dept. of State Pub. 339 (1932), 71–2.

Military Staff Committee, and the pledged national contingents are in a state of readiness to act in such cases, but the Charter contemplates that international action shall be timely as well as powerful. The use of air-force contingents, which are specially provided for in Article 45 of the Charter, suggests an instance in which modern military science may prove effective as an instrument of international measures for the preservation of the peace.

It might be argued that the provisions of Chapter VII of the Charter, relating to Action with Respect to Threats to the Peace, Breaches of the Peace, and Acts of Aggression, were drafted with an eye to cases in which it was necessary to apply collective measures of force against a state which had begun or was about to begin a forcible attack on another state's territory, and that they are not applicable to a situation such as the Nicaraguan incident of 1926, where the territorial safety of the United States was never endangered. But the language of the articles in Chapter VII is not so limited, and significance may be attached to the use of the term "threats to the peace" and "breaches of the peace" in addition to the term "acts of aggression." Peace may be threatened by the need of the individual state to use self-help for the protection of its nationals as well as by the aggression of one state against another. It would be a narrow and stultifying interpretation of the Charter to assert that "peace" is used in that instrument only as the antonym of "war" and that therefore peace is not threatened or breached unless war is in the offing or has broken out. It should not be anticipated, therefore, that a Committee of Jurists appointed by the Security Council of the United Nations would need to be evasive, as was the similar Committee appointed by the League Council to report on the Corfu case in 1923. It will be recalled that, after the assassination of Italian members of the group charged with the delimitation of the Greco-Albanian frontier, Italian forces bombarded the Greek island of Corfu and then occupied it. The Committee of Jurists was asked the question: "Are measures of coercion which are not meant to constitute acts of war consistent with the terms of Article 12 to 15 of the Covenant when they are taken by one Member of the League of Nations against another Member of the League without prior recourse to the procedure laid down in those articles?" The Jurists replied that such coercive measures "may or may not be consistent with the stated articles of the Covenant." [29] Reading the Charter as a whole, it is impossible to escape the conclusion that the Organization is responsible for the substitution of collective measures for the individual measures of self-help which were legalized by international law before the world community was organized. The one exception is the case of self-defense, already discussed.

In Chapter V attention was drawn to the special case of international loans and the effect of the Drago Doctrine and the Porter Convention. It was there pointed out that, since under Article 103 of the Charter the obligations of that treaty take precedence over any conflicting obligation, the loophole in the Porter Convention could now be considered to be filled. In other words, states are not now free to use force for the collection of contract debts, even where the resort to arbitration fails to bring about a settlement.

It may accordingly be stated as a conclusion that the Charter has already achieved a modernization of the international law relative to the use of armed forces by a state for the protection of its nationals abroad. The generalization of the treaty rule embodied in the Charter under traditional international legal concepts would need to await the Organization's approach to universality, but from the standpoint of the acceptance of the hypothesis of community interest the Charter rule may be posited as a rule of the modern law of nations.

INTERVENTION

As already suggested, the term "intervention" may be used broadly to cover cases of the use of armed forces for the protection of nationals and other cases of self-help, as well as instances of actual interference with the political independence of another state. Professor Hyde's limitation of the term to embrace only the last category of acts is useful and is adopted for the purpose of this discussion.[30] Intervention may or may not involve the use of force. It is frequently possible for a powerful state to impair the political independence of another weaker state without actually utilizing its armed forces. This result may be accomplished by lending open

[29] League of Nations, *Off. J.* (1924), 524.
[30] See 1 Hyde, 146.

approval, as by the relaxation of an arms embargo, to a revolutionary group headed by individuals ready to accept the political or economic dominance of the intervening state.[31] It may be accomplished by the withholding of recognition of a new government, combined with various forms of economic and financial pressure until the will of the stronger state prevails through the resignation or overthrow of the government disapproved. Examples of such intervention may be found in the history of various parts of the world and rather particularly in the history (fortunately now ancient history) of the relations between the United States and the Republics of the Caribbean area.

Because interventions have played so vivid a part in inter-American relations, the movement to secure agreement by treaty on the illegality of intervention gathered momentum in the Inter-American Conferences. In 1928 at Havana the United States was not prepared to agree to the renunciation of what it considered its right under international law, but with the development of the Good Neighbor Policy under the administrations of President Franklin D. Roosevelt agreement was finally secured. When Secretary Hull first gave consent at the Seventh International Conference of American States in 1933, he attached a reservation couched in broad and rather indefinite language. This reservation was not repeated at the Buenos Aires Conference of 1936 in accepting the Additional Protocol Relative to Non-Intervention, which provides in Article 1 that "the high contracting parties declare inadmissible the intervention of any one of them, directly or indirectly, and for whatever reason, in the internal or external affairs of any other of the parties." [32]

The latest formulation of this doctrine is contained in the Report on the Draft Declaration of the Rights and Duties of American States approved by the Governing Board of the Pan American Union on July 17, 1946. It reads: "Intervention by any one or more states, directly or indirectly, and for whatever reasons in the internal or external affairs of another state is inadmissible." One of the first tasks of the General Assembly of the United Nations in discharging its duty to encourage "the progressive development of international law and its codification" (Article 13 of the Charter)

[31] Cf. 1 Hyde, 271, for a discussion of the Nicaraguan situation in 1926–27.
[32] See 1 Hyde, sec. 83B.

might be to secure the universalization of this inter-American agreement. But the phraseology of the text approved by the Governing Board of the Pan American Union stands in need of revision to avoid the implication that, in its reference to action by "one or more States," it contemplates a limitation on the powers of the United Nations under the Charter. Collective intervention by the United Nations itself is contemplated by the Charter in the Sixth Principle, stated in Article 2, relative to exacting the compliance of non-Members in the interest of the maintenance of peace. As already explained in Chapters III and VI, the League Covenant afforded a precedent in this respect.[88] Without repeating what has already been said on this point, the conclusion may be stated that the acceptance of the hypothesis of community interest contemplates the admission of the right of the organized international community to intervene in the general interest. The discussions in the Security Council and in the General Assembly of the position of the Franco Government in Spain are illustrative of the point. Intervention in the affairs of a Member state which had brought about a condition threatening the peace of the world would also be possible under the Charter, as in situations such as those to be discussed in the following Chapter.

RETALIATION OR REPRISALS

International law has recognized the right of a state to resort to reprisals or retaliation as a means of vindication of rights infringed by another state. The early history of the development of the law of reprisals shows the rigid formalism of the law. In the sixteenth and seventeenth centuries, for example, when wars were constantly recurrent and there was no suggestion except in the books of jurists that the waging of war might itself be illegal, there developed a practice regarding reprisals which was highly legalistic. If, for example, the Spanish fleet seized the ships of an English merchant, he might apply to his king for letters of reprisal which authorized him in meticulous legal terms to go forth and seize Spanish ships of equal value to compensate him for his loss. If after the seizure of such Spanish ships as he could lay his hands on, their value was in excess of his claim, the balance had to be accounted for, turned over to the

[88] See 2 Oppenheim, 131 ff.

English Government, and returned by it to Spain. The remarkable fact is that the requirements of this law of reprisals were observed with all the punctilio of the *coda duello*.[34] The practice, in its highly organized form, fell into desuetude with the growth of national navies, which substituted state action for the action of the individual.[35] Perhaps it may be said that the international society is now entering on the third period, wherein collective international measures are taking the place of state action. Certainly all that has been said in regard to other forms of self-help under a modernized law of nations applies equally to the use of reprisals or retaliation. An aggrieved state is now under a duty, if it is a Member of the United Nations, to refer its case to the Security Council and not to take forceful action on its own behalf.

The practice of the Governments of the United States and Great Britain since the formation of the United Nations contains notable examples of respect for the new procedures. In August 1946 the United States protested to Yugoslavia regarding aggressive action taken against American aircraft flying over Yugoslav territory when forced out of their courses by stress of weather. The United States made certain demands relative to planes and their crews which had been forced to land and couched its demands in the form of an ultimatum, requiring compliance within forty-eight hours. However, instead of the traditional threat of forceful action in case of noncompliance, the United States declared that if its demands were not complied with it would "call upon the Security Council of the United Nations to meet promptly and to take appropriate action." [86] The matter was adjusted by direct negotiations between the two governments and therefore did not come before the Security Council.

On December 9, 1946 the British Government addressed a note to the Albanian Government concerning incidents in Corfu Channel; on May 15 British warships had been fired on by Albanian coastal batteries, and on October 22 two British destroyers struck mines with serious damage to both vessels and with the loss of the lives of

---

[34] See Clark, "The English Practice with Regard to Reprisals by Private Persons," 27 *Am. J. Int. L.* (1933), 694.

[85] *Neutrality: Its History, Economics and Law*, Vol. I: Jessup and Deák, *The Origins* (1935), 12 ff.

[86] 15 Dept. of State *Bulletin* (1946), 417.

forty-four officers and seamen. After arguing the liability of the Albanian Government under international law, the British Government demanded an apology, reparation for the damage to the ships, and full compensation for the relatives of the men killed. The note continued: "If no satisfactory reply is received within fourteen days of the delivery of this note, His Majesty's Government will have no alternative but to bring the matter before the Security Council of the United Nations as a serious threat to, and a breach of, international peace and security, showing criminal disregard of the safety of innocent seamen of any nationality lawfully using an international highway." The reply of the Albanian Government, dated December 21, not being considered satisfactory, the British representative on January 10, 1947 transmitted the correspondence to the Secretary-General of the United Nations for submission to the Security Council under Article 35 of the Charter.[37]

PACIFIC BLOCKADE

Pacific blockade is another form of self-help regulated by international law. Its use has illustrated the old bilateral nature of international law. An aggrieved state might seek to bring another state to terms by blockading its ports "peacefully"; that is, without declaring war and establishing a belligerent blockade. If the latter course were followed, the blockading state would be vested with the rights of a belligerent, which include the privilege of intercepting and condemning the vessels of third states or neutrals which might attempt to run the blockade. In a pacific blockade the blockader had no such privilege and was bound to confine its efforts to the interception of the vessels of the blockaded state. Thus when in 1902 Great Britain, Germany, and Italy sought to compel Venezuela to honor its financial obligations, they established a pacific blockade of the Venezuelan coast. The United States gave notice that under such a blockade there was no right to interfere with vessels flying the flag of the United States. The blockading powers, yielding to

[37] UN Doc. S/247, 10 January 1947. For the suggestion that resort to an international authority should not be used as a "threat" in the course of diplomatic negotiations, see the authorities discussed in Morgenthau, "Diplomacy," 55 *Yale L. J.* (1946), 1067, 1072.

the United States view, thereupon asserted that their blockade "created *ipso facto* a state of war" and thus gave them belligerent rights.[38] This action well illustrates the point made earlier that international law regulated lesser uses of force but not the resort to war itself.

The affair led to an interesting case submitted to the Permanent Court of Arbitration. The three blockading powers as well as the United States, France, Belgium, Mexico, the Netherlands, Spain, Sweden, and Norway signed agreements with Venezuela concerning the satisfaction of their respective claims against the latter state. Arrangements were made for the application of certain Venezuelan revenues to the discharge of the claims. The three blockading powers claimed preferential treatment in the allocation of the funds available, on the ground that their blockade had brought about the settlement. This claim to preferential treatment was contested by the other states and submitted by agreement to the Permanent Court of Arbitration. The tribunal carefully avoided committing itself on the question of the legality of the blockade, but decided in favor of the claim of the blockading powers.[39] It has been natural for commentators to deduce an implied approval of the blockading act, and this point of view was foreshadowed in the arguments before the tribunal. According to the Report of the Agent of the United States: "The force and value of the award as a precedent cannot yet be justly measured. By some it may be approved as giving to the blockading powers the just reward of their military exertions by securing the prompt payment of their claims, while leaving the other creditor States free to secure in their own way the payment of their claims. By others the award may be regarded as a premium on war, as inconsistent with the spirit of the Hague Convention, and as tending to incite armed conflicts between creditor States having claims against a common debtor. If the latter view, which was urged to the tribunal by the counsel for the United States, is correct, the injurious effects of the award as a precedent will be limited by other and later arbitral decisions and by the action of public opinion." [40]

[38] See 2 Hyde, 1669.

[39] Scott, *Hague Court Reports* (1916), 55.

[40] *The Venezuelan Arbitration before the Hague Tribunal, 1903*, Sen. Doc. 119, 58th Cong. 3d Sess., 15.

USE OF FORCE BY INDIVIDUALS

The acceptance of the hypothesis that individuals are subjects of international law and are bound directly by it necessitates the consideration here of certain examples of the use of force by individuals.

The matter of piracy, as already mentioned, is the one case in which it has been generally said that international law imposed duties directly on individuals, but the actual legal situation has been also explained in terms of state rights. The explanation is that international law in case of piracy removes usual limitations on the jurisdiction of states and permits any state which apprehends a pirate to punish him.[41] With the acceptance of the hypothesis that the individual is a subject of international law, such reconciliation with the traditional basis of international law is no longer necessary. Accordingly it may be stated that under a modernized law of nations unauthorized acts of violence on the high seas committed by individuals are violations of international law. On the procedural side, practice already provides a solution in that each state remains free to inflict such punishment as it may choose to provide by its local law. International law might itself assert the death penalty, or life imprisonment in states where capital punishment is forbidden.

The basic theoretical hurdle having been jumped, there would be no obstacle in the way of agreement on other individual acts which should be assimilated to acts of piracy or treated in the same way. The Washington Conference on Limitation of Armaments in 1922 proposed a convention which would have used this formula for sinkings of merchant vessels by submarines, but the convention never entered into force. The problem of international law would be to catalogue those acts of individuals which have sufficient international significance to warrant placing their punishment under international auspices. Some of these would involve the illegal use of force and others would not. They might include terroristic activities, assassination of heads of states, counterfeiting of foreign currencies, the slave trade, traffic in narcotics, and unauthorized manufacture of atomic or other weapons.

[41] "Harvard Research in International Law, Draft Convention on Piracy," 26 *Am. J. Int. L. Supp.* (1932), 743.

It has already been noted that the trial of the major war criminals has set a pattern for the future in regard to the substantive law and the general theory in accord with which procedures will need to be established.[42] Among the precedents which will be utilized will undoubtedly be the conference convened under League of Nations auspices to study the international suppression and punishment of terroristic crimes. This effort was the result of the assassination of King Alexander of Yugoslavia in Marseilles in 1934. It led to the drafting of two conventions dealing with the definition of such crimes and the trials of their perpetrators before an international criminal court, but the conventions were never brought into force.[48]

One of the difficulties which will confront the enforcement of an international criminal code will be the fact that punishment cannot take place until the criminals have been detected and apprehended. If they are successful in initiating a war, they must first be defeated by the use of collective international action. If their conspiracy to initiate a war is to be detected before the war breaks out, one must contemplate the existence of an international Bureau of Investigation and international power to arrest persons who may be directing the government of one of the states which is a member of the international organization. It is hardly necessary to point out that the organization of the world for peace has not yet progressed to the point at which a solution of such difficulties seems feasible.

Antiforeign sentiment has inspired numerous instances of mob violence against particular alien groups. Some of the most lamentable cases have taken place in the United States with Chinese and Italian nationals as the victims.[44] Such cases have been considered in inter-

---

[42] In view of the position taken in this book, as explained in the Introductory Chap. and Chap. II, it is unnecessary to argue here the accuracy of the statement of the Nurnberg Tribunal that it has long been recognized that international law imposes duties and liabilities on individuals as well as on states. The Tribunal cited in support of its view the decision of the Supreme Court of the United States in *Ex parte* Quirin, 317 *U.S.* 1 (1942); see Fite, *op. cit.,* *supra* note 18, p. 12.

[43] See League of Nations Doc. A.24(b). 1936. V., V. Legal 1938. V. 2. and C. 94. M. 47. 1938. V., V. Legal 1938. V. 3; Hudson, *International Tribunals, Past and Future* (1944), 185; Sottile, "Le Terrorisme international," 65 *Recueil des cours* (1938), 91.

[44] See 2 Hyde, sec. 290.

national law with reference to the responsibility of the state in whose territory the atrocity takes place. The state is considered responsible when it has failed to use the means at its disposal to prevent the outrage or to punish leaders of the mob. The question of state responsibility for injury to aliens has been considered in Chapter V and will not be reconsidered here. The procedure for the punishment of the individual leaders of the mob would not be different in principle from the procedure for punishing individuals for violations of other rules of international law. In mob violence cases, where the mob is definitely inspired by hostility to persons of another nationality, international law should posit the liability of the individual for a breach of that law. The practical difficulty is that in such cases it is frequently difficult to identify the members of the mob or to find witnesses who are willing to testify to such identity. The established procedure of holding the state responsible in such cases is probably the only way in which atonement can be made to the injured individuals or their families. In most countries it may be assumed that if the guilty individuals can be identified, the injured person or his representative can institute a civil suit and may recover damages. The problem from the point of view of a revised international law recognizing the position of the individual is rather one of the jurisdiction of the courts of other countries on the principle of universalism which is utilized in case of piracy, or one of the establishment of international criminal courts. The general arguments in favor of the territorial theory of criminal jurisdiction, such as the availability of witnesses, lose their force when it is apparent that an antiforeign bias pervades a community and makes it impossible to find locally a jury which will convict or even a judge who will impartially preside and sentence in case of conviction. But given the difficulties of proof and the natural reactions of judge or jury in the state of which the victims were nationals, it is by no means certain that a fair trial would be obtained in that state if the crime of mob violence were made an extraditable one from the state where the outrage occurred to the state of which the victims were nationals. It is, indeed, the distrust of the impartiality of the courts of other states that frequently inspires the unwillingness of governments to remit their citizens to the final judgment of such courts. The problem of the establishment of international criminal courts has already been considered, and nothing needs to be added with reference to this particular type of international crime.

Where antiforeign bias results in outbreaks of mob violence, there is little occasion for sympathy with the members of the mob or the motives that inspire them. The situation is different in a number of historic instances of boycotting foreign goods and commercial establishments. The most familiar cases are those of the Chinese boycotts of Americans, British, and Japanese and the Turkish boycotts of Austrians and Greeks.[45]

There seems to be general agreement that where individuals merely exercise their liberty to refrain from buying particular goods or from working at particular tasks, and do not accompany their acts with violence or intimidation, international law cannot characterize the acts as illegal or hold the government responsible. If the government supports or instigates the action, it may be responsible, particularly under usual obligations expressed in treaties of commerce. In 1901 Secretary of State Hay denied liability of the United States for injuries suffered by Chinese in boycotts in Montana on the ground that the remedies available through the courts were adequate.[46] Chinese boycotting of Japan was found by the League of Nations Committee of Nineteen to be justified as a legitimate use of reprisals.[47] Incidents have been reported in the press of longshoremen declining to load ships with cargoes for the Franco Government of Spain or for the British and Dutch forces engaged in hostilities with the nationalists in Java, a type of pressure used in the Turkish boycotts of 1908 and 1909. From the standpoint of new international law characterizing certain violent acts of individuals as criminal, it may be suggested that an appropriate standard would be that which the local law utilizes for determining illegality in such cases. In Anglo-American law the

[45] The cases are all reviewed in Takayanagi, *Comparative Study of Boycotts* (Tentative Draft), Japanese Council, Institute of Pacific Relations (1933). The Chinese boycotts are discussed by Bouvé, "The National Boycott as an International Delinquency," 28 *Am. J. Int. L.* (1934), 19. The Turkish boycotts of 1908 and 1909 are described in Laferrière, "*Le Boycott et le droit international*," 17 *Revue générale de droit international public* (1910), 288; see also Séfériadès, *Réflexions sur le boycottage en droit international* (1912).

[46] 6 Moore, *op. cit., supra* note 15, p. 675.

[47] League of Nations, Doc. A (Extr.). 22. 1933. VII, VII. Political 1933. VII. 2.

criterion is the use of coercion of other individuals to bring about a loss of trade.[48] The injured individual may bring a civil action for damages and may secure an injunction to restrain the conspiratorial action; but unless violence is used the boycotting action will probably not be the basis of a criminal prosecution.

From the viewpoint of international relations it is clear that organized boycotts are generally likely to be attended by violence and to have a directly injurious effect on international relations. It is doubtful whether in such cases a modernized international law should seek to distinguish between tort and criminal law. If individuals resort to any form of violence inspired by hostility to another people or government, their acts should be characterized as illegal and they should be subject to trial in whatever international forum is established for that purpose. In the case of a boycott, procedures might be adopted whereby the action could be instituted by the persons damaged, and if the boycotters were found guilty any fine assessed might be collected for the benefit of the injured party. Realistically, however, it must be recognized that in cases of boycott and of mob violence the guilty persons may be judgment-proof so far as adequate compensation to the damaged party is concerned, and that if punishment is to serve as a deterrent some penalty other than a fine may be necessary.

On the substantive side it is necessary to ask whether a modernized international law should content itself with cognizance of cases of violence inspired by an antiforeign bias. The international repercussions of such cases give them a special character, but history indicates that anti-racial bias as the instigation of group violence is equally likely to rouse international issues irrespective of nationality. This has been due in part to a general humanitarian sentiment which is shocked by such outrages and in part to the distribution of members of racial groups through a number of countries. Thus the lynching of Negroes in the southern states of the United States may arouse a humanitarian revulsion in other countries as well as in the United States itself, but there are not large, organized, politically active groups of Negroes in other states to take up the cudgels on behalf of the fellow members of their race. On the other hand, anti-Jewish pogroms in any part of the world stir other Jewish groups sufficiently

[48] Bouvé, *op. cit., supra* note 45, p. 24.

well organized to make their voices heard. Aside from any racial bond, the religious factor may have the same consequences, as in the response of Christian groups in various countries to the massacres of Christian Armenians in Turkey.

Granted the acknowledgment of individual rights protected by international law, all such cases must be considered to be matters of international concern, and those who use violence against national, racial, or religious minorities should be considered "violators of the laws of nations," to use the old phrase of the famous Act of 7 Anne, which in 1708 provided penalties for those who violated the immunities of ambassadors and other public ministers.

A major step was taken in this direction by another resolution of the General Assembly of the United Nations adopted on December 13, 1946 relative to the crime of genocide. This term has attained wide currency since it was coined by Dr. Lemkin and described in his book "Axis Rule in Occupied Europe," published by the Carnegie Endowment for International Peace in 1944. Lemkin defined the term as meaning "the destruction of a nation or of an ethnic group." The General Assembly expanded the definition in declaring:

> Genocide is a denial of the right of existence of entire human groups, as homicide is a denial of the right to live of individual human beings; such denial of the right of existence shocks the conscience of mankind, results in great losses to humanity in the form of cultural and other contributions represented by these human groups, and is contrary to moral law and to the spirit and aims of the United Nations.
>
> Many instances of such crimes of genocide have occurred when racial, religious, political and other groups have been destroyed, entirely or in part.
>
> •The punishment of the crime of genocide is a matter of international concern.
>
> The General Assembly therefore
>
> Affirms that genocide is a crime under international law which the civilized world condemns, and for the commission of which principals and accomplices—whether private individuals, public officials or statesmen, and whether the crime is

committed on religious, racial, political or any other grounds
—are punishable;

Invites the Member States to enact the necessary legislation for the prevention and punishment of this crime;

Recommends that international cooperation be organized
between States with a view to facilitating the speedy prevention and punishment of the crime of genocide; and, to this
end,

Requests the Economic and Social Council to undertake
the necessary studies, with a view to drawing up a draft convention on the crime of genocide to be submitted to the next
regular session of the General Assembly.[49]

The fact that this resolution mentions "political groups" as well
as racial and religious groups among those which may be the victims
of genocide suggests very broad applications of the principle. There
is also much significance in the fact that the task of elaborating a
convention on the subject is entrusted to the Economic and Social
Council, perhaps for consideration by its Commission on Human
Rights. But it is also notable that at this stage the General Assembly
suggested that enforcement and punishment should be left to the
states, which are urged to enact national laws on the subject. It is
true that "international cooperation" is also recommended, but there
is no repetition of the language used in the resolution on the crime of
aggressive war relative to an International Criminal Code. It remains
to be seen whether proposals will be submitted for the trial before
an international tribunal of persons or groups accused of committing
or plotting genocide.

CIVIL WARS AND REVOLUTION

As suggested in Chapter III, the problem of international legal
regulation of civil war and revolution is a difficult one. As organized
societies gain in stability the suppression of forcible changes in government becomes a normal and natural task of the community. Thus,
in the United States, political leaders no longer repeat the words of
Thomas Jefferson: "I hold it that a little rebellion now and then is a

[49] *UN Journal*, No. 58 Supp. A-A/P.V./55, 476.

good thing. . . . God forbid we should ever be 20 years without such a rebellion." [50] But the right of resistance against autocratic suppression is deeply ingrained in the human spirit and has had the blessing of great political theorists such as Vattel and Locke.[51] Should it be an international crime, like piracy, for an individual to revolt against oppression? To answer this question in the affirmative is to assert that the international community should be based on the principle of mutual assistance to suppress internal disturbances of the magnitude of revolution or civil war. The Havana Convention of 1928 on Rights and Duties of States in the Event of Civil Strife is a partial acceptance of that principle, although the treaty does not go so far as to provide for collective intervention.

The problem may be examined from the point of view of the establishment of a world state. When this result is achieved the world government, unless it presents a complete reversal of all its human prototypes, will enact law and will take steps to suppress armed rebellion against its authority. As is sometimes said, after the establishment of a world state all war would be civil war, and in such a world civil war the power of world government would be directed to the suppression of all resistance against its authority. The right of resistance would not be recognized. The denial of the right of resistance must be predicated on the same consideration that attends the outlawing of war in an international community of sovereign states: namely, provision of peaceful substitutes for war. The establishment of world government assumes the creation of governmental organs and processes adequate to remedy wrongs and to provide justice for all people. The law of a world state would therefore deny the "right of revolution."

In the present state of the world in which the sovereign state persists, albeit each state is bound to the others through a still primitive form of international governmental organization, it must be held that the interest of the world community in peace is greater than the assertion of an individual or group of individuals that his or their

[50] Ford (ed.), *The Writings of Thomas Jefferson*, Vol. IV, 1784–1787, (1894), 362, 467; see Goebel, *The Recognition Policy of the United States* (1915).

[51] Lauterpacht, *An International Bill of the Rights of Man* (1945), 43, 46, 58.

rights are being disregarded. If the state has relinquished its right to resort to war, so the individual must relinquish any right to overthrow his own government by force. This, in pragmatic terms, means merely that he adds to the usual risks of rebellion the risk of international aid to the government he attacks. From the point of view of the ethical right of revolution, the right is inalienable; its exercise is forgone when government provides the processes for correcting abuses by nonviolent means. Such a conclusion would throw upon the international community, now organized in the United Nations, a heavy burden. The international community would have to take cognizance of and remedy situations within states which are provocative of rebellion. It would have to be prepared, as the federal government of the United States is prepared, to render armed assistance to any of its members whose local forces are inadequate to preserve domestic peace and tranquillity. But, as has been pointed out in Chapter III, the history of the recognition policy of states, and particularly of modern trends toward collective interest in the nonrecognition of governments which assume or maintain power by violence, teaches that international interference in such matters may lead to undesirable domination of the internal situation in a state and be productive of more international friction than it eliminates. The difficulty is one of organization and procedures; as these develop, desirable international results may be achieved through such collective interventions. The United Nations as now organized is not capable of exercising such a role. The recent debates on Franco Spain are illustrative of this weakness. Until international organization or international government reaches a stage of greater political maturity, international law must avoid stretching its arm into a state in case of civil war. As under traditional international law, the situation may come under legal regulation when in its preparation or in its operation it projects its disturbing influence outside the boundaries of a single state. Such a situation may be said to exist where a territory is already under a form of delegated international control —e.g. the mandated territory of Palestine—or where the case involves nonself-governing peoples to whom the obligations of Chapter XI or XII of the Charter apply. Even the first rudimentary forms of world government, as that term is commonly used by its proponents, would necessarily leave to the subordinate political units a large measure of responsibility for the maintenance of local peace. In a political unit as large and complex as is this terrestrial globe, a local civil war might well be conceived to have only the magnitude of an individual murder in the United States today.

CHAPTER VIII

RIGHTS AND DUTIES IN CASE OF ILLEGAL USE OF FORCE

IN THE PRECEDING CHAPTER an attempt was made to indicate the instances in which, under a modernized law of nations, force may be lawfully used by a state. It was concluded that force could be used only in self-defense and then only as a preliminary matter until the organized power of the international community could be brought to bear. If the resort to force in self-defense is of a high order of magnitude, involving the use of air, land, and sea forces, even though it continue for only a short period of time before the international forces begin to operate or obtain the victory, the position of third parties may be affected. Armed forces of the state acting in self-defense may need to continue their operations under the International Staff Committee of the United Nations or with its authority in order to avoid giving military advantage to the aggressor. After the national contingents made available to the United Nations are put into the field against the aggressor, it is necessary to envisage the duration of conflict over a period of time sufficiently prolonged to involve the conduct of individuals and states indirectly affected. Commercial intercourse may be interrupted, damage may be inflicted by inaccurate bombing or on property in the line of fire, property may be requisitioned for the use of the international force. It is a mistake to assume that the acceptance of the concept of international police forces and their use against an "outlaw," with its consequent abolition of the concept of "war" in a legal sense, eliminates the necessity for the legal regulation of the rights and duties of those who are active participants in the struggle and of those who for geographical or other reasons are not called on to take an active part. The need is clouded by the metaphor of "the policeman," as if some single strong-armed guardian of the law could pick a nation up by the scruff of its neck and haul it to the lockup. If a nation goes berserk. force is let loose.

and if the international community seeks to restore order, it must use greater force. We may cease to call it war, but there will be fighting, and people will be killed. The analogy is not to the single citizen who assaults and kills, but rather to major rioting or civil war which requires the troops to be called out.

This picture is not changed if one envisages the creation of a world state with organized forces for the suppression of violence. John Bassett Moore pointed out in 1924 that the elimination of international war could not be expected until the world had ceased to see recurrences of civil war.[1] Civil war, revolution, mob violence are more frequent manifestations of man's unruly and still savage will than are wars between states. It may well be, as advocates of world government are wont to maintain, that it is better to have blood spilled to preserve and perfect the union than merely to shift once again the balance of power among sovereign states, but this fact does not alter the point under consideration here, which is the determination of legal rights and duties when sizable armed forces are fighting.

When the United States was torn by civil war lasting four years there was some tendency to argue that all the soldiers and officials of the Confederacy were rebels and traitors and should be dealt with as such, but actually so severe a policy was not followed consistently. The Federal Armies promulgated General Orders 100 for the Conduct of the Armies in the Field, embodying the suggestion of Francis Lieber, Professor of International Law at Columbia University, and thus laid the foundations of the modern rules of international law on belligerent occupation. The Supreme Court of the United States acknowledged that the Confederacy was a *de facto* government whose status of belligerency was recognized by the Federal Government.[2]

As the Civil War cases signalized, the gradual advances of the armies representing established government led to the occupation of territory which was held while the war still went on. Assume such an occupation by international "police" forces, and a multitude of legal problems arise at once: What law applies in the occupied territory—is the law of the group in revolt to be re-established at

[1] Moore, *International Law and Some Current Illusions* (1924), 37.
[2] Cf. *inter alia*, U.S. *v.* Pacific Railroad, 120 U.S. 227, 233 (1887); Thorington *v.* Smith, 8 *Wall.* 10 (1868), and other citations in 2 Hyde, sec. 48.

once, even if it contains such provisions as those of Hitler's Nürnberg laws? If it is not, what law is to apply to determine the rights and duties of the people—inheritance, purchase and sale, marriage, civil rights? Are the local officials to continue to function, the postmen, the firemen, the mayors and city magistrates? Can the international police forces requisition private automobiles and trucks to transport men and matériel, and if so are they to make compensation, and when and how? Can the residents of a town be turned out of their homes to afford billets to the international police? Are the sins of their leaders to be visited on all the population, or how are the latter to be treated? All these and many more are problems which commonly confront the military occupant, and for convenience in meeting them international law has developed rules which secured a large measure of codification in the Hague Conventions. The same type of factual problems would confront an international police force; and a modernized law of nations will need to provide rules for their orderly and equitable solution. Similar are the problems of the treatment of prisoners: is an international police force to be governed by the Geneva Conventions, which had remarkable vitality even during World War II? Municipal police in the United States are subject to laws concerning abusive use of force and third-degree methods;[a] are international police forces to be governed by rules designed to check needless suffering and excessive violence? Is it to be understood that international police forces may follow recent precedents and engage in indiscriminate aerial bombardment which cannot distinguish between innocent civilians and guilty leaders or combatant troops? Are they to use gas and bacteria? Are women and children to be raped and killed and their homes looted, or are the traditional rules regarding the sanctity of the home and the person to be re-enacted and actually enforced by the world authority?

It has been argued that atomic warfare has brought about such a change that there is no longer any reality in talking in terms of old-fashioned drawn-out struggles. The international police force is envisaged as swooping down on the people who have resorted to arms in defiance of world government and with one or two shatter-

[a] Bonahoon v. Indiana, 178 N.E. 570 (1931); Brooks v. Fidelity and Deposit Co., 147 Md. 194 (1925).

ing blasts eliminating the evildoers and all their works. Two points need to be considered in contemplating such a picture, which is far more horrible than encouraging. In the first place, the highly indiscriminate nature of atomic bombing suggests that any world government to which decent people would wish to owe allegiance would not lightly resort to this most potent weapon, but would hold it in reserve for the most serious of outbreaks.[4] In the second place, assuming that the territory of the "rebels" has been seared and devastated and their whole organization of local government and supply utterly crushed, is the world government to set up a cordon around the area and allow it slowly to fester away, or will occupation forces then move in to restore normal life to the area? One may argue again that world government contemplates national disarmament to such low levels and international armament of such superior might as to make impossible a full-scale military operation of long duration. But surely human history does not teach that it is fantastic to assume that some officer of the international forces might betray his trust and carry with him to the revolting party a contingent of air or other forces, perhaps including atomic bombs.

All of these considerations are advanced, not as arguments against the continuous effort to achieve world government, but merely to point out the need for law to govern men and armies when armed force is being used, no matter whether that force is wielded by a municipality, a member of a federal state, a national state, or a world government. Since that is the topic being discussed here, consideration is not devoted to that vital problem of the veto under the Charter of the United Nations. It must be assumed for the purposes of this discussion that this problem did not arise, or that it has been solved, and that international forces are put into the field against a lawbreaking state in the present world of the United Nations, or against some local governmental group under a world government.

The preceding part of this discussion has dealt with the need for law to govern the conduct of international forces in their relations with individuals who may be residents of the territory in which the illegal use of force erupts or of other territory utilized or affected by the international military operations. A modernized law of nations

[4] Brodie (ed.), *The Absolute Weapon: Atomic Power and World Order* (1946), 98.

must also review and develop the law defining "war crimes" and fixing the penalties for their punishment.[5] Perhaps the precedents of the war trials in Germany and Japan are to be adopted en bloc; perhaps, in view of their rather hasty improvisation, they stand in need of revision. In any case it may be asserted that just as the Federal Government during the Civil War in the United States found it necessary to have relationships with the organized rebels governed by rules, so the international community will find it necessary to have laid down in advance rules determining the liability of leaders of the revolting group and of the subordinate officers and individuals engaged in the conflict.

An attempt was made by the Harvard Research in International Law from 1935 to 1939 to suggest, in the form of a Draft Convention with Comment, certain rules of law which might be made applicable in cases where a state resorted to the use of armed force in violation of a treaty agreement.[6] The proposals were companion pieces to a Draft Convention on Rights and Duties of Neutral States in Naval and Aerial War.[7] The latter draft dealt in terms of the traditional law, with certain suggestions for its development within the framework of the classical system of war and neutrality. The Draft on Aggression frankly spoke *de lege ferenda*, and was written in terms of the progress which seemed to have been made up to the time of its drafting by the community of states. Its publication actually occurred a few weeks after the outbreak of World War II, but the work had been completed before that conflict broke out and according to a prefatory note "is not to be attributed to the international events of that period." Contenting itself with a legal sample, it concentrated chiefly on events which might be anticipated in war at sea, although certain more general rules were also included. The Draft Convention took as its starting point the hypothesis that a resort to force in violation of a treaty obligation of the type which it defined would not result in war in the old legal sense, with its consequent legal conditions of "belligerency" and "neutrality." In that respect it is similar to the approach utilized here. It also assumed

[5] See Chap. VII.
[6] "Harvard Research in International Law, Draft Convention on Rights and Duties of States in Case of Aggression," 33 *Am. J. Int. L. Supp.* (1939), 823 ff.
[7] *Ibid.*, 175 ff.

(properly for its purposes) that the hypothetical agreement not to resort to the use of force was accompanied by a further treaty provision for the determination by a "competent international authority" of the fact that there had been an "aggression" as that term was used in the Draft Convention. It was envisaged that such an authority might be the Permanent Court of International Justice or the Council or Assembly of the League of Nations or some similar body. It was not assumed that the League of Nations had a universal membership, and provisions were included to define the rights and duties of states which were neither "aggressors" nor participants in the international measures of suppression of violence. The discussion in this book, it must be recalled, rests on the two hypotheses of the acceptance of the doctrine of community interest and the acceptance of the doctrine that individuals are subjects of international law. It would no doubt be convenient if there were an automatic test of aggression which would enable or require the Security Council to act promptly when a predefined condition existed. Numerous attempts were made in the interwar period to agree upon a satisfactory definition. The attempt was renewed at the United Nations Conference in San Francisco, but no formula was found to be acceptable and none was included in the Charter.[8]

The Harvard Research Draft on Rights and Duties of States in Case of Aggression properly envisaged two stages after fighting had commenced. The immediate stage would necessarily precede the determination of the "competent international authority" as to whether there had been an illegal resort to force. The second stage would commence when that determination had been made. It was suggested that during the first stage the traditional law governing the rights and duties of neutrals would perforce apply; the suggested new rules would become applicable when the second stage was reached. Here also two such stages must be contemplated. It may be assumed that, when fighting breaks out, one or both parties will assert that action has been taken in self-defense. There may be a

[8] *Report to the President on the Results of the San Francisco Conference by the Chairman of the United States Delegation*, Dept. of State Pub. 2349 (1945), 91. For the use of the term "aggression" in treaties and for bibliographical references, see "Harvard Research in International Law, Draft Convention on Rights and Duties of States in Case of Aggression," *op cit., supra* note 6, p. 848 ff.

lapse of time before the Security Council convenes, discusses, and decides. The Comment on the Harvard Draft noted with reference to this time lag that "It was twenty-nine months after the outbreak of the war in the Chaco before the League decided that Paraguay was the aggressor. The Japanese attack on Mukden occurred on September 18, 1931; the League resolution which censured Japan was adopted on February 24, 1933. In the Greco-Bulgar frontier incident of 1925, the Council of the League appointed a commission of investigation seven days after the first outbreak. The report came before the Council about five weeks later." [9]

The Charter of the United Nations seeks to minimize such delays. According to Article 28 "The Security Council shall be so organized as to be able to function continuously. Each member of the Security Council shall for this purpose be represented at all times at the seat of the Organization." The Military Staff Committee provided for in Article 47 is designed to enable the Security Council to act quickly. The agreements of the Members under Article 43 for the supplying of contingents of armed forces and other facilities have a similar aim. Article 45 states that "In order to enable the United Nations to take urgent military measures, Members shall hold immediately available national air-force contingents for combined international enforcement action." Most important are those provisions in Articles 24, 25, 41, and 48 which require the Members to act on the decision of the Security Council. These are enormous advances over the old system of the League of Nations, but possibility of delay has not been eliminated. The veto power of the five permanent members of the Security Council hangs over its deliberations, and it may be assumed that the representatives of these five members will want information before they decide whether or not to exercise their power. If the Security Council wishes to utilize the pledged forces of a Member not represented on the Council, that Member must, under Article 44, be given an opportunity to participate in the decisions concerning the employment of those forces. Amendments to the Charter eliminating the veto may be envisaged, or one may contemplate the transformation of the Security Council into a still more powerful executive agency of the world community with its own forces at its call. Unless one anticipates the election of

[9] *Ibid.*, 877. Cf. Jessup, *International Security* (1935), 145-47.

a world president who, like the governor of one of the states of the United States, may call out the militia or, like the President of the United States, may call out the federal forces in an emergency,[10] one must still contemplate the need for deliberations of a group of men drawn from different parts of the world and perhaps sitting at a spot thousands of miles from the scene of the conflict.

Recently the Siamese Government appealed to the United Nations in connection with clashes between French and Siamese forces on the border of Indo-China.[11] Neither party admitted that it was the aggressor; detailed information was not available in New York, where the Security Council sat. Even if there were a world government, the same factual difficulties would be present. The international authority might issue a cease-and-desist order; airborne divisions might be flown to the spot; but short of indiscriminate and overwhelming aerial bombardment of both parties (one of whom presumably is acting innocently in self-defense) the time lag will not be absent. Is the merchant in San Francisco or London or Paris or the state corporation in Moscow subsequently to be held guilty of a war crime if he or it does not interrupt an aerial shipment to Saigon or Bangkok of raw materials which might normally have an innocent character? What is the legal position of a Belgian mining company or a scientific expedition from the University of Copenhagen whose representatives find themselves in the midst of the troubled area, faced with military requisitions of men and transport equipment or accidentally injured by chancing to be in the line of fire?

Perhaps the answers to all such questions are simple. It may be easy later to assess responsibility and require compensation; but the readiness with which the answer comes does not mean that no answer should be provided in advance. The history of private law shows that it should. No attempt is made here to write an exhaustive treatise on the law which might be made applicable in all such situations. The attempt is to take certain illustrative examples to suggest certain underlying principles and specific rules that might be useful. For convenience two time-situations are envisaged: the first begins

[10] See Rankin, *When Civil Law Fails* (1939); Corwin, *The President: Office and Powers* (1940); Fairman, *The Law of Martial Rule* (1930).
[11] UN Doc. A/93, 3 Oct. 1946.

with a resort to force and ends when some decision has been made by the Security Council or other "competent international authority"; the second begins when that decision has been made and ends when peace is re-established. In order to deal with a precise and known situation, the existing structure and functioning of the United Nations will be utilized for illustrative purposes.

THE SITUATION BEFORE ACTION BY THE INTERNATIONAL AUTHORITY

Let it be assumed that armed forces of State *A* attack the frontier guard of State *B* in a remote region of the world. Assume that *B* immediately radios the Secretary-General of the United Nations asserting that the attack has been made without provocation and appealing for help. Nothing is said as to whether its frontier guards are resisting in self-defense. The Secretary-General receives the message on Saturday, March 1, and a meeting of the Security Council is called for March 3. The message from *B* is immediately considered and *A* is instructed to desist. At the same time representatives of the Military Staff Committee are ordered to proceed to *B* to investigate on the spot. The representatives leave on March 4 and arrive in *B* on March 6. The nearest available landing field is separated by fifty miles of mountainous terrain from the frontier. En route the representatives have flown over the frontier and identified the spot at which fighting is taking place, but are able to determine little from their aerial observation. They reach the spot on March 8 and find sizable forces engaged on both sides. They are able to get into contact with the commanders on both sides and are told by each that the other party began the attack. They get a message back to the Security Council on March 10. Meanwhile *A* has informed the Security Council that *B*'s forces began the attack on February 28 and that *A*'s forces are resisting in self-defense. These messages are considered by the Security Council on March 11. It is still impossible to decide whether *A* or *B* is in the right. A warning is sent to *A* and *B* that international forces will bombard both positions on March 14 unless word is received that both parties have withdrawn behind their frontiers and have ceased fighting. This warning would constitute a "provisional measure" under Article 40 of the Charter, which is "without prejudice to the rights, claims, or position of the

parties concerned." On March 13 messages are received from both
A and B that the orders of the Security Council have been complied
with; but that night a radio from the representative of the Military
Staff Committee advises that fighting still continues. International
air contingents are dispatched on the 15th and bomb the positions
on the 17th. On the 18th the representatives of the Military Staff
Committee report that fighting nevertheless continues. Eighteen days
have already elapsed since the first outbreak, and the international
machinery has worked with all possible dispatch; the conflict is still
unchecked, and there is as yet no information which would enable the
Security Council to decide in favor of A or B.

Without continuing such specification of detail, it may be concluded that the lapse of three or four weeks before a decision could
be reached would be by no means abnormal and might even represent remarkably rapid action. If the disturbance broke out in Europe,
the facilities for rapid investigation and action would be greater and
international decision might be quickly reached. Yet in the current
situation in Greece, where disturbed conditions were alleged to exist
along the frontiers with Bulgaria, Yugoslavia, and Albania, the time
lag was much in evidence. The Greek appeal to the Security Council
was dated December 3, 1946; on December 19 the Security Council
adopted a revised resolution for the appointment of a Commission
of Investigation. The resolution provided that the Commission should
proceed to the area not later than January 15, 1947 and should
report its findings to the Security Council at the earliest possible
date.[12] At this writing it would not appear possible that the report
could be received until some ten weeks after the date of the Greek
appeal; this would be twice the time which elapsed before the League
of Nations Council received a report on the Greco-Bulgar frontier
incident of 1925 to which reference has already been made, but in
that case the circumstances demanded and stimulated most urgent
action.

It may be suggested that the Security Council might develop a
procedure somewhat as follows: Immediately on the receipt of such
a notice as that from State B in the hypothetical case, the Security
Council might announce the existence of a state of emergency. Such

[12] See UN Doc. S/214, 13 Dec. 1946, par. 7; 15 Dept. of State *Bulletin*
(1946), 1172; 16 *ibid.* (1947), 23.

an announcement would be made under Article 39 of the Charter,
which empowers and requires the Security Council to "determine
the existence of any threat to the peace, breach of the peace, or act
of aggression" and to "make recommendations, or decide what measures shall be taken in accordance with Articles 41 and 42, to maintain
or restore international peace and security." It would be a reasonable
conclusion that the sending of such a notice as that from State *B*
established at least the existence of a "threat to the peace," even if it
should later be established that *B*'s allegations were not true. The
receipt of the report on March 10 from the representatives of the
Military Staff Committee would establish that there was an actual
breach of the peace. Since the bare fact of conflict might be established by the first preliminary aerial survey it might be argued that
the Security Council should not issue the announcement of a state
of emergency until it is possible to assert that there has been such
a breach of the peace. Such announcement would not in any way
seek to assess responsibility, but would merely indicate the location
and the parties involved.

The legal consequence of such an announcement would be to
put all states on notice. The announcement should indicate the
geographical area affected. In such a case as that of the Greco-Bulgar
frontier incident of 1925 the area would necessarily include the entire
territory of the two states involved. In a case like that of the
Siamese frontier incident of 1946 the area would include all of Siam
and Indo-China, but not metropolitan France or other French colonies. The Security Council might make, under Article 41 of the
Charter, a general decision of automatic application [18] that on the

---

[18] Even though the Security Council has broad powers under Art. 41, it
might be desirable in so vital a matter to embody the proposed rules in an
international convention submitted to the Members of the United Nations for
ratification. That such a convention is not, however, necessary is indicated by
legislation already passed in the United States which declares that "whenever
the United States is called upon by the Security Council to apply measures
which said Council has decided, pursuant to Article 41 of said Charter, are to
be employed to give effect to its decisions under said Charter, the President
may . . . investigate, regulate, or prohibit, in whole or in part, economic
relations or rail, sea, air, postal, telegraphic, radio, and other means of communication between any foreign country or any national thereof or any
person therein and the United States or any person subject to the jurisdiction
thereof or involving any property subject to the jurisdiction of the United
States." United Nations Participation Act of 1945, 59 Stat. 619, 620 (1945).

announcement of a state of emergency it should become unlawful for any state (including the two states involved) or for any individual to deliver any goods to the area defined. It should also be unlawful for any person to enter the area. The elaborate mechanics devised to meet the requirements of modern total war should be utilized, including the freezing of foreign balances, prohibition of loans and credits, shutting off of radio, cable, and postal communications, and access by rail, ship, or airplane. All ships, aircraft, or trains would be required to turn back or deviate. Exception would have to be made for agents of the United Nations, such as the representatives of the Military Staff Committee. This same exception should extend to accredited representatives of the world press and radio. Special provision would need to be made for the exception of the transportation used by such exempted persons. Exception might also be desirable for diplomatic and consular representatives of other states whose presence might be needed to assure the welfare of their nationals, but the dispatch by other states of special military observers should not be authorized, for in this respect the agents of the United Nations should be able to serve the needs of all. When committees of the League of Nations considered the measures necessary to establish a blockade against a Covenant-breaking state, there was difference of opinion concerning the severance of "personal" relations. The International Blockade Committee thought that it would not be necessary, for example, "to forbid a father whose daughter might have married an inhabitant of the defaulting state to hold a communication with her on purely personal affairs." But the Third Committee of the Assembly thought that even such contacts should be cut off.[14]

In short, a blockade by land, sea, and air would be established. This blockade would be in the first instance what used to be known as a "paper blockade," with no validity under the traditional law of war. Since in this state of emergency there is no question of balancing the convenience of belligerents and neutrals, but merely a question of taking the first steps toward bringing about general co-operation in the maintenance or restoration of peace, the bare notice is sufficient. All states should be required to enact in advance appropriate laws, comparable to the neutrality statutes of the United

[14] Jessup, *American Neutrality and International Police* (1928), 78–80.

States and other countries,[15] which would take effect on the issuance of the Security Council's announcement of a state of emergency. Such laws should provide appropriate penalties under the national law for any individual contravening the regulations of the Security Council. They should provide that compliance with the "blockade" would constitute a defense in any civil action, as for breach of contract to deliver goods within the defined area. At this stage the old problem of "continuous voyage," involving a delivery of goods to adjacent territory for transshipment to the blockaded area, should be handled through the duty imposed on adjacent states.

It is to be remarked that under the traditional law of neutrality a neutral state was not under a duty to prevent its nationals from engaging in the contraband traffic or running a blockade. Under the proposed plan all states would have such a duty, and moreover all individuals would be bound both by the international rule and by the national law. Thus voluntary enlistment of an individual from State C in the armed forces of A or B would constitute both a national and an international offense.

It may well be objected that any elaborate system of controls of trade which would take effect automatically on the declaration of a state of emergency would be unduly complicated and would place undue limitations on world commerce if the conflict which evoked the declaration was of a minor nature or so located geographically as to justify more limited measures. This objection might be met by provision for flexibility under special rules to be adopted by the Security Council; but it should also be pointed out that minor conflicts have frequently developed into major ones and that even considerable sacrifices endured for the sake of avoiding a general war are justifiable.

Obviously such a blockade, applied impartially to the area where

[15] For the type of statutes in force under the traditional system of neutrality, see Deák and Jessup, *A Collection of Neutrality Laws, Regulations and Treaties of Various Countries*, 2 vols. (1939). It may be pardonable for one of the editors of these volumes to recall that Alwyn V. Freeman, in reviewing them, suggested that they might some day contribute to the development of an organized system of law for the international community that would supersede the traditional law of neutrality; 89 *U. of Pa. L. Rev.* (1941), 414–15. The positions taken in this chapter are inspired by the view that the historic experience with neutrality may now be utilized to assist in meeting the new situations envisaged.

the conflict is located and to both parties, would be hard on the state which is actually fighting in self-defense. But until there has been time for determination of the right and wrong of the case, no alternative is possible. The parallel must be the situation within a state in which police or militia restore order before the rights of the parties can be determined.[16] Under Article 40 of the Charter "The Security Council shall duly take account of failure to comply with such provisional measures" as the parties have been called on to take. Account might be taken by imposing on the party ultimately determined to be the aggressor full responsibility to make compensation for all damage and injury caused to the attacked state and its nationals and to third states and their nationals by the unlawful use of force. Granted that the state actually defending itself against an attack may be put at a military disadvantage by the blockade order, justification must be found in the anticipation of the subsequent and early availability of international forces sufficiently powerful to redress the balance.

Another legal consequence of the announcement of a state of emergency would be that neither contending party would possess a right of military requisition; either would be held to full accountability for any damage to persons or property injured. The liability of the party ultimately found to be acting in lawful self-defense would subsequently have to be assumed by the aggressor as part of the damages it would be required to pay.

The state of emergency should be terminated by the Security Council as soon as it is satisfied that order has been restored and that the situation is under control. In reaching such a decision it would presumably act on all available evidence, including especially the report of its representatives on the spot. The question of modifying the announcement to make measures applicable to only one party after a decision is reached on the merits will be considered below. *

The foregoing hypothetical situation does not consider the

---

[16] Corwin, *op. cit., supra* note 10, pp. 167-70; Rankin, *op. cit., supra* note 10, p. 204. Although the current controversy in the state of Georgia regarding the governorship did not lead to federal intervention, it recalls earlier instances of a similar type, especially that in Arkansas in 1872; Secretary of War, *Annual Report, 1873-74*, H. R. Exec. Doc. No. 229, 43d Cong., 1st Sess. (1874). Cf. *New York Times*, Jan. 17, 1947, p. 10.

added involvement of "regional arrangements or agencies for dealing with such matters relating to the maintenance of international peace and security as are appropriate for regional action," which under Articles 52 and 51 of the Charter are legitimate. For example, if the supposed conflict between A and B takes place in the Western Hemisphere and if the American Republics perfect a permanent treaty for mutual assistance along the lines of the Act of Chapultepec, all of the parties to such a regional arrangement will be entitled to resort to "collective self-defense," "until the Security Council has taken the measures necessary to maintain international peace and security." It is doubtful whether the announcement of a state of emergency would constitute such necessary measures. Whether or not logical, it would hardly be practicable to have the suggested blockade made applicable to the whole Western Hemisphere in case joint action were taken in such a conflict. The alternative would be to consider the states parties to such a regional pact, aside from the two states immediately involved in the conflict, as agents of the Security Council and therefore exempted from the blockade. This would be consistent with the general intent of the provisions of the Charter concerning regional arrangements, since those provisions contemplate that the regional group would act on behalf of the world community or the United Nations.

THE SITUATION AFTER DECISION BY THE INTERNATIONAL AUTHORITY

I. Negative Decisions

In terms of this discussion, the decision of the international authority, that is of the Security Council, may be either affirmative or negative. A negative decision would result if one of the permanent members of the Security Council, for reasons which seemed good to it, chose to exercise its veto, thus preventing the Security Council from taking enforcement action or even from reaching a decision that State A or B was the aggressor. The power of the veto may stretch farther back into the time sequence and prevent the Security Council from ordering an investigation on the spot. It cannot prevent the consideration and discussion of the question in the Security Council. The situation has already been illustrated by the Iranian question before the Security Council,[17] and the point here made is clear from the Joint Statement of the Sponsoring Powers, with which France associated herself at San Francisco. The statement notes that beyond the point of consideration and discussion "decisions and actions by the Security Council may well have major political consequences and may even initiate a chain of events which might, in the end, require the Council under its responsibilities to invoke measures of enforcement. . . . This chain of events begins when the Council decides to make an investigation, or determines that the time has come to call upon states to settle their differences, or makes recommendations to the parties. It is to such decisions and actions that unanimity of the permanent members applies, with the important proviso . . . for abstention from voting by parties to a dispute." [18] The abstention from voting by parties to a dispute, be it noted, does not apply to decisions regarding measures of enforcement under Chapter VII of the Charter.

This is the gap in the Charter which may become as notorious as the gap in the Covenant which, under Article 12, left the Members of the League free to go to war three months after an arbitral award, a judicial decision, or a report by the League Council. It must always be borne in mind that the veto may be exercised not only when one of the permanent members of the Security Council is a party to a dispute, but also in any case in which such a member desires to block action, perhaps because of sympathy with one of the parties.

If the veto is exercised and action by the United Nations is thus blocked, completely or for a period of time, fighting between the parties may continue over a period of any duration permitted by the conditions of the contest and the contestants. During such a period, what is to be the legal position of third states and their nationals?

The official British commentary on the Charter suggests that in such cases "the Members will resume their liberty of action." It is further stated that if "a Great Power refuses to accept a judgment concurred in by all the other Great Powers not parties to the dispute and at least three other Members of the Security Council, and resolves to defy the public opinion of the world which such a

[17] See Eagleton, "The Jurisdiction of the Security Council over Disputes," 40 *Am. J. Int. L.* (1946), 513, 516 ff.
[18] *Report to the President, op. cit., supra* note 8, p. 74.

judgment would express, it is impossible to predict the outcome or to lay down rules as to what ought to be done." [18a] The view taken here is the opposite of the conclusion reached by the British Secretary of State for Foreign Affairs. It is not likely that the "gap" in the Charter will soon be filled. Neither, it is believed, is it likely that the United Nations will soon collapse through a crucial exercise of the veto. But the possibility should be envisaged, and those who are, in the words of the Foreign Secretary, "working together in close co-operation for the maintenance of international peace and security," should predetermine the rules that should be applicable in such a tragic event.

One possible solution would be to say that in such circumstances it must be recognized that war exists and that the traditional law concerning the rights and duties of belligerents and neutrals, with such changes in detail as might be agreed on through general convention, would be in force. That traditional law was on the whole well adapted to the situations which existed when the resort to war was unregulated by law. But it cannot be assumed that a return to that traditional law would recommend itself to the peoples of the world. The hopes which the Charter has raised would be dashed if there were agreement now that war retains its old position in the international community, even in what one may hope would be the exceptional case of the use of the veto. Although the efforts of such stalwarts as the Australian Minister for External Affairs, Mr. Evatt, will not be immediately productive of any amendment to the Charter modifying the veto power, the problem can be handled by supplementary convention, just as the proposals of the United States with regard to the control of atomic energy contemplate such a device for regulating that danger through agreement supplementary to the Charter.[19] Aside from the question of the veto it would presumably be necessary in any body to muster a majority vote, and the possibility of a deadlock cannot be ignored. In any case proposals looking toward a modern law of nations must rest on the illegality of resort to war. The problem is far broader than the defects in the Charter. Because

[18a] *A Commentary on the Charter of the United Nations*, Cmd. 6666, Miscellaneous No. 9 (1945), 16 and 17.

[19] *The International Control of Atomic Energy: Growth of a Policy*, Dept. of State Pub. 2702 (1946), 58.

of the sheer size and complexity of the world treated as a single political unit, the problem would not be obviated by the establishment of world government, with the qualification already noted.

· If the legal position of nonparticipants in the conflict is to be regulated by some international agreement short of a return to the old status of war and neutrality, it would be disastrous to agree that every state may decide for itself which of the two contestants is in the right and may govern its conduct according to its own decision, even if it were agreed that they would not actually support one or the other side by force. The ensuing conflict among Members of the United Nations would be destructive of the ordered world community which the Charter and any modern law of nations must seek to preserve. State C would be shipping or permitting its nationals to ship war supplies to A, while State D would be assisting State B. The history of neutrality teaches that out of such situations conflict between nonparticipants and contestants readily results,[20] and it would not be long before C and D would be enmeshed in the struggle out of "self-defense." If the Security Council had been unable to act on the respective merits of A and B, it is hardly to be anticipated that it would secure the necessary unanimity as to the position of C or D.

There is no alternative except to extend throughout the duration of the conflict the system of impartial blockade against both parties to the fighting. The problems then arising would differ in magnitude but not in principle from those already discussed. This difference in degree may, however, entail serious consequences. If, for example, the conflict between A and B continues over a long period of time and the international blockade of both parties is stringently enforced, it may well be anticipated that sympathizers with A or B throughout the world will become agitated by reports of starvation conditions in the one or the other country. Heart-rending accounts of the condition of innocent civilians will appear in the press of the world. Famine and its attendant diseases and all the horrors of civilian life under conditions of modern war will be graphically portrayed. Committees and Associations of the Friends of A (or B) will be

---

[20] The history of the period of American neutrality from 1914 to 1917 is illustrative; see Morrissey, *The American Defense of Neutral Rights, 1914-1917* (1939).

formed. Pressure will be brought to alleviate the blockade by permitting shipments of food, medicines, and medical personnel. If the blockade system be adopted under rules of the Security Council, the pressures will be directed toward inducing the members of the Council to modify those rules. If the system has been set up under general convention, the General Assembly, perhaps meeting in special session, may recommend modification of the convention, a slow and laborious process at best. Perhaps a resolution of the General Assembly passed by a large majority might declare that the parties to the convention were justified in making an exception for humanitarian reasons. The Economic and Social Council, or a specialized agency such as the Food and Agriculture Organization or the World Health Organization, might be charged with the duty of bringing in supplies and supervising their distribution. Such action of the General Assembly would probably be at best extralegal; it might well be a violation of Article 12 of the Charter, which forbids the General Assembly to make any recommendation with regard to a dispute or situation which is under consideration by the Security Council unless the Security Council so requests. Under the stresses of a situation such as that here envisaged, it is not unlikely that seven members of the Security Council might insist that such a request is a procedural matter to which the veto power does not apply, notwithstanding the view of the Four Sponsoring Powers and France at San Francisco that "the decision regarding the preliminary question as to whether or not . . . a matter is procedural must be taken by a vote of seven members of the Security Council, including the concurring votes of the permanent members." [21] Over the protest of one or more dissident members of the Security Council a resolution containing such a request might be passed and the General Assembly might act on it. It may well be that the Charter and the system of the United Nations as a whole will develop and evolve through some such emergency steps in time of crisis, but the crisis might also culminate in the destruction of the Organization.

It is worth noting at this point that generalizations on hypothetical disputes between A's and B's necessarily eliminate the im-

[21] UNIO, 11 Documents of the United Nations Conference on International Organization, San Francisco, 1945 (1945), 714; Conf. Doc. 852, III/1/37 (1), June 8, 1945.

portant factor of the factual differences between actual cases. Without any invidious implications, the hypothetical situation may be tested by identifying *A* and *B* in terms of historic cases or current points of friction. For example, if *A* were identified as Paraguay and *B* as Bolivia, and conflict again broke out in the Gran Chaco as it did in 1928, world opinion would probably not reach fever pitch, because the interests of the countries of the world at large would not be vitally affected and because there are not important groups throughout the world with close familial, national, or economic ties with Paraguay and Bolivia. On the other hand, if *A* is identified as Italy and *B* as Yugoslavia, brought into conflict over the disposition of Venezia Giulia, the international repercussions would be violent. Moreover, access to the two countries is such that unless there were international supervision of enforcement of the blockade, violation of it would be relatively easy. Given the deadlock in the Security Council that has been assumed, it is not to be supposed that international enforcement of the blockade would be ordered.

It might well be that in such situations the provisions of the Charter concerning regional arrangements for the maintenance of international peace and security would prove to be the best solution. It has already been suggested that a regional agency might be considered the agent of the United Nations in these cases. Such a regional agency might be able to function without encountering the obstacle of the veto and might operate throughout the conflict as the international body charged with the duty of enforcing the blockade or of alleviating it and supervising any permitted passage of food and medical supplies. Again, for the sake of illustration, it may be suggested that the world community would not be averse to allowing an inter-American regional agency of this type to assume and discharge such responsibilities in a situation in the Western Hemisphere. But in the hypothetical case of an Italian-Yugoslav conflict so facile an answer might not be given, even assuming that some comparable European regional agency is established. The breakdown of such a system might be envisaged if there should come into existence a regional arrangement for Western Europe and another regional arrangement for Eastern Europe; the two regional agencies might clash with each other and precipitate world conflict. It is true that, under Article 53 of the Charter, regional agencies may not take "enforcement" action without the authorization of the Security Council except in the case of action against the "enemy" states in World War II. While this transitory provision is still in force, action might be taken against Italy, but not against Yugoslavia. It would remain true that a regional arrangement such as that contemplated by the American Republics might justify its action on the basis of collective self-defense so long as the Security Council found itself unable to act.

The so-called Non-Intervention System of 1936 developed among twenty-eight European states with reference to the Spanish Civil War is an experiment of unhappy memory, since it is now generally regarded as having assisted the Axis Powers in their preparations for the international war which began in 1939. It has a certain illustrative value.[22] In the first place, it is an instance of joint action designed to impose an international quarantine on a conflict without judgment as to the merits of the cause of either contending faction. If it had been rigorously carried out and the actual intervention of third states had not actually taken place, it might have localized the conflict, and the outcome might have been different. It developed certain international procedures for the supervision of the plan of nonintercourse with Spain, such as the presence of "neutral" observers on vessels and the Nyon agreement concerning submarine activities. It was accompanied by such policies as those of Great Britain in declining to recognize the belligerency of either party. In the second place, it reveals the human difficulty of administering any such plan when emotions are involved and when there exists in other parts of the world a passionate conviction of the righteousness of one cause and the iniquity of the other. No plan should be suggested as a desideratum which fails to take into account this emotional factor.

The difficulties envisaged justify a reconsideration of the argument against a return to the traditional system of neutrality. The theoretical, and in some cases the practical, advantage of that system was that it drew a line between the rights and duties of states and the rights and duties of individuals. A neutral state was bound to use

---

[22] For a detailed description, see Padelford, *International Law and Diplomacy in the Spanish Civil Strife* (1939), Chap. III.

the means at its disposal to prevent certain acts, such as those which would make its territory a base of operations for a belligerent. A neutral state was not bound to restrain its nationals from dealing in contraband, running a blockade, or individually enlisting in a belligerent army. Theoretically, the conduct of the individual in assisting one side or the other would not involve the state, but actually the state's interest in protecting the interests of its nationals and its own commercial interest, broadly viewed, frequently brought the neutral into conflict with the belligerent. The question is whether the risk of generalization of the conflict would be greater under such procedures or under the suggested international blockade of both parties. Even under the traditional law of neutrality the individual could be penalized for the acts which his state was not bound to prevent him from performing, as by the seizure and condemnation of his ships and cargoes. Under the suggested law of international blockade one of the fictions of the old law would be removed, and it would be acknowledged that the individual was directly bound by the international law and could be penalized for a breach of the rule.

It was suggested in the preceding chapter that a modern law of nations operating in a world organized for collective enforcement of the law is compelled to characterize a resort to civil war as an illegal use of force. If this be true, at least until an international authority may have reviewed the situation and reached a contrary conclusion, then the same international measures should be applied to civil wars as to armed conflicts between states. This means a utilization of the device employed so unsuccessfully in the Spanish Civil War, 1936–39. The emotional factor to which attention has been called would operate powerfully. But again it is a question of choice between unhappy alternatives. In the history of labor relations in the United States the employment of federal troops for the suppression of conditions of violence with which the state forces have been unable to cope has generally been denounced in labor circles as being inspired by antagonism to the rights and interests of labor.[23] The denunciation may be historically true in some cases and false in others. It remains true, however, that when violence breaks out forces of government frequently see it as their first duty to restore and maintain peace in order that peaceful processes of

[23] See 13 *Neb. L. Bulletin* (1934), 291, 301; 36 *Col. L. Rev.* (1936), 494.

negotiation, mediation, arbitration, and the like may be utilized. Judgment on the merits cannot precede the use of police forces. If this analogy be followed, the rule of law in international relations, and the inevitable international interest in civil strife because of its international repercussions, suggest that the policy of suppression of force must be followed in the first instance. As in the illustrative cases of international conflict, if the international authority is prevented by failure to secure the necessary unanimity or majority from ordering investigation and the dispatch of international contingents—that is, from actually intervening in the struggle with adequate force—the alternative is the resort to collective blockade or quarantine of the state in which the civil war has broken out. The factual circumstances of each case will vary, and such quarantine may in some cases sustain the "right" and in some cases the "wrong." How can it be otherwise until right and wrong are identified in terms of the clashing factions? As already suggested, the general interest of the world community, and therefore eventually of the "right," would not be better served if each outside state or each group of individuals in such outside states were free to reach its own conclusion and to intervene on one side or the other.

THE SITUATION AFTER ACTION BY THE INTERNATIONAL AUTHORITY

II. Affirmative Decisions

The preceding discussion has concerned itself with the problem that might arise where the international authority is unable to act because of a split in opinion blocking the necessary vote. Such inaction has been termed a negative decision. An affirmative decision would be made where the necessary majority could be secured. Such a decision might involve several stages—investigation, orders to the contending parties, orders to all other Members of the United Nations, use of international forces. It has been suggested that as soon as a threat to the peace is found to exist through an appeal to the Security Council alleging an armed attack, a state of emergency might be proclaimed, and the legal consequences of such a condition have been sketched. The stage that will now be considered is that which begins with the operations of international forces. What are the rights and duties of those forces in carrying out their mission? This discussion is not concerned with the obligation of states to contribute contingents to such forces.

Under Article 43 of the Charter one of the facilities which Members are to accord to the Security Council in the agreements to be concluded with that body are rights of passage.[24] If international land forces, for example, need to proceed over the territory of a state adjacent to an aggressor, they will be accorded permission to pass. Traditional international law has asserted that in case of the permitted passage of the armed forces of one state across the territory of another those forces enjoy an immunity from the jurisdiction of the state traversed.[25] The same rule would be applicable to armed forces composed of national contingents under international command./There will be need to state the rule precisely and to ensure its application to the flight of military aircraft and to the free admission of war vessels, transports, and supply ships and their cargoes to the ports of a state. It makes no legal difference whether immunities are extended to them because they are national forces despite their international command, or because they are United Nations forces despite their composition from national contingents. As a matter of precedent and principle it would be preferable to agree that the immunities are accorded to and for the Organization. The recognition of the international personality of the Organization [26] would remove any theoretical obstacle to such an agreement.

While operating in the territory of an attacked state or of an adjacent state through which the international forces pass and in which they may be compelled to resist counterattack by the "aggressor," the international forces must have the usual freedom of an army to disregard private rights which might otherwise hinder military operations. Thus there would be a right to cross private property, even though it involved destruction of crops. Buildings might be utilized as cover, as artillery posts, or as billets; they might be

[24] Cf. the special position of Switzerland in the League of Nations as illustrated in her refusal to allow the passage of international contingents at the time of the Vilna incident in 1920; Bonjour, *Swiss Neutrality, Its History and Meaning* (1946), 115.

[25] The Schooner Exchange v. McFaddon, 7 Cranch 116 (1812); Hudson, *Cases and Other Materials on International Law* (2d ed. 1936), 526, note 12.

[26] See Chap. II.

destroyed to clear a line of fire. Under traditional international law, damage resulting from necessary military operations does not subject the state whose forces do the damage to responsibility to pay compensation, but requisition of property, as for billets or food, involves a liability to pay.[27] It is unnecessary to discuss the distinctions which exist under the traditional law, since under a modern law of nations it should be agreed that the burden should be shared and should not fall upon the hapless individual or state. The international forces should be required to keep careful account of all such damage, and machinery should be provided for the proof of claims at the earliest possible date. There should be delegated to responsible officers the power to pass on and settle claims in the field up to a specified amount, as was authorized for United States Military Government detachments.[28] Payment should be made by the United Nations as part of the cost of the enforcement measures. If some authority under the Charter is needed, although it probably is not, reference may be made to Article 50, which suggests that the Security Council shall aid any state to solve "special economic problems" arising from the carrying out of enforcement measures. The destruction of buildings and crops in a state whose territory is a field of military operations may be deemed to be such a special economic problem, although the article relates more generally to measures of blockade and other economic and financial controls. In this respect the Charter will need to be supplemented by a convention along the lines of the Convention on Financial Assistance drafted by the League of Nations.[29]

Problems which arose during World War II as the result of the occupation or use of allied territory by armed forces of various countries could not be solved by automatic application of the Fourth Hague Convention, which was drafted with an eye to the occupation of enemy territory. A convention will need to be drafted dealing with such questions as the continued functioning of local courts and the jurisdiction of military tribunals for the trial of offences by and against members of the international force. The several agree-

[27] 2 Hyde, sec. 295; Feilchenfeld, *The International Economic Law of Belligerent Occupation* (1942), 32.

[28] *United States Army and Navy Manual of Military Government and Civil Affairs*, FM 27-5, OPNAV 50E-3 (1943), 58-61.

[29] 5 Hudson, *International Legislation* (1936), 751.

ments on this subject concluded by the United States during World War II may offer precedents.[30]

When operating against the "aggressor" or in its territory the international forces should be governed by rules relating to the conduct of hostilities and the treatment of prisoners of war. This is not a matter of sentiment, but of military necessity. A restudy and revision of the Fourth Hague Convention would be called for in any case, as experience during World War II demonstrated. In 1907 the members of the Hague Conference did not have in mind the complex problems involved in modern industrial organization and in the participation of the state directly or indirectly in many forms of commercial and financial transactions and enterprises.[31] Among other types of problems, it should be agreed that the traditional rules concerning the sanctity of the home and of the individual should be respected. Exceptions in terms of requisition of billets and supplies and services will need to be restated. Particularly, it should be determined whether the ancient practice of taking hostages is to remain legal and whether hostages may be shot or placed in positions of danger or must be treated as prisoners of war. The United States Army Manual was not clear on this point and seemed to recognize the legality of putting hostages to death,[32] but killing hostages was listed as a war crime in the Charter of the International Military Tribunal for the trial of the major war criminals.[33] There will also be need to reconsider the rule of Article 52 of the Hague Convention relative to the use of civilian personnel on tasks contributing directly to military operations. Under traditional law enemy

[30] For discussion of the applicable law and citations to the applicable documents, see King, "Jurisdiction over Friendly Foreign Armed Forces," 36 *Am. J. Int. L.* (1942), 539, and "Further Developments Concerning Jurisdiction over Friendly Foreign Armed Forces," 40 *id.* (1946), 257.

[31] See Feilchenfeld, *op. cit., supra* note 27, and Freeman, "General Note on the Law of War Booty," 40 *Am. J. Int. L.* (1946), 795.

[32] *War Department, Basic Field Manual, Rules of Land Warfare,* FM 27-10 (1940), states in sec. 358 on reprisals: "Hostages taken and held for the declared purpose of insuring against unlawful acts by the enemy forces or people may be punished or put to death if the unlawful acts are nevertheless committed. Reprisals against prisoners of war are expressly forbidden by the Geneva Convention of 1929." But in the comment on the Geneva Convention in sec. 76 of the *Manual* it is said: "When a hostage is accepted he is treated as a prisoner of war."

[33] *Trial of War Criminals,* Dept. of State, Pub. 2420 (1945), 16.

civilians could be required to work on roads and railroads used exclusively for military transport, but they could not be required to build fortifications. There was no certainty as to whether they could properly be forced to labor on the construction of a military airport.

Agreement should also be reached as to the legitimacy of various means of conducting hostilities. Much of the opposition to the attempts to frame such regulations has stemmed from the belief that the attempts were futile and that since war itself was a lawless situation it was illogical to provide that it should be waged "lawfully." These arguments have no applicability to the regulation of the conduct of international forces. The occasion for their use will be determined by the Charter or other applicable convention, and there is no reason to assume that the United Nations should be impotent or unwilling to govern its forces by such rules as are found suitable. The applicability of the same or even more stringent rules to the state against which the international forces are being used would have the sanction of regulations for the trial of war criminals. Such trials could be conducted more efficiently and more justly if the crimes are clearly defined in advance.

It is to be noted that the regulations to govern the conduct of international forces of the United Nations need not be embodied in a convention requiring the ratification of the Members. The Security Council, on the recommendation of its Military Staff Committee, might adopt regulations to govern such forces. It is true that Article 47 of the Charter places on the Military Staff Committee under the Security Council responsibility only for the strategic direction of the forces placed at the Security Council's disposal and that "Questions relating to the command of such forces shall be worked out subsequently." The phrases used in this book suggesting international command may therefore be premature, although in one sense it may be said that there is international command even if actual command of the various contingents is entrusted or delegated to national officers. If the regulations governing the conduct of such forces in the field were drawn up by the Security Council and submitted by it to the General Assembly and approved by that body, there would be no reason to question their legal efficacy for the purpose. The General Assembly might well recommend to the Members that they adopt such regulations for the governance of any contingents which they might subsequently supply, and that, *mutatis mutandis*, they make them equally applicable to the conduct of their forces should these be used in self-defense.

It is to be anticipated that as the work of the United Nations Atomic Energy Commission progresses and the use of atomic weapons by a single state is outlawed, agreement will also be reached on the use of such weapons by international forces. Such agreement might include the principle that atomic weapons are never to be used, or that they are not to be used except in case of great necessity; that before the dropping of atomic bombs, reasonable notice shall be given so as to afford opportunity for the evacuation of civilians from the area. Such bombs would presumably be utilized for the destruction of industrial buildings, docks, fortifications, supply dumps, and the like rather than primarily against bodies of troops except as these might be massed in a fortified area. Notice would therefore not be inconsistent with military effectiveness.

The experience of World War II suggests that, so far as general aerial bombardment is concerned, attempts to define objectives in terms of their military use or by the old test of "fortified" places will not be continued, and that the indiscriminate killing of civilians in a state that has resorted to force in violation of the law, and against which international enforcement measures are taken, must be anticipated. It is erroneous to deduce from this conclusion, as is sometimes done, that the old distinction between civilians and military personnel has been abandoned. Women and children are not deliberately shot when an attacking force enters a town, as are members of the enemy armed forces who do not surrender. In general, such civilian personnel are not made prisoners of war, although some civilians may be.[84] The distinction never did exist when a city was under siege, in the sense that the starvation of civilians and their destruction by gunfire was not a violation of the rules of war. The distinction did not exist in World War II in case of aerial bombardment; it is unnecessary here to discuss whether allied bombardments were justified by the right of reprisal. But there are still limits which a modern law of nations should impose on man's inhumanity to man. International forces should be forbidden to use poison gas or bacteriological warfare. Poisoned weapons, dumdum and explosive

[84] *Basic Field Manual, op cit., supra* note 31, p. 18.

bullets, and the poisoning of wells should be banned. Despite the discussion above, the possession or use of atomic bombs, even by an international authority, may also be prohibited. Previous regulations on some of these subjects have been sustained and widely observed because of the hard-boiled military conclusion that their military efficiency did not overweigh the possible disadvantages of retaliation and the needless additional suffering caused. The military efficiency of the modern flame-thrower apparently does overweigh the opposing considerations, and it is to be anticipated that its use will be permitted to international forces. But in regard to any particular weapon, the decision will be made by the military expert, whose decision will be reviewed by civilians into whose final conclusions will enter countervailing considerations of humanity. Three principles might be accepted as the basis for final decision:

1. An illegal use of force should be suppressed with the utmost dispatch by the international forces.

2. In the observance of the first principle, international forces should refrain from measures which cause additional suffering to military and civilian personnel without compensating military advantage to an overwhelming degree.

3. International enforcement measures should be carried out under the first principle with a view to the earliest possible resumption of normal civilian life in the "aggressor" country after the illegal use of force has been suppressed.

The adoption of such principles would deny the propriety of purely punitive measures or steps taken in revenge. The punishment of the guilty should be in accordance with procedures for proper trial by military courts in the field for individual atrocities and by appropriate international tribunals for the subsequent punishment of war crimes.

Among other existing rules for belligerent occupation there should be retained those which dictate that the normal life of the occupied area should continue in so far as it is not inconsistent with military necessity. This conclusion, dictated primarily by military convenience, is in accord with the third principle stated above. Thus the local law would continue to govern normal civilian transactions, save as the occupant expressly modifies such laws. Subordinate local officials should continue to discharge their civil functions unless replaced. So far as is consistent with any necessity for limiting large assemblies of persons, religious life and instruction in schools and universities should not be interrupted. The right of requisition, it has been noted, would need to be retained as well as the right of billeting. Because the international forces are operating for the entire world community, attempts to defray the expense of the military operations through forced loans and similar devices should be prohibited. Available assets should subsequently be marshaled under international auspices and the various states that contributed forces should receive pro rata shares. Local taxes might, however, be collected by the occupant and utilized, as required under the Hague Convention, for local purposes.[85] The old relic of the ancient right of booty which is found in the stipulation that the occupant may take property of the enemy government, should similarly be waived in favor of such subsequent international steps as may be taken. This would eliminate the present difficult legal problems of determining whether property belonging to corporations over which a government exercises varying degrees of control is to be considered public or private property. The old safeguards surrounding historic monuments and charitable, religious, and philanthropic enterprises should be maintained. There is some doubt of the importance of the old rule which included municipal property in this classification.[86] In general, the principle of respect for private property and the sanctity of the home should be observed.

Although it may seem futile to prescribe that the same or similar rules shall bind the forces of a state which has already revealed its lawlessness by resorting to the illegal use of force, experience does not indicate that it is actually futile. The same arguments of military convenience and necessity which underlie existing rules will be applicable to the aggressor's forces, and the relative assurance of punishment for defined war crimes may act as an additional deterrent. It must be contemplated also that such rules will be binding on the forces of a state which resorts to war in self-defense before the inter-

---

[85] Art. 48 of the Hague Regulations; cf. Feilchenfeld, *op. cit., supra* note 27, p. 48.

[86] Franklin, "Municipal Property under Belligerent Occupation," 38 *Am. J. Int. L.* (1944), 383.

national decision prerequisite to international enforcement measures has been made.

If the Security Council should decide to establish a blockade as a measure of enforcement, the application of blockade measures might be left to the Member states, each of whom would be obligated to embargo shipments from its ports or in its vessels or aircraft to the blockaded state. The co-operation of non-Member states might be obtained, as that of Egypt and the United States was to some extent in the application of League sanctions when Italy attacked Ethiopia in 1935.[37] To ensure effectiveness, however, the Security Council might call on certain Members to supply naval and air forces to patrol the blockaded area. Such enforcement measures are not considered to be "war" under the Charter, and the blockading forces would not be entitled, by invoking traditional international law, to claim the belligerent rights of visit, search, and capture. But comparable rights would have to be given to such blockading forces, or their presence would be futile. As among Members, it should be agreed that these rights exist. If that be the international rule and if it be accepted that the rule binds individuals as well as states, the situation presents no special difficulties. Ships approaching the blockaded area could be stopped and their papers and cargo examined. If there were suspicious circumstances which, under traditional prize law, would constitute "probable cause" for capture, the ship might be seized. The question would then arise whether each state contributing forces to the blockading squadron would set up its own prize court to determine whether the ship and cargo should be condemned and forfeited. If forfeited, should the prize go to the capturing state? What rules would the prize court apply in reaching its decision?

The most equitable and satisfactory solution would be to have a condemned prize sold and the proceeds placed in a special fund to be turned over to the United Nations. At the close of the enforcement measures the fund might be used as partial compensation to the states which had supplied the blockading forces. If the Court determined that the captain or other personnel had been guilty of par-

---

[37] See "League of Nations," *Official Journal, Spec. Supp.* 151 (1936), 83–91. At least "passive co-operation" might be secured; see Jessup, *op. cit., supra* note 14, p. 103.

ticipation in the attempt to breach the blockade, such persons might be turned over to the authorities of the state of which they were nationals, or to the state whose flag the captured ship flew, for trial and punishment. A record of the prize proceedings with all pertinent evidence would be turned over at the same time. Such results might be achieved if the trial of the case were conducted in a national prize court. It would be more generally conformable to an organized world community to establish in convenient locations international prize courts, which might be composed of a bench of judges recruited from the several states participating in the blockade. The arrangement would be similar to that under the convention of 1862 between the United States and Great Britain for the suppression of the African slave trade.[88] Under that agreement the two parties agreed to allow their respective war vessels to seize suspected slave ships and send them in for adjudication before mixed courts. The experiment was short-lived, and subsequent conventions, both bipartite and multipartite, reverted to the more usual procedure utilized in several fishery conventions, whereby the right of search and capture was, so to speak, internationalized, but the captured vessel in each case would be delivered to the authorities of its own country for adjudication.[89] At the present time international organization has progressed to a point at which the establishment of international courts of the type indicated would be practicable.[40]

The rules of law to govern the right of visit, search, and capture and to guide an international prize court in its judgments would need to be restated. As in the case of the rules governing the conduct of hostilities on land, the Hague Conventions and, in this case, the Declaration of London of 1909 would be a convenient basis for discussion. With the elimination of the old clashes between neutral and belligerent interests, agreement should be much more readily reached than in the past. The doctrine of contraband might be eliminated in favor of an expanded doctrine of blockade. Destruction of

[88] 1 Malloy, *Treaties*, 674; 2 Moore, *Digest of Int. L.* (1906), 946.
[89] 1 Hyde 756; Leonard, *International Regulation of Fisheries* (1944), 144.
[40] The failure to create an International Prize Court in 1907 was due chiefly to the inability of the principal maritime states to agree on what law it would apply; see Hudson, *International Tribunals Past and Future* (1944), 166. The experience emphasizes the necessity for agreement on the substantive law before appropriate procedures are developed.

prizes at sea should be prohibited. The manner in which aircraft might be utilized against surface merchant ships and against other aircraft attempting to breach the blockade needs technical study and careful statement. The rules suggested on these still novel points by the Harvard Research Draft Convention on Neutrality may merit consideration.[41] Attention may be directed especially to the proposals there made for a system of neutral certificates designed to meet some of the traditional difficulties in visit and search on the high seas.[42]

It should be agreed that the state against which international enforcement action is taken shall have no right of interference with ships or aircraft of other states. Any act of force by the war vessels or aircraft of that state on or over the high seas should be considered an act of piracy. It is to be assumed that the blockading forces would have the right and the duty to prevent by force the commission of any such act of piracy.

These situations seem simple enough when the "aggressor" state is a minor power and overwhelming force can be mustered against it. If on the other hand that state is a major power and ways are found to secure international enforcement measures, it is clear that conflict on a large scale may result.[43] This would probably mean a widening of the field of action, with a necessity for action by the blockading forces at considerable distances from the state blockaded. As history shows, this expansion would increase the number of cases in which overzealous blockading vessels would interfere with innocent commerce, and the task of the international prize court would be greater; but the principles would not be altered, and the same rules could be applicable.

If enforcement measures are being carried on by a regional group acting under the right of self-defense as determined by the Charter and as discussed earlier in this Chapter, the group might establish mixed prize courts on the model already envisaged. Here the need for detailed rules of substantive law and of prize procedure would

[41] "Harvard Research in International Law, Draft Convention on Rights and Duties of Neutral States in Naval and Aerial War," 33 *Am. J. Int. L. Supp.* (1939), 175.

[42] *Ibid*, 505 ff.

[43] A major power would in all probability marshal satellites or allies in its train; Lippmann, *New York Herald Tribune*, Dec. 31, 1946.

be the greater, for the commerce of several great powers not engaged in the blockading effort would be involved. The situation may be pictured as one in which an inter-American regional group, utilizing chiefly United States forces, would interrupt the commerce of such states as the Soviet Union, the United Kingdom, and France, not to mention the large merchant fleets of such states as Norway, Sweden, and the Netherlands. If it be agreed that the regional group is acting as the agent of the United Nations, the principles remain the same, although the practical difficulties are much greater.

As in other situations described, the lack of universality of the United Nations presents the problem of the rights of third states. Under the hypothesis of the acceptance of the principle of community interest, the proposed law would be considered to be law of general application, and non-Member states might be invited to adhere to the conventions embodying the rules. But, for the reasons explained in Chapter VI, the rules should be deemed applicable to third states even if they do not adhere.

The development of the United Nations into a World Government would facilitate measures of enforcement but would not eliminate the need for law governing the conduct of the international forces. As, under the law of the United States, the individual is protected against unreasonable searches and seizures, so the individual ship- or aircraft-owner would need like protection against an abuse of power by international forces. The limitation of national armaments and the development of a standing international force would eliminate such problems as the distribution of prizes and would reduce the scale of operations, but there would still be activities which may be likened rather to smuggling than to blockade-running. Again the operations of government on a world scale would result in factual difficulties so different in magnitude as to be different in character from those confronted in the law within national states today.

Law and governmental organization are interdependent. A modern law of nations cannot function without proper organization. Even world government cannot function without proper law. "The law, like the traveler, must be ready for the morrow. It must have a principle of growth." [44]

[44] Cardozo, *The Growth of the Law* (1927), 20.

INDEX

Lightning Source UK Ltd.
Milton Keynes UK
UKOW02n0139170117
292190UK00001BA/95/P

9 781340 638320